Looking for the Last Percent

HARVEY M. CHOLDIN

Looking for the
Last Percent

THE CONTROVERSY OVER
CENSUS UNDERCOUNTS

RUTGERS UNIVERSITY PRESS
New Brunswick, New Jersey

Library of Congress Cataloging-in-Publication Data

Choldin, Harvey M.
    Looking for the last percent : the controversy over census
undercounts / Harvey M. Choldin
        p.   cm.
    Includes bibliographical references and index.
    ISBN 0-8135-2039-8 (cloth) — ISBN 0-8135-2040-1 (pbk.)
    1. Census undercounts—United States. 2. United States—Census.
3. United States. Bureau of the Census. I. Title.
HA214.C57   1994
304.6'0723—dc20   93-24224
                                                                       CIP

British Cataloging-in-Publication information available

Contents

Preface and Acknowledgments

During the spring semester of 1983, I had the double good fortune to be on sabbatical leave from my regular responsibilities and to be a visiting scholar at Georgetown University's Center for Population Research. I was in Washington to gather information about "the politics of the census." Georgetown's population center proved to be an ideal vantage point. Three members of the center's senior staff, demographers Henry Shryock, Jacob Siegel, and Conrad Taeuber, had held pivotal positions at the Census Bureau, and all of them were well connected in Washington's network of statisticians. They were generous with their time, introducing me to knowledgeable colleagues throughout the city. In particular, Conrad Taeuber, retired Associate Director of the Census, who had been responsible for the 1960 and 1970 enumerations, helped me in every conceivable way.

I interviewed dozens of individuals at the Census Bureau, and others who had retired from it; all of them had been deeply involved in censuses. I also interviewed persons outside of the bureau who had been closely associated with the census controversies of 1980. They included congressional staff members, Department of Commerce officials, members of Census Bureau's "minority advisory committees," and various others. These were committees created in 1975 to advise the director of the census about dealing with particular minorities. There were committees on blacks, Hispanics, and Asian-Americans and Pacific Islanders. I spoke with lobbyists who were concerned with population and statistics. I particularly enjoyed talking with attorneys on both sides of census related lawsuits. In my interviews I asked people to relate their personal experiences and also to explain and interpret what had happened. I consistently found that people loved to talk about the census. For everyone inside and outside of the bureau it had been an engrossing experience for months or even years of their lives.

I talked at first with "friends of the Census Bureau," but eventually I got both sides of the story. My bias was toward the bureau, and this was reinforced by the professional network I entered from Georgetown University. Eventually I overcame my hesitation to interview people who were critical of the Census Bureau.

Seven years later, in fall 1989, I returned to Washington to collect more information while final preparations for the 1990 census were underway. Once again I was on sabbatical leave, and luckily I had an appointment as the Population Reference Bureau's visiting scholar for 1989–1990. Located in downtown Washington, PRB is a not-for-profit organization that prepares educational materials on population problems. PRB provided a supporting, congenial atmosphere for which I am grateful.

My plan was to collect more information about the 1990 census and about continuing controversies over undercounting and adjusting. To my surprise, I found it almost impossible to conduct effective interviews in 1989–1990. The Census staff had been instructed by their superiors and attorneys not to discuss undercounting and adjusting since they were the subject of pending litigation. Consequently, interviewing became more or less useless for me, except with a few staff members who were oblivious to bureaucratic orders. I interviewed former staffers and individuals who were close to the bureau. I relied on legal documents. Staff members who refused to talk with me had already told their stories in the form of depositions, which I read. I also collected Census Bureau documents on how they planned and executed the census. I attended congressional and judicial hearings and meetings of advisory committees and panels. Whenever a census staffer spoke at a university or professional meeting, I tried to be there.

Finally, I was pleased to be sworn in as an unpaid special employee of the census. That appointment allowed me to visit census field offices in 1990. Visitors are ordinarily excluded from those offices because the Census Bureau assures the public that their personal information will be held in confidence. As a sworn employee, I accepted a staff member's obligation not to disclose personal information, and I was able to enter the offices. In 1990, I visited a processing office, a regional census center, and three district offices at different stages of the census. It was exciting to see how the data are collected and processed. Altogether this book represents a ten-year project, based upon a variety of kinds of data. I conducted scores of interviews, observed dozens of meetings and hearings, visited several census offices, and studied innumerable documents. This book brings together information from all those sources.

Sociologist Howard Becker explains that writing is not a solitary activity. Working on this book and receiving help from dozens of colleagues, friends, and even strangers, I relearned that lesson. I appreciate all their help.

I am grateful to all who agreed to be interviewed in 1983 and 1989–1990. Employed by the Census Bureau at the time of their interviews were Fred Bohme, Peter Bounpane, Bill Butz, Theodore Clemence, Donald Dahmann, Don Dalzell, Marshall deBarry, Phillip N. Fulton, Howard Hogan, Michael Levin, Robert W. Marx, J. Gregory Robinson, Rich Takei, Janet Tippett, Silla Tomasi, Marshall Turner, Jim Wetzel, and Karen A. Woodrow.

Interviewees who had retired or resigned from the bureau included Barbara Bailar, Vincent Barabba, Charles Cowan, Ross Eckler, Edwin Goldfield, George Hall, David Kaplan, Daniel Levine, David McMillen, Jeffrey Passel, Jacob Siegel, Kirk Wolter, and Arthur Young.

There seems to be a national network of professionals who are involved with the census. I wish to thank several members for their help: Patricia Becker, Kimball Brace, Carolee Bush, Eugene Ericksen, Leo Estrada, David Fein, Jean Griffith, Robert Hill, Benjamin King, William Kruskal, TerriAnn Lowenthal, Evelyn Mann, William O'Hare, Courtenay Slater, Michael Stoto, Seymour Sudman, and Katherine K. Wallman.

I interviewed attorneys who represented the government in 1980; they included Douglas Letter and Shiela Lieber at the Department of Justice as well as Assistant United States Attorneys Mike Dolinger and Steven Obus. On the opposing legal team, representing New York in 1980, attorneys Alan Glickman and Mary McCorry explained their case to me. Robert Sedler and James Tuck represented Detroit in 1980. I spoke also with Vilma Martinez and Eddie Williams as well as other members of minority advisory committees.

Finally thanks to the following who agreed to be interviewed or supplied useful reports: Roger Conner (Federation for American Immigration Reform), Mike Ferrell (House Subcommittee on Census and Population), David C. Huckabee (Congressional Research Service), David Jones (City of New York), Daniel Melnick (Congressional Research Service and National Science Foundation), Mark Plant (Department of Commerce), and Jennifer Williams (Congressional Research Service).

Five individuals at the bureau repeatedly and patiently answered my questions and supplied me with documents. They are Valerie Gregg, Janice Guinyard, Thomas A. Jones, Bobbi Milton, and David Pemberton. Charles O. Jones, who was in charge of the 1990 census, permitted me to be sworn in for a few months in 1990 as an unpaid census employee. At the Census Bureau's Chicago regional office I was assisted by Mary Grady, Audrey Iverson, Stanley O. Moore, and Margaret Ururoglo.

I want to thank four organizations that supported my work materially. Georgetown University's Center for Population Research graciously housed me as a visiting scholar during spring semester 1983. The University of Illinois's Institute for Government and Public Affairs, Robert Rich, director, provided grants in 1987 and 1988 to support travel and the purchase of a computer. The Population Reference Bureau, Inc., Thomas Merrick, director, brought me in as Mellon Foundation Visiting Scholar, 1989–1990. The University of Illinois provided sabbatical leaves for spring semester 1983 and academic year 1989–1990. Thanks also to the wonderful librarians of the University of Illinois Documents Library, especially Susan Bekiares and John Littlewood.

Friends and colleagues have read and criticized drafts of these chapters. These patient souls include Margo Anderson, Rena Cheskis-Gold, Constance Citro, Omer Galle, Carole Horwitz, Bill O'Hare, Daniel J. O'Keefe, Anthony M.Orum, Bryant Robey, Alan Schnaiberg, and Conrad Taeuber. Many thanks to all of them. My brave friend statistician Robert Bohrer died in November 1993; he was an advisor and an inspiration. Elizabeth "Betty" S. Barlow skillfully typed and copy edited these pages. My mother, Hannah W. Choldin, and my aunt, Mildred Spector, teamed up as an informal clipping service to supply me with dozens of useful news clippings on the census. Finally, love to my daughters, Kate Choldin and Mary Choldin, and my wife, Marianna Tax Choldin, for their constant good humor and encouragement.

Looking for the Last Percent

1 Introduction

My goal is to tell the story of a conflict that pitted census administrators against mayors, governors, and others with primarily political concerns. They clashed over the question of what to do about undercounts in the 1980 and 1990 censuses. As in all disputes, they were pulling in different directions, and had different definitions of the problem. My story tells how the census administrators, many of whom were technical-scientific specialists, dealt with "outsiders" who got powerfully involved in the census process.

As early as 1970, almost 1,900 municipal officials, including mayors of many big cities, complained to the Census Bureau, claiming in each case that the decennial census had undercounted their people (Panel on Decennial Census Plans, 1978). In 1980, the mayors of Detroit, New York, and Chicago sued the federal government, alleging again that the census had undercounted their cities. Altogether there were fifty-four lawsuits over the 1980 census, mostly about undercounting and adjustment (Mitroff, Mason, and Barabba, 1983). In 1988, anticipating an undercount in the 1990 census, a new coalition filed another lawsuit. This coalition included the cities of New York, Chicago, and Los Angeles; Dade County, Florida; the states of New York and California; the U.S. Conference of Mayors; the National League of Cities; the League of United Latin American Citizens; and the National Association for the Advancement of Colored People, among others.[1] This time the plaintiffs demanded in advance that the Census Bureau introduce certain statistical procedures to correct the 1990 census counts, thereby compensating for an undercount.

In this book I will explore these complaints against the census. Why have mayors and minority leaders complained so loudly? What is at stake in the results of the decennial census? What are the roles of mayors, Congress and its committees, federal courts, and the Department of Commerce, which is parent agency to the Bureau of the Census?

What is an undercount and what is at stake? An undercount indicates those persons who are missed in a census, usually between 1 and 3 percent of the whole population. (I will explain in chapter 4 how demographers estimate the size of the undercount.) Typically, the undercount represents a disproportionately large fraction of poor, urban, and minority populations, so it has its biggest impact upon large cities where they are found in greater numbers. What is at stake? For mayors and leaders of minority organizations, the census results represent state and federal dollars and political representation. Many governmental programs rely upon numerical formulas in order to distribute funds to localities, and often those formulas are based upon population numbers. If a state or federal program used a formula that allocated dollars proportionately to population, a city that did not have all of its people counted would not get all of the dollars to which it was entitled. Likewise, following a precept of the Constitution, seats in the House of Representatives are reallocated after every census. Seats in state legislatures are also reallocated after national censuses. Electoral districts in all states are redrawn every ten years, based upon new census data. Mayors and leaders of minority organizations know that their constituents will lose full representation if they are undercounted. As I will show in chapter 2, controversy over both of these processes, formula-funding of grant programs and legislative apportionment and redistricting, intensified after 1964. By then city governments were dependent upon grant programs as their economies deteriorated and federal programs for cities expanded. Many of the programs were formula-funded. Also, midwestern and northeastern cities began to lose population after 1950, and many mayors, unwilling to face this fact, blamed such losses on undercounts.

The Supreme Court established the one person, one vote principle in 1964 in its decision in *Baker* v. *Carr*. That decision represented a turning point because the new principle governed the process of redistricting. When districts were created according to the one person, one vote principle, states could no longer sustain the inequitable pattern that prevailed through most of the twentieth century in which cities were underrepresented and rural areas were overrepresented in Congress and in state legislatures. Enforcement of the new principle had to be based upon census results, which made those numbers into powerful political tools. Passed in 1965, the Voting Rights Act and subsequent legal decisions based upon it, made census numbers even more valuable, particularly those representing black and Hispanic neighborhoods. This explains in a nutshell why many mayors and leaders of racial and ethnic organizations were motivated to go to court to protest undercounts. Census numbers had become valuable.

How did this contentiousness affect censustakers? How did census administrators, whom I perceived as scientific-technical specialists, behave in this political environment? Officials of the Census Bureau were not newcomers to political controversy—running an agency of the federal government, they had always worked with Congress and the administration. The framers of the Constitution deliberately introduced a mandatory census as a solution to the political problem of balancing power between large and small states. In the course of American history, political controversies over censuses have erupted from time to time, but those experiences did not prepare census administrators for the volatile and all-consuming controversy over undercounting and adjusting. At stake for the censustakers has been their own claim to impartiality, their reputation for being conscientious producers of unbiased numbers. Their claim to being statistical scientists rather than part of a politically motivated government has proven to be vulnerable. The lawsuits in 1980 represented strong political pressure on the Census Bureau, which it has resisted. Since then the mayors have kept up their pressure to influence census procedures and leaders of racial and ethnic groups, congressional committees, and agencies of the administration, especially the Office of Management and Budget and the Department of Commerce, soon followed suit. These pressures created a new political environment for the Census Bureau. Much of this book will be about the Census Bureau and how its statisticians, social scientists, and administrators have conducted themselves in this new environment.

Census officials have done their usual work, conducting decennial censuses according to their best plans and methods. They have met with groups that use the census (data users) to ascertain their needs and wishes. Census officials have employed expert consultants—advisory committees and the like—to contribute to their decisionmaking. They have conducted surveys, tests, and evaluations to improve their methods. And they have carried out their censuses in a timely manner. Officials have also conducted demographic and statistical research. At first that research was aimed at more accurate measurement of undercounts themselves. It attempted to ascertain the characteristics of the undercounted and where they were located. At the same time, researchers explored new or modified census techniques that might be introduced to count these persons. Since 1980, though, the research has gone toward devising statistical techniques with which to adjust census counts in order to correct for undercounting. The story of that research and development effort is recounted in chapter 8.

This story is timely; the undercount/adjustment issue is still unresolved and indeed contentious. The secretary of commerce decided in 1991 that there would be no adjustment to the 1990 census counts. A large coalition of plaintiffs, led by the city of New York, sued the government, demanding a statistical adjustment to the results of the 1990 census. The defendants, led by the Department of Commerce, have rejected that demand. A federal district judge ruled in favor of the Department of Commerce and the plaintiffs have appealed. If the plaintiffs win and the court of appeals orders an adjustment, we can anticipate another appeal on the part of the government to the Supreme Court, probably supported by rural and suburban interests. If the lawsuits over the 1980 census are any guide to the pace at which the courts will adjudicate the 1990 disputes, we can expect long delays: The biggest case concerning the 1980 census was not decided until 1987! And now there is an ancillary issue, whether the population estimates that the Census Bureau prepares annually for states, counties, and cities should be adjusted to reflect the 1990 census undercount. While many demographers and statisticians have supported such an adjustment, many politicians, including governors of states that would stand to lose federal dollars if the estimates were adjusted, are on record as opposing it. Barbara Bryant, director of the census bureau for the 1990 census, announced in December 1992 that she would not adjust the estimates. Since then a number of governors and members of Congress have asked the secretary of commerce to reverse that decision. So, adjustments to census estimates may represent another ongoing controversy. Here again, we find census officials in the political arena, making a decision that would have been considered technical in a quieter time.

This quick summary indicates this book's main themes. The census of population, which once appeared to be an innocuous bookkeeping exercise to count the American people, has been drawn into a forceful political controversy. The census fails to count all Americans, and those whom it misses are likely to be members of poor minority groups who live in cities. That differential undercounting creates an issue at the center of the nation's social problems. From the point of view of the big city mayors, the leaders of racial and ethnic organizations, and their advocates, the census undercount represents a form of injustice, or at least it represents a statistical mechanism that supports injustice. They demand statistical adjustments to correct for undercounts. But under Presidents Reagan and Bush, federal officials tended to view statistical adjustment as an unproven modification to the traditional way of conducting the census. They contend that statistical adjustment would introduce more problems than it would solve. In general the controversy over undercounting puts census officials under great political pressure and threatens to undermine their reputation for producing high-quality numbers in an impartial manner.

A few words on the vehemence of this controversy. In the course of my research, I met people who were severely critical of the Census Bureau. I heard people characterize census administrators as "bureaucratic hacks." Perhaps most articulate were two lawyers who represented the mayors of Detroit and New York in 1980. Seeing injustice in America—poor minority groups in urban slums, lacking federal benefits and proper political representation—they identified the Census Bureau as one of the instruments of oppression insofar as it failed to supply the numbers that would help these groups. Furthermore, since they felt the bureau had the ability to make those statistical adjustments that would create better numbers, they saw its leaders as unhelpful and intransigent. These lawyers developed persuasive arguments in favor of adjusting census results. They sought to right the wrong done to the cities in terms of political representation and federal dollars. The mayors' attorneys singled out the constitutional requirement that congressional seats be assigned according to the numbers of persons in the states, as determined by decennial censuses, and the Supreme Court decisions that established the one person, one vote principle. The lawyers contended that the Constitution's requirements could not be fulfilled if the census undercount were not remedied. In addition to the lawyers, there were respected statisticians and demographers who argued passionately in favor of adjusting the census counts.

Others who explained the census to me were strongly committed to the Census Bureau, its accomplishments and traditions. Many of the people I interviewed expressed intense feelings about the issues. In the course of my research, I met retired census officials Conrad Taeuber, David Kaplan, and Daniel Levine, who together had devoted about one hundred years to the census. Even after retirement, each of them continued an intense involvement with the census and exhibited enormous pride in the Census Bureau. Kaplan regaled me with stories of the bureau's "good old days," of starting during the depression, of working with great statisticians, of the accomplishment in finishing the census each time. Kaplan believed the census recorded the history of the country. He recalled a time when he showed a shelf of census volumes to his grandson. Kaplan opened a volume and showed where his name was printed as a census official; he had contributed to writing this great history! Obviously, he cherished that memory. Likewise, younger census officials expressed pride in their agency. They were proud of the history of the census, its origin in the Constitution, its essential role in government. They were proud of the agency's close connections with the social science and statistical professions. They were proud of the agency's international prestige, its central function in the national statistical system, and its reputation for producing high-quality, accurate, impartial numbers.

This book can be situated in a small but growing literature

about statistics in the sociopolitical context. Over the decades there have been very few books describing the Census Bureau and its history. A notable addition to that literature is *The American Census: A Social History* (Anderson 1988), which emphasizes nineteenth-century developments. From time to time, the Director of the Census Bureau has commissioned the National Academy of Sciences—National Research Council (NRC) for advice on difficult technical census questions. NRC has convened committees of statisticians and social scientists to consider the bureau's questions, and these groups have published valuable reports, most recently *The Bicentennial Census: New Directions for Methodology in 1990* (Citro and Cohen 1985). Three volumes of conference proceedings are central to the literature on statistics and politics. *Social Statistics and the City* (Heer 1968), opened the issue of the importance of statistics, especially the census, to poor, urban minorities. More than twenty years later, in the midst of the fray over the 1980 census, the *Conference on Census Undercount* (U.S. Bureau of the Census 1980) presented central statements on the controversy over adjusting census counts. Both works ask the question, how can census takers more effectively count the "difficult to enumerate," meaning poor, urban, minority males. Both works also discuss the impact of deficient statistics on urban communities. *The Politics of Numbers* (Alonso and Starr 1987) is the first book to attempt generally to frame the issues of statistics in their sociopolitical context.

Before getting into my main story, I will explain how and why I got interested in the issue of the census undercounts, what my attitudes were as I studied this issue, and how they changed. As a sociology major in college and in graduate school in the early 1960s, I had been taught that the U.S. Census represented *the* standard of excellence in data collection, tabulation, and presentation. The Census Bureau was our oldest and largest data collection agency, a cornerstone of the social scientific edifice. In my imagination, the Census Bureau was a kind of scientific institute comprised of statisticians, demographers, and others.

In 1979, I began to read stories in the *New York Times* about problems at the Census Bureau as it prepared for the 1980 decennial census. One story reported that the bureau's main computers had been destroyed accidentally when sprinklers drenched them. Another said that the bureau's director was being replaced abruptly.

A third article told how a contractor had been applying mailing labels to census envelopes in such a way that people would inadvertently destroy valuable information when they tore open their census packets. In the spring and summer of 1980, when the decennial enumeration was actually taking place, the *Times* ran more stories about the census, covering the lawsuits against the government. The census was getting bad press. One writer labelled it "the bad news census." Strangely enough, I took this news personally. I saw it as a repudiation of social science, my profession. I was frustrated to see that the Census Bureau was not explaining itself effectively in the press.

Ten years later, as the 1990 census got underway, the *New York Times* revived the same story. Once again the paper emphasized glitches and shortcomings in the census: The post office failed to deliver millions of forms. The nighttime effort to count homeless people failed to count many of them. The census could not hire temporary workers quickly enough. Too few people were mailing back their questionnaires. So 1990 became the second bad news census.

At the beginning of my research, I tended to be unsympathetic toward the municipal officials who challenged the census, especially the New Yorkers. Perhaps I should have sympathized with the mayors; as a Chicagoan and an urban sociologist I have always resented anti-urbanism. Nonetheless, I suspected the mayors of political grandstanding based upon ignorance. They were unwilling to admit that their communities had lost people. Furthermore, in claiming that their cities had lost hundreds of millions of dollars because of census undercounts, they failed to acknowledge that some governmental funding formulas were written in such a way as to protect them from the undercount, so they really would not lose much money, regardless of census results. Furthermore, I was concerned that the mayors' attacks would serve to undermine people's confidence in the census, thereby helping to destroy the census itself.

As I got deeper into the subject, I discovered that the issues were not so one-sided. Lawyers representing the cities had some strong arguments. The differential undercount was harmful to the cities; the statisticians were making progress toward a method for correcting the census counts. Furthermore, I came to see a few actions and arguments of the census officials that I considered to be less than admirable. I thought that they had argued too strongly in 1980 that adjustment was impossible, although they convinced me that they were correct not to adjust at that time. They protested too vehemently that they had come to the decision not to adjust by purely rational processes. They faced a difficult situation, and did their best to make a rational decision, but they never admitted that, from the outset, they had staked out a position that they were determined to defend. Nonetheless, my sympathies were with the census officials, and I believe that they behaved responsibly. As they saw it, they had a serious responsibility: They had to conduct the census properly and to maintain the Census Bureau's reputation for producing high-quality, dependable data. They contended that in 1980 it would have been premature to adjust the census counts.

In 1987 the politics of the census became more complicated than they had been in 1980. The Department of Commerce, which is responsible for the Census Bureau, became actively involved in the undercount adjustment dispute. They took control over the bureau, especially with regard to census undercounting and adjustment. Officials of the department proceeded to micromanage important parts of the 1990 census. They contended that a decision about census adjustment was so important in public policy that it could not be delegated to mere technicians, an argument that failed to recognize the long history of responsible decision making within the bureau. I consistently resented the arrogation of power by the Commerce officials, particularly because their inflexible position against adjustment was so obvious. In the late 1980s I changed my mind about adjustment. I had, at first, been skeptical about the wisdom of adjusting census results, but I became convinced that the Census Bureau's statisticians had developed new techniques that were adequate to the task of adjusting the counts.

In telling the story of these issues I will endeavor to present both sides accurately. There were highly committed lawyers and social scientists working on behalf of the cities. The lawyers articulated powerful arguments in favor of adjustment, and the social scientists pushed the methodology of adjustment forward. Nonetheless, it will not be hard for readers to detect my admiration for the social scientists and administrators of the Census Bureau.

The overall design of the book is as follows. Chapter 2 offers a general discussion of the roles played by science and politics in the census. Chapter 3 initiates a chronology, presenting a series of events starting in the early 1960s that set the stage for the main conflict over the 1980 census. The rest of the book is divided into two sections: Chapters 4 through 7 refer to the 1980 census, telling how census officials planned it and carried it out, and relating the stories of two major lawsuits against the government, the "Detroit Case" and the "New York Case." Both of those 1980 cases highlight the political and scientific issues of undercounting and the demand for statistical adjustment. The remainder of the book, Chapters 8 through 12, is devoted to the 1990 census. They tell the story of research and development at the Census Bureau toward the goal of measuring census coverage and adjusting census counts. That is followed by the story of political maneuvers, starting in 1987, that preceded the 1990 census. Chapters 10 and 11 describe the design and execution of the 1990 census, followed by a year of evaluating and decisionmaking, culminating in a decision by the secretary of commerce not to adjust the 1990 census counts.

2 Science and Politics in the Census

CENSUS OFFICIALS live at once in two worlds, the world of science and the world of politics, and each places certain demands on the other. Many top census officials are scientifically trained, holding higher degrees in such fields as statistics, sociology, and economics. They use scientific standards of judgment, such as accuracy in measurement and control or elimination of bias, as technically defined. Individually they belong to their professions, which serve for them as reference groups. As members of these professions, they interact and communicate with their peers, nationally and internationally, at conventions and conferences, committee meetings, and through published journals as well as through the exchange and review of manuscripts. This communications system gives census scientists access to up-to-date theories, methods, and techniques. It also exposes their work to scrutiny by colleagues outside of the bureau. Census people don't see themselves merely as members of these professions; they see the bureau as having a great scientific tradition, as playing a central role in the national scientific enterprise, and in setting standards. Furthermore, like all other scientists, they require a sheltered environment, like a laboratory or institute, in which to work.

The Census Bureau has played a central role in the development of certain sciences, most notably statistics and demography, but also economics, sociology, and geography. Census officials from all over the world have traveled to the bureau's headquarters at Suitland, Maryland, a Washington suburb, to study the techniques of censuses and statistics in the bureau's international training program. Three notable examples of scientific and technical advances that originated or grew in the census are punchcard data processing; the acquisition of UNIVAC, the first electronic computer in a non-military agency; and survey sampling.

Punchcard data processing, was invented around 1880. By 1870 the census had grown so big that the government could not readily tabulate the data. The U.S. population had grown to approximately 39 million, and the census consisted of eighteen questions. Using ordinary methods of manual tabulation, the 1870 census took two years to tally. Herman Hollerith, a young engineer working as a special agent in the census office, invented a machine to count and tabulate records (Eckler 1972). He then devised punched cards that could be sorted and counted. His new apparatus was used to tabulate information in the census of 1890, by which time Hollerith had left government service to start his own company, International Business Machines (IBM).

The second example of the bureau's scientific-technical leadership is the acquisition of UNIVAC, literally the first large-scale computer outside of the military. In the winter of 1945–1946, engineers finished building ENIAC, "the first electronic computer to function dependably" (Duncan and Shelton 1978:120) for the War Department. Even before it was completed, one of its designers had begun to talk with Morris Hansen at the Census Bureau. They continued their discussions after the war, in an expanding circle of participants, which drew in officials of the National Bureau of Standards, additional census scientists, and representatives of the Department of Commerce. Despite the fact that some congressmen, along with the solicitor general of the Department of Commerce, saw the project as a "harebrained scheme," the bureau got authorization in 1946 to plan and design an electronic computer for census use. Planning and design continued for two years, and in 1948, the National Bureau of Standards contracted for the computer. The machine was installed in 1951 when the bureau was still tabulating 1950 data, for which it was first used. The agency continued to utilize the computer for several years on many survey projects. In acquiring UNIVAC, the bureau was years ahead of science and industry in computer applications.

The third innovation, the introduction and promotion of sampling, made a major scientific contribution to the nation's capacity for gathering information. Arriving in the late 1930s and early 1940s, as a new development in statistical science, sampling found a multifaceted economic and political context. The nation was in a deep economic depression and the federal government was introducing major new programs. Political leaders and program administrators needed timely information that simply did not exist. In the mid-1930s they did not even know how many people were unemployed. Administrators believed that the best way to collect information about a population was to make a complete enumeration of everyone in it, regardless of how large the number might be. This approach to collecting data was likely to be inaccurate and expensive. Also, complete enumeration is usually cumbersome and slow, and was therefore incapable of generating information quickly for decision-making purposes. Nevertheless, by 1933, the Census Bureau was operating more than fifty periodic surveys, based upon "intuitive" sampling, designed without knowledge of the laws of probability (Duncan and Shelton 1978:36). Other agencies, including the Internal Revenue Service and the Department of Agriculture, were doing the same.

At this time , the Census Bureau was at a low ebb (Duncan and Shelton 1978:43). As a consequence of budget-cutting legislation in 1932, the agency reduced its staff drastically. "This left the bureau with only a skeleton staff, many of whom had joined the agency in 1902 and had little technical training in statistics. In 1933, the bureau had only three Ph.D.'s and only one professional man under forty-five years of age" (Eckler 1972:19). In June 1933, a new committee was formed in Washington. The Committee on Government Statistics and Information Services (COGSIS), which was to have a powerful effect on government statistics. The committee was composed of leading social scientists, and its key members had good relationships with several cabinet secretaries. Utilizing statistical expertise from universities and elsewhere, COGSIS advised various departments as they attempted to develop new statistical programs. The committee's members and consultants promoted the use of new ideas in mathematical statistics which had been developed in England. "Unquestionably, this group had tremendous effect on switching the point of view within federal agencies from compilation to professional design and analysis of statistics" (Duncan and Shelton 1978:30). By working so closely with the agencies, COGSIS also influenced the organization and staffing of federal offices and helped the agencies to establish research units. This was accompanied by a new staffing pattern that allowed college graduates to be hired rather than clerks. There was an abundance of graduates available in those depression years.

Probability sampling was one of the new ideas strongly promoted in the statistical network in those years. In 1934, Jerzy Neyman, a leading European mathematical statistician, published a paper that proved that randomness in a sample was more important than large size in determining accuracy. Prior to Neyman's proof, it was popularly believed that in order to get good results from a sample, the most important thing was to obtain a very large number of cases. Neyman demonstrated that a random sample, even if it is small, yields a more accurate estimate than a large non-random one, an idea that flew in the face of common sense. The fiasco of the *Literary Digest* 1936 presidential poll demonstrated the fallacy in this reliance upon large samples. The magazine had conducted public opinion polls before each election from 1920 to 1932, correctly predicting the winner each time. In 1936, they mailed 10 million ballots and received more than 2 million returns. With great confidence they predicted that Roosevelt would lose the election. Unwisely and unwittingly, though, the *Literary Digest*'s pollsters had built certain biases into their procedure so that their returns came mostly from upper-income households and grossly underrepresented a large segment of the populace that voted for Roosevelt. As one textbook on social research says, "The most obvious conclusion from this case is that a huge sample is no protection against error" (Simon 1969:114).

In the mid-1930s, the Census Bureau began to hire a few statistically trained professionals who wasted no time in applying Neyman's new ideas. In 1934–1937, federal agencies attempted to conduct sample surveys, with varying degrees of success. The first large-scale successful application came in the 1937 enumerative check census of unemployment. As late as 1937, the nation's level of unemployment was unknown. President Roosevelt commissioned a voluntary census of unemployment, which was conducted by leaving a form at every residential mailbox in the country. Recognizing that this method would fail to count all unemployed persons, three social statisticians, Calvin Dedrick, Samuel Stouffer, and Frederick Stephan, prevailed upon the director of the national project to authorize a "check census" of unemployment. They argued that "a check census by a probability sample . . . would provide for the United States and for major population segments reasonably accurate estimates of unemployment and partial unemployment" (Duncan and Shelton 1978:44). Using a 2 percent sample, they produced results much more quickly than did the total enumeration. They showed a higher proportion unemployed than did the total enumeration. Their results were widely accepted by governmental administrators, thus boosting the acceptability of sampling. In the same year, W. Edwards Deming, who headed the statistical program at the Department of Agriculture's graduate school, arranged for Neyman to come to Washington to hold a Conference on Sampling Human Populations. This meeting effectively brought Neyman's article to the attention of Washington's statisticians.

Around 1940, the Census Bureau added staff members who were experts on sampling, including Deming, Philip Hauser, who had directed a sample survey on unemployment for the Works Progress Administration (WPA), and William N. Hurwitz. These men, who eventually became internationally known leaders in the field, were ready to handle sampling in the 1940 census. In order to accommodate additional questions, the bureau's leadership decided to incorporate sampling. They devised a system in which there would be extra questions for 5 percent of the people. The sampling process worked successfully, yielding more information than past censuses. It also yielded unanticipated benefits as well: sample results were tabulated months ahead of the full count, and sample data permitted more detailed cross-tabulations for large areas than was possible with full-count data (Duncan and Shelton 1978:46).

A third success of sampling was the Monthly Report on the Labor Force, developed in 1943. This ongoing survey picked up the WPA's Sample Survey of Unemployment when WPA was abolished; initially, the new survey was needed for wartime manpower planning. The Census Bureau took responsibility for the Monthly Report on the Labor Force, with Hansen and Hurwitz designing a new sample based upon their original theoretical work, which Duncan and Shelton call "a major breakthrough in the theory as well as in the practice of finite sampling in the social and economic fields" (Duncan and Shelton 1978: 55). In 1947, the survey was renamed the Current Population Survey (CPS), which has been conducted uninterrupted for more than four decades.

The bureau took the lead in the field of sampling human populations. In 1953, Hansen, Hurwitz, and Madow published *Sample Survey Methods and Theory*, which stood for decades as the subject's premier text. Deming made numerous contributions to sampling theory. He also applied sampling concepts to manufacturing processes for quality control. Those applications were widely adopted in Japan, where they contributed to that country's reputation for excellent products, and where Deming's contribution is widely recognized (Mann 1988). In the realm of statistics, the bureau conducted pioneering work on the concept of error. It set a new standard by publishing in every survey report an estimate of the study's margin of error.

Every modern nation has a statistical system to produce information on the economy and the people—their health, education, and the like. Most nations assign this task to one agency, a central statistical bureau, but the United States has a decentralized system. The United States' national statistical system consists of several disparate agencies, including the National Center for Health Statistics, which collects reports on births and deaths from the states and produces national vital statistics; the Center for Education Statistics in the Department of Education; the Bureau of Labor Statistics in the Department of Labor; and the National Agricultural Statistics Service in the Department of Agriculture. The Paperwork Reduction Act assigns to the Office of Management and Budget (OMB) the responsibility for coordinating the work of the various statistical agencies. In recent years OMB has devoted relatively few resources to this task.

The Bureau of the Census may be considered the cornerstone of the statistical edifice. It is the oldest and largest agency, with a regular staff of more than 5,000 persons. That number swells to more than 300,000 every ten years in the midst of a population census. The bureau has a highly educated, experienced, professional statistical staff, who are members of the civil service; the bureau's director is a presidential appointee, confirmed by the Senate. There is usually one other political appointee in the bureau, the chief of congressional liaison. Each incoming president appoints a new director who, in recent terms, has been an individual with some professional involvement in political polling or market research and has had some connection either with the president's campaign or at least with his party.

The bureau conducts economic censuses, the Census of Governments, and the Census of Agriculture. It conducts large ongoing surveys such as the Current Population Survey and the Survey of Income and Program Participation. Also, on contract with other agencies, it conducts large surveys in the fields of health, housing, and criminal victimization. Most crucially, however, it conducts the decennial census of population, which produces basic numbers upon which all the other statistical agencies depend. So, for example, when demographers at the National Center for Health Statistics determine how many deaths occurred in a year, they cannot calculate the nation's death rate without using the census population figures. (In calculating that rate, the deaths are the numerator, but the population is the denominator.) Likewise, if researchers at the National Center for Education Statistics plan to conduct a survey of teenagers, they cannot draw a sample without consulting the census figures showing the geographical distribution of the population by age. The main function of the Bureau of the Census is to produce accurate data for governmental purposes. This is where politics enters the scene. The bureau is charged with producing accurate data about several subjects, including businesses, farms, and local governments, but we will be concerned only with its original and ongoing subject, the American people.

Population data are used at every level of government. Localities use them for city planning, school administration, health services planning, and other purposes. States use them to divide communities into size categories. The federal government uses them to reapportion the House of Representatives and to plan for military manpower. Governments use census data for hundreds of other purposes. The census itself has a unique function within the social sciences. It is the disciplines' oldest and largest data-collection instrument. Social scientists in universities and elsewhere rely upon the census for basic data. Geographers and sociologists use census data descriptively, for example, mapping differences in housing quality, education, or race. Social scientists can follow trends over long periods of time in such variables as the educational attainment of the people. Using census data, analysts make sophisticated statistical inquiries into social and economic questions such as what is the trend in occupational attainment among whites and blacks, taking account of the differences in their age composition and educational background. Survey researchers, including market researchers in the private sector, rely upon the census as a "frame" within which they can design and draw randomized samples. But all of these uses of census data in government, science, and private industry rely upon a widely held, implicit belief that the data are unbiased and accurate (President's Commission on Federal Statistics 1971). Fortunately, there has been consensus on that point over the decades.

Within the statistical profession, it was taken for granted that statistical agencies should stand apart from politics. It was assumed that politics was inimical to the production of high-quality statistics. Two historical episodes stood as glaring examples of what could happen when politics intruded into national statistics. One was the complete suppression of the results of the Soviet national census of 1937, presumably because the results were unacceptable to Stalin. That census revealed high mortality levels in the country, so he forbade its publication. The other was the Nigerian national census of 1962. Nigeria became independent in 1960, at which time the data from the last census, taken in 1952, was too old to be used for fundamental governmental purposes, including, for example, parliamentary representation and "government amenities" (Ekanem 1972:42). There was intense rivalry between the peoples of the new nation's two regions. When the 1962 census was taken, "people not only ensured that they were not left out of the census but hundreds saw to it that they were counted at least twice. . . . When Northerners heard that the population of the South was slightly larger than their own, a supplementary count was made which resulted in an addition of nine million people to their figures" (Ibid.: 43–44). Wisely, the government "cancelled" the results and conducted a new enumeration in 1963 with better results. Both episodes, Soviet and Nigerian, were well known to American demographers and statisticians, who smugly pointed to their own Census Bureau as a model agency, undisturbed by national politics.

Given its political origins and its situation in the government, one might not have predicted that the U.S. census would develop into an impartial, scientific organization. From its beginnings, the U.S. census has been situated in the political system. Several early censuses were conducted out of the office of the president or, more frequently, that of the secretary of state. The censuses of 1790–1870 were conducted by assistants to the federal marshals. The first twelve censuses were taken without the existence of a permanent federal agency. Before each census, the government set up a temporary agency that was dismantled after the project was finished. This system was not congenial to the development of a strong national statistical system and, beginning in 1840, advocates of improved national statistics such as the American Statistical Association advocated the establishment of an ongoing census agency. Finally, in 1902, the government created a permanent Census Bureau. After a year in the Department of the Interior, the bureau was placed in the newly established Department of Commerce and Labor. When those two fields were divided, the census stayed in the Department of Commerce where it remains today.

Title 13 of the U.S. Code governs the census. It assigns responsibility to the secretary of commerce, who has authority to determine the procedures used in conducting the census. In practice, the secretary traditionally delegates that authority to the bureau's director. At present the director of the census reports to the deputy undersecretary for economic affairs of the Department of Commerce. This means that there is an undersecretary and a deputy undersecretary between the director and the secretary. Title 13 also requires all census employees, including the director, to protect the confidentiality of records. Census employees are subject to a fine if they disclose information about an individual person or firm. The bureau has scrupulously conformed to this rule over the years.[1] The rule is fundamental to the conduct of the census because it enables the bureau to assure people that they can provide personal information about themselves without fear that anyone else will learn it. Any person may get information from his or her own census records. No other person or agency, including federal agencies, can get information from the Census Bureau. The records of censuses are disclosed seventy-two years after each census, so as of the writing of this book the latest census to have been "opened" was the one conducted in 1920.

In recent decades the Senate and the House have each assigned oversight of the Census Bureau to one of its own subcommittees. The House has a Subcommittee on Census, Statistics, and Postal Personnel (known previously as the Subcommittee on Census and

Population) under the Post Office and Civil Service Committee; the Senate has a Subcommittee on Energy, Nuclear Proliferation, and Government Processes under the Committee on Governmental Affairs. The House subcommittee is usually more active than the Senate in its oversight. It is also generally considered to be a low-status subcommittee, an assertion substantiated by the fact that the subcommittee often gets a freshman congressperson as chair. When, in perhaps one or two terms, that individual's seniority is sufficient to merit a more attractive committee assignment, the leadership of the Subcommittee on Census and Population devolves once again upon a novice. Another House unit that is important to the census is the appropriations committee, which determines the bureau's budget.

In the executive branch, the OMB exercises a considerable degree of control over the bureau. In 1939, the Bureau of the Budget, OMB's predecessor agency, took responsibility for statistical policy coordination and forms clearance (Wallman 1988). Statistical agencies had to submit their questionnaires and other data-gathering instruments to the Bureau of the Budget for approval. The bureau's coordination function was intended to prevent different statistical agencies from collecting the same data from the same respondents and to work toward the standardization of various concepts. Standardization would ensure that all statistical agencies define categories such as industries or racial groups in the same way. A lack of such uniformity can make it impossible to combine information gathered by different agencies. The Bureau of the Budget made a considerable investment in forms clearance and statistical coordination, developing a staff of sixty-nine persons by 1947. OMB, by comparison, has neglected these functions, shrinking the staff to as few as nine at its smallest.

Nonetheless, OMB's influence over the Census Bureau has increased since the passage of the Paperwork Reduction Act of 1980. That Act requires OMB to scrutinize all federal questionnaires to insure that they do not place an excessive response "burden" on the public. The Act is based upon the premise that governmental agencies impose an undue burden upon businesses and individuals by frequently asking them to fill out forms to provide information about themselves. Small businesses, in particular, have often complained about this nuisance. The Paperwork Reduction Act gives OMB the authority to scrutinize the forms (questionnaires) that federal agencies, including statistical agencies, use in their data collection. OMB may approve or disapprove whole surveys and questionnaires or they exercise a sort of line-item veto, allowing certain questions and disallowing others. Since the goal of the act is to minimize burden, officials at OMB may take it as their mandate to cut back on questions. That posture places the burden of proof on the administrators of statistical agencies to justify every question they ask.

Social scientists contend that the statistical agencies are not major culprits in imposing a burden on the public. Businesses must fill out forms for many nonstatistical agencies, but individuals do not. Furthermore, participating in a decennial census or an occasional survey should not be seen as much of a burden (Rockwell 1989). Nonetheless, the OMB has forms-clearance authority over the statistical agencies and pursues its mandate to lessen the burden upon the public. The Reagan administration also favored the private sector over the public in the field of statistics. This policy says that government should not perform functions that could be done equally well or better by private companies. Thus, for example, if private companies are capable of disseminating statistical information in printed or electronic form, then the government should not compete with them. This policy has not had a major impact upon the census of population.

In sum, the director of the Census Bureau operates in a governmental context that requires him or her to comply with the provisions of Title 13, to report to the secretary of commerce and to the congressional oversight committees, to get a budget cleared by the secretary and OMB and funded by Congress, and to seek approval of questionnaires and other matters from OMB.

Despite this multitude of superordinate authorities, census directors and their agency have traditionally enjoyed a considerable degree of autonomy. Presumably, there was an amicable relationship between the chair of the House oversight subcommittee and the director of the bureau, in which the chair accepted the director as a responsible professional who could be trusted to make defensible decisions. From the director's point of view, that grant of autonomy represented the optimal situation, particularly if it was accompanied by sufficient funds for the agency's needs. Nonetheless, over time the relationship between the subcommittee and the bureau has had its ups and downs.

In the decades of the 1930s through the 1960s the agency did its work with little interference. To deal with the problems they confronted, presidential administrations needed particular sorts of information from time to time, and they prevailed upon the bureau to collect it. For example, during the depression they needed unemployment data for economic programs, and during World War II they required manpower data for the military. But, assuming they would get the information they required, apparently they left census officials considerable discretion regarding data collection and other technical matters. Occasional political controversies impinged upon census administrators. In 1940, for example, several senators opposed the introduction of new income questions as an invasion of privacy. A group of senators reopened the privacy issue in 1960, but their protests failed to catch fire.

There is another way to present the history of the census, featuring politics rather than science. Historian Margo Anderson has studied the United States census from its inception. She explains that the census was born as a solution to a political dispute and that it has always been influenced by politics (Anderson 1988). In the Constitutional Convention, delegates attempted to balance the future influence of large and small states. Delegates from smaller states contended that, if congressional seats were allocated proportionally to population size, slaveholding states would acquire undue influence. States with slaves claimed that they were entitled to count them. A compromise was reached such that every slave would count as three-fifths of a person. In order to implement this allocation scheme, the census was devised to count all the persons and slaves.

Repeatedly thereafter, politics entered into censuses. One constant theme was that census jobs were traditionally assigned as spoils, through incumbent political parties. There was a series of flare-ups, as well. Three examples will suffice to show how politics has been involved with the census. The first example is the census of 1840, when the State Department conducted the nation's sixth census. The project became politicized in two ways. The secretary of state appointed chief clerk William A. Weaver to superintend the census. Weaver had no apparent qualifications for the job, but he turned the census into a "family enterprise" by hiring four relatives as staff (Cohen 1982:191). Weaver got into a dispute over which of two printers would legitimately hold the contract to print a statistical compendium to the census. Weaver gave the work to the Congress's official printer. But during the census, a new administration came to office, including Daniel Webster as the new secretary of state. Webster wished not to favor that printer, who had criticized him in print. He gave the contract to a new printer, although the first printer had already begun the job. Thus, two printers were at work producing the same compendium volume. This generated an imbroglio that resulted in a congressional hearing, after which Weaver was forced out of office.

Then, after the 1840 census, there was an argument over a set of findings that purported to show a high rate of insanity among free blacks in northern states. Indeed, the further north the state, the higher the black insanity rate, which peaked in the state of Maine, with one out of fourteen blacks shown to be insane or an "idiot" (Ibid.:192).

Edward Jarvis, a statistically minded physician in Massachusetts, who was a specialist on insanity, scrutinized the census results and discovered all sorts of simple mistakes. He found, for example, that in Worcester, Massachusetts, there was an asylum housing 133 white persons, who were shown in the census to be black. Unable to track down more errors of that sort, however, the physician began to look for some possible cause of systematic error. He found numerous cases where towns shown in the census to be all white also showed insane black persons. Focusing on the black insanity question, Jarvis published a series of magazine articles on the problems of the census. Despite Jarvis's careful research, "the correlation was put to use politically. The material on insanity from the census had enormous appeal for proslavery advocates. . . . Not only did it appear to substantiate the argument that slavery was good for the blacks; it also called up vivid images of maniacs at every northern crossroads and lent itself perfectly to the kind of emotional hyperbole that was so often employed by defenders of slavery" (Ibid.:195).

Finally, in 1844, John Quincy Adams delivered a resolution to the House of Representatives asking the secretary of state to look into allegations of errors. He also delivered a memorial to the same effect from the newly formed American Statistical Association. The House had just formed a Select Committee on Statistics, where Adams expected to find a sympathetic hearing. Adams had shown an interest in the census as early as 1841, when he prodded the secretary of state to produce census results more quickly. In 1844, though, Adams was concerned about the proslavery uses to which census statistics were being put. Adams failed to get an effective inquiry. The new secretary of state, John C. Calhoun, had no interest in discouraging the proslavery uses of the statistics and told Adams that there was no problem with the census because its many small errors simply cancelled each other out. Neither the House Select Committee on Statistics nor a senate committee to which Calhoun's request was referred chose to investigate problems in the census.

Skipping a half-century, we can see a second political census controversy around 1890, although there were others in the intervening years. Once again the controversy swirled about a superintendent of the census, Robert P. Porter (Lee 1984). Porter had headed a section in the administration of the 1880 census, then served in the controversial position of secretary of the protectionist Tariff Commission. He was also co-owner and editor of a New York newspaper. Porter was indeed a prominent figure. At the time of his appointment, the *New York Times* editorialized that "nobody can have any confidence in statistics gathered by so insincere a person for the express purpose of making out a party case." There were several kinds of complaints against the census of 1890. One newspaper complained that membership in the Republican Party was the main qualification for a census job. A magazine wrote that in Louisiana there was racial discrimination in hiring such that whites were underrepresented among enumerators and that unqualified blacks had been hired. There was a complaint that new questions on health and mortgages represented an invasion of privacy.

When census results began to emerge, they failed to show that the country's population had grown as rapidly as some might have hoped or expected, and the census was attacked for conducting an inaccurate enumeration. *The Nation* wrote of the "utter worthlessness of the census of 1890." Another magazine carried an article entitled, "A Defective Census." Finally, "By April 1892, the House drafted a resolution calling for a special investigation because it had been charged through the columns of the public press and elsewhere that the Census Bureau had been wrongfully conducted under Superintendent Porter" (Lee 1984:13). When the House conducted a hearing, it strangely failed to discuss allegations of an undercount. It did look into "paying for positions, reasons for dismissal [of employees], editing of schedules, and questionable operations within the Washington offices" (Ibid.). Despite the controversy, in the ensuing years, the 1890 enumeration came to be accepted as a decent census. Walter Willcox, a leading statistician of his day, wrote that he believed that the eleventh census was "well within one percent of the truth in its statement of the total population," (Ibid., 14). Nonetheless, when it was being conducted, it was buffeted by strong political winds from the press, and to a lesser extent, from Congress.

Our third statistics-politics episode erupted after the 1920 census. In the midst of a period of great population growth, the urban areas were outstripping the rural, and the census showed for the first time an urban majority. The census "showed that population growth of the previous decade would add representatives to those urban industrial states with large foreign-born populations" (Conk 1987:163) while taking seats from rural states with native-born people. In response, "Congress balked at passing reapportionment legislation." Some congressmen proposed excluding unnaturalized aliens from the counts, but this proposal failed passage. Eventually, the Congress simply failed to act. It never reapportioned in response to the 1920 census. The legislature passed a new census law in 1929 and waited to reapportion until after the 1930 census. Conk argues that for decades thereafter (until the one person, one vote decision), politicians lost interest in precise local population counts. They had learned a set of tricks with which to enforce rural domination, especially in state legislatures, so that aspect of the census lost salience to them.

Anderson's conclusion to her history of the census is that the United States has continually experienced a growing population which has shifted in its geography and its racial-ethnic makeup. These demographic changes, which have been revealed definitively by the censuses, have frequently required reallocation of congressional seats. Those states that failed to benefit from growth were not always amenable to such reallocations. Thus from time to time the census has been connected with fundamental political controversies. The controversies around the censuses of 1840, 1890, and 1920 may be seen as worst-case illustrations of the conjunction between politics and the census.

3 Prelude to the 1980 Census: Issues in the 1960s and 1970s

THE POLITICAL salience of census statistics began to rise in the 1960s. In 1962, the Supreme Court's decision in *Baker* v. *Carr* established the "one person, one vote" principle. Prior to this decision, for more than a half century, the political system was tilted toward rural America, with congressional and state legislative districts apportioned such that rural residents were overrepresented and city residents were underrepresented (Anderson 1988). The more the urban majority grew, the more apparent this inequity became, and the more intolerable it was to urban leaders. After *Baker* v. *Carr*, though, federal courts applied the one person, one vote principle of equal representation with increasing rigor in cases referring to distortions in congressional districts and state legislative districts. In such cases judges frequently required that the size differences between districts had to be extremely small, sometimes as small as three or four persons. Then, in 1965, the Voting Rights Act went further in helping to outlaw those forms of gerrymandering that had the effect of creating districts that undermined black voting power (Thernstrom 1987). The act plus the court decisions bestowed a new political potential upon small-area statistics since they could be utilized in struggles over legislative redistricting.

Privacy reemerged as an issue in the late 1960s (Conk 1987). Beginning in 1967, Congressman Jackson Betts promoted the idea that the census was overly intrusive, containing too many questions, some of which were of no concern to the government

(Eckler 1972). He contended that it was wrong to compel people, by force of law, to answer census questions. Representative Betts promoted legislation to cut the number of census questions severely and to remove criminal sanctions from the refusal to answer. He was joined in 1969 by conservative senators who introduced equivalent legislation in their chamber. In 1969, there were hearings on these bills in both houses of Congress. Census administrators along with data users defended the existing system, and eventually, the restrictive legislation failed (U.S. Congress, 1970). So, once again, invasion of privacy failed to catch hold as a major issue.

The rise of poverty and race relations as major national issues was a much more prominent sociopolitical development of the 1960s. There were the civil rights movement and its offshoots such as the Mexican-American Brown Power movement. In addition, the federal government initiated the War Against Poverty and the Great Society programs. These movements and programs stated clearly that poor minority groups had a legitimate claim to better conditions in cities. Several of the social welfare programs of President Johnson's Great Society distributed dollars by means of statistically driven grant-in-aid formulas. The proliferation of federal grants programs and the cities' increasing dependence upon them tended to heighten the political salience of census statistics. Such formulas often incorporated population size, as measured or estimated by the Census Bureau, as a major factor. By 1978 there were more than one hundred such programs, covering a wide range of concerns, from preschool education (Headstart) to urban mass transportation (U.S. Congress 1978). The formulas themselves ranged from the simple to the complicated. For example, a program that distributed assistance to states for schools used a simple formula: each state's grant was "based on the ratio of the population in the State to the population of all the States" (U.S. Congress 1978:23).

On the other hand, Community Development Block Grants were distributed to large urban jurisdictions by means of a much more complicated process. The program had two different formulas and each jurisdiction got its grant from the one that gave a larger allotment. "The first formula is based on each jurisdiction's percentage share of three weighted factors: population (25 percent), population below the poverty level (50 percent), and the number of housing units in each jurisdiction with 1.01 persons per room [an indicator of overcrowding] (25 percent)" (U.S. General Accounting Office 1987:143). The alternate formula also had three factors, but instead of using population, it used "growth rate lag," defined as "the lag in a jurisdiction's population growth between 1960 and 1980 in relation to the total growth of all jurisdictions in that period." This version was intended to protect the interests of cities and counties that were losing population. Thus their lack of growth was used as an indicator of their need for funding under this program.

In the 1970s and 1980s, the federal government continued to distribute grants to states and localities by means of formulas, and in 1987 the General Accounting Office released a comprehensive analysis of the formulas themselves. Analyzing data from fiscal 1984, the GAO discovered that there were 142 programs that accounted for the distribution of almost $85 billion per year (U.S. General Accounting Office 1987:11). There were thirteen categories of data that were used in the various formulas, ranging from environmental features through health levels, but the most frequently used category was population. "Of the 142 formula grant programs, 93 (65 percent) used some measure of population to allocate funds" (Ibid.:384). Furthermore, the single most commonly used data source was the decennial census.

These formula-funded grant programs became politically important because of the big cities' increasing dependence on federal dollars. During the twenty-five years following World War II, the cities of the northeastern quadrant of the United States fell upon hard times. Rapid suburbanization cost them large segments of their middle-class and working-class populations. As commerce and industry suburbanized, the cities also lost jobs and enterprises, so their tax bases were weakened. Retaining substantial numbers of poor people along with old, deteriorating infrastructures, municipalities had enormous expenses for which they could not pay. Cities faced economic troubles that were so severe that some, including Cleveland and New York City, came to the brink of bankruptcy. The cities' dependency on federal aid was accentuated by the General Revenue Sharing program, initiated by President Nixon in 1972. Revenue sharing, which became the largest and most pervasive formula-funded program, sent monthly checks to every county and local government in the country, approximately 39,000 in all. The program's allocation formula was heavily weighted toward current population. By 1976, the government was distributing $6.2 billion per year via this program, roughly $30 for every man, woman, and child. The program expired in 1986 when the last payments were made. Nonetheless, general revenue sharing had the same effect as the one person, one vote principle: it heightened the political value of small-area statistics.

In 1967, social scientists took cognizance of the new political relevance of statistics. Daniel Patrick Moynihan, then director of the Harvard-MIT Joint Center for Urban Studies, asked David Heer, a sociologist-demographer on the Harvard faculty, to organize a conference to explore the problems of statistics pertaining to urban black populations. As Heer wrote, "Moynihan asked me if I would plan a conference that would (1) publicize the fact that many Negroes had not been counted in the 1960 census, and (2) attempt to arouse national concern about the matter" (Heer 1968:2). The conference, which was held in Washington, D.C. in June 1967, brought together fifty-seven individuals including government officials, mostly from the federal statistical agencies, municipal officials, university professors, foundation administrators, and others with backgrounds in statistics or extensive knowledge of the situation of the black population. The conferees heard and discussed seven technical papers on such topics as "Procedural difficulties in taking past censuses in predominantly Negro, Puerto Rican, and Mexican Areas." Papers and discussions explicitly noted the nexus between statistics and certain problems in the real world. The conference passed a set of resolutions, based upon the following assumptions:

Specifically, we hold that where a group defined by racial or ethnic terms and concentrated in specific political jurisdictions is significantly undercounted in relation to other groups, then individual members of that group are thereby deprived of the constitutional right to equal representation in the House of Representatives and, by inference, in other legislative bodies. Further, we hold that individual members of such a group are thereby deprived of their right to equal protection of the laws as provided in Section I of the 14th Amendment to the Constitution, in that they are deprived of their entitlement to partake in federal and other programs designed for areas and populations with their characteristics. (Ibid.:176)

Then they made a plea to Congress for funding:

We feel it is incumbent on the Congress to provide the Bureau of the Census, the National Center of Health Statistics, the Bureau of Labor Statistics, and such other agencies as are concerned, with the funds necessary to obtain a full enumeration of all groups in the population. (Ibid.:177)

The rest of the resolutions made specific technical recommendations for improving the census as well as vital statistics (birth, death, marriage, and divorce) by race, across the nation. Overcoming the undercount meant counting better.

When the 1970 census was taken, the bureau was deluged by complaints. By November of that year, the number of complaints had grown to almost 1,900 (Panel on Decennial Census Plans 1978:11). Most of the complaints said that the introduction of the mailout-mailback procedure, which had been used to cover 60 percent of the nation, had been a mistake. Mailout-mailback was the bureau's radically new way of collecting information. Instead of sending enumerators to conduct an interview at every household, the census mailed questionnaires for "self-enumeration." Someone at each household was supposed to supply information for everyone in the group; the respondent was supposed to fill in the blanks. Mailout-mailback was based on residential address lists. Critics of this new procedure said that the commercially prepared mailing lists, purchased from the Donnelly Corporation, were far from complete and that postal workers in many places had failed to work diligently to bring them up to standard. Furthermore, the critics said that people in general were disinclined to fill in and mail back questionnaires.

By September 1970 the bureau had released preliminary population counts for localities and, in response to complaints from municipal officials, the House subcommittee on census and statistics held hearings on the accuracy of 1970 census enumeration (U.S. Congress 1970). In addition to census officials, fifty-one individuals testified before the subcommittee at a hearing that met for seven days. The subcommittee received 102 written communications. Members of Congress spoke at the hearing along with mayors from small towns and big cities. New York's Mayor John Lindsay, Chicago's Richard J. Daley, and Detroit's Roman S. Gribbs complained to the subcommittee about the undercount in

1970. Speakers at the hearings included representatives of organizations such as the Puerto Rican Association for Community Affairs and the National Urban League, Mexican-Americans and Chinese-Americans. All of the minority spokespersons complained about the ill effects of disproportionate undercounts of their groups, and they demanded improved procedures. Whitney M. Young, Jr., executive director of the National Urban League, submitted a position paper which began with a riddle: "[Question] What comes once every ten years and can't count? [Answer] The United States Census" (U.S. Congress 1970:107).

A typical grievance came from a mayor who maintained that his community had more people than the census counted. I suspect the mayor had not anticipated a loss in population or had anticipated much more growth than the census indicated. Often municipal administrations had analyzed the numbers of new houses and apartments constructed, utility hookups, telephone connections, and drivers licenses, and used the growth of these numbers to show that population must have grown. Apparently these municipal officials were unaware of the falling size of American households. In 1960, the average household was composed of 3.33 persons. By 1970, this number had fallen to 3.14. This decline meant that a community could perhaps add housing units and households without adding population. At this time the end of the postwar baby boom and the fact that young adults were leaving home at a younger age contributed to the reduction in household size. Most communities were enjoying the postwar prosperity, which generated certain trends, such as an increase in the numbers of telephones, that erroneously implied population growth.

Other complaints were made by mayors of university towns like Champaign, Illinois and Eugene, Oregon. In those cases, city officials contended that the university's own records of students in dormitories exceeded the census numbers. However this did not necessarily mean that the college officials had better counts than those of the census officials. In the case of Champaign's complaint,

The Chicago Regional Office [of the bureau] obtained a roster of students at the University of Illinois. After checking this roster against census enumeration records, the initial accuracy of the student enumeration was confirmed. The 7,000 students were living in housing units not owned or operated by the university and were, therefore, counted as part of the general population, rather than as students residing on campus. The 7,000 shortage . . . was, therefore, not an undercount. (U.S. Congress 1970:437).

The complaint resulted from ignorance of the census Rules of Residence.

Other complaints were based upon the plaintiffs' ignorance of other census technicalities, particularly those of census geography. For example Huntington, West Virginia complained that the census must have been wrong when it announced a preliminary total of 72,970 which represented a loss of population. With the help of their congressman and the local census office, the community organized a volunteer group to recanvass Huntington's households. They produced forms for 732 households that the census allegedly missed. Altogether, these forms might have added between 1,000 and 2,000 individuals to the city's total. The census office then checked all of those new forms. "By comparing these 732 forms with data already recorded, it was discovered that all but 71 households (representing 183 persons) were either outside the city of Huntington or duplicated households and individuals already counted." Then there was a field check which determined that

four addresses were nonexistent, three were in the county and outside the Huntington city limits, two had the wrong name entered, and eight were households which had moved into Huntington since April 1 and knew they had been counted elsewhere.

So this boiled down to 30 households and 90 people. . . . They were living in the rear or over commercial buildings or were transient or floater population that simply had not been caught in the census. (U.S. Congress 1970:219)

Altogether, this extraordinary check yielded an increment of approximately one-tenth of one percent to the city's population, but it also validated the quality of the original enumeration.

Several complaints against the 1970 census went directly into the courts (U.S. Congress 1970:13–16). By the time of the September congressional hearings, five suits had been filed. One case (*Davis et al.* v. *Stans et al.*) pertained to voting rights, saying that an undercount defeats the one person, one vote principle. Two suits, one representing Chinese-Americans and another representing Chicanos (*Quon et al.* v. *Stans et al.* and *Prieto et al.* v. *Stans et al.*), demanded face-to-face enumeration because the mailout-mailback system would fail to count poor minority groups accurately. In another case (*Borough of Bethel Park* v. *Stans et al.*) several Pennsylvania municipalities challenged the census' residence rules. The plaintiff said that the bureau was using inappropriate rules for determining state of residence for college students, members of the armed services, inmates of institutions, and Americans overseas.

The government (i.e., the bureau) won all of the cases. In one group of cases, the courts held that the mayors lacked standing to sue. The courts held that the mayors could not demonstrate injuries caused directly by the bureau's actions. In another group of cases, judges relied upon a basic principle of administrative law which states that administrators' decisions may not be arbitrary or capricious; judges are to assume that administrators' decisions are not to be second-guessed in the courtroom if it can be shown that those decisions were made by a reasonable process. Years later, census officials discovered that not all judges would apply this particular principle. Despite their victories, census administrators learned from the 1970 cases that their actions could be reviewed by the courts (Harvard Law Review 1981).

In late 1971, Congressman John Dellenback of Oregon became involved in the census controversy. As mentioned above, the city of Eugene, which was in his district, challenged the accuracy of its census count. Representing the city of Eugene, Dellenback made inquiries at the bureau. In this context he became familiar with the census procedure known as imputation, by which statisticians handle the problem of missing data by creating and filling in numbers on some justifiable basis. Representative Dellenback inquired about the addition of persons to census totals at the state level and in particular, he asked about two new imputation procedures used in 1970: the postenumeration post office check (PEPOC) and the national vacancy check. While Representative Dellenback did not directly challenge the validity of imputation, he continued for several months to press the director for numbers and explanations (Dellenback 1991). The question of imputation came up repeatedly in census controversies for more than a decade thereafter.

The Nixon administration became concerned with the political uses and effects of statistics and attempted to influence the statistical agencies. They took a number of actions that disrupted the normal workings of the Census Bureau and threatened its own conception of itself as nonpolitical. Apparently, the administration viewed the bureau's leadership as liberal Democrats, especially the senior professionals, the so-called "class of '40," who had joined the civil service around the time of the 1940 census and who were therefore considered to be vestiges of the New Deal (Taeuber 1987).

After his election in 1968, Nixon brought in George K. Brown as director of the bureau. Nixon also brought Lance Tarrance from the Republican National Committee to the bureau to serve as special assistant to the director. According to former Acting Director Daniel Levine, "Lance set up an organization within the bureau, a small group. . . . They were concerned about the order in which small-area data were released. Republicans were the first to computerize the ways in which to redistrict a state. The order of release was important to them—who gets it first, who got it altogether. They wanted to expedite it for certain users" (Levine 1983b). In addition to the distribution of small-area data, the Nixonians were concerned with the "messages" attached to statistical reports. Based upon results from current population surveys, the bureau's population division had reported that "the number of 'persons living in poverty' had increased under President Nixon" (Magnet 1981). This was not the sort of message the administration wanted to promote. The White House assigned a public relations officer to the population division who came to meetings to monitor the proceedings and to review (or censor) reports. According to Conrad Taeuber, then associate director for demographic fields, "Nothing was suppressed. It was more a matter of emphasis—'why go into the unpleasant aspects of life in the U.S.?' " (Ibid.:89). The Nixon administration reorganized the statistical programs of the Department of Commerce into a new unit called the Social and Economic Statistics Administration (SESA). The Census Bureau was placed in the new agency, which meant that the bureau's director would have to report to its head. The Senate held a hearing to confirm the agency's first head. At that hearing, Senator William Proxmire said of the nominee, "Mr. Edward Failor is totally unqualified to head SESA. He has no professional statistical background whatsoever. He comes to the position directly from the Committee to Re-Elect the President, where he wrote canned partisan speeches for congressional candidates" (U.S.

Congress 1973:40). Apparently this political involvement in the bureau's affairs demoralized the professional staff and lead to the resignation of several key staffers, including the widely respected Conrad Taeuber.

By the winter of 1971–1972, the statistical profession had become concerned about this series of events. At the 1972 meeting of the American Statistical Association, Philip Hauser spoke on the subject of "Statistics and Politics." He recounted the sequence of events that led to the "premature retirement" of several senior officials of the bureau; "the order to the Bureau of the Census to stop using 'Poverty' in the title of its annual report on the poor"; and the placement within the bureau of five persons whom he called "political commissars" (Hauser 1972). He referred to "the collapse of morale among statisticians in a number of agencies by reason of 'the reign of terror' generated by the presence of political functionaries placed at the statistical operating and analytical levels." In his conclusion, Hauser said, "Never have I witnessed as widespread and insistent efforts to politicize the statistical enterprise" (Hauser 1972:96. See also American Statistical Association-Federal Statistics Users Conference, 1973, and U.S. Congress, 1972).

The Federal Statistics Users' Conference, which represented companies and universities that used federal statistics, appointed a committee to obtain "details and information concerning the personnel reassignments and reorganization of federal statistical agencies." The American Statistical Association joined with the Conference to form a "Committee on the Integrity of Federal Statistics," which issued a report (American Statistical Association, 1973). Their report was more moderate than Hauser's, but appeared to be equally concerned about the reports of political involvement in the federal statistical agencies. The committee's principal concern was that, even though it had not been demonstrated that anyone had "fudged" any statistics, a continuing pattern of political appointments and other unseemly involvement would undermine the public's confidence in the impartiality and accuracy of federal statistics (Ibid. 1973).

In 1972, the House subcommittee on census and statistics also conducted an inquiry into politicization of federal statistics. The House subcommittee looked specifically at the discontinuation of press conferences at the Bureau of Labor Statistics and at the planned reorganization of the federal agencies, as prescribed by the Office of Management and Budget. The subcommittee's staff conducted dozens of interviews with present and former employees of the main statistical agencies as well as with journalists, outside statisticians, and others. The subcommittee's report referred to events at the bureau, saying,

There appeared to have been two political appointments at census. One was to an administrative position at the top management level. This individual's effect on census operations has been insulated against by the integrity and professionalism of the long-term key professionals responsible for census operations. However, the individual has attempted on many occasions to politically influence the course of events at the Bureau of the Census. (U.S. Congress 1972:5)

Nonetheless, the subcommittee concluded that government statistics had not been corrupted. They reported that their informants were "practically unanimous" in saying that "the gathering, assembling, and reporting of the statistical data was free of politics." They were confident of the quality of the products of the statistical agencies.

Overall, the actions of the Nixon administration showed the officials of the statistical agencies that when a presidential administration gets concerned about statistics, it may attempt to gain control over them. While it was never shown that any statistical products were compromised, the administration's actions in the early 1970s demoralized the statisticians and made them defensive. Also, particular personnel actions in the bureau resulted in the losses by resignation of experienced, valuable individuals.

After Richard Nixon was elected to his second term, he accepted a letter of resignation from George H. Brown as director of the bureau. The president then nominated Vincent Barabba as a replacement. Barabba's qualifications for the directorship were slim. At the time of his appointment, he was chairman of the board of Decision Making Information, Inc., a market research firm. He had conducted polls for Nixon's reelection campaign. When he was nominated to be director, he had served on the American Marketing Association's Census Advisory Committee for twenty months. At Barabba's Senate confirmation nomination hearing, Senator Proxmire said that Barabba's experience was only marginally involved in professional statistical activities and that he was generally unqualified. At that same hearing, the president of the American Statistical Association testified in opposition to Barabba's appointment. Several other professional associations, including the American Economic Association and the American Sociological Association, went on record as favoring nonpolitical appointments of statistically qualified individuals as heads of federal statistical agencies. But Barabba was appointed and went on to become an outstanding director.

In 1976, Jimmy Carter was elected president and he nominated a new director, Emanuel "Manny" Plotkin, who was a marketing executive at Sears and "a strong favorite of the President's own pollster, Patrick Caddell" (Yagoda 1980). This proved to be an unfortunate appointment. Plotkin was inept at running the agency, he kept his office closed, and generally failed to develop a good working relationship with the senior staff. Plotkin was also ineffectual in dealing with Congress, which turned out to be a serious liability to the bureau in 1977 when it was struggling to defeat the Census Reform Act.

Before each census, the bureau conducts surveys, "pretests," and "dress rehearsals," to test their procedures and materials. In 1976 and 1977, they conducted pretests in Oakland, California, and Camden, New Jersey. Unlike the pretests of previous decades, these two attracted considerable political attention. In response, Representative William Lehman, chairman of the subcommittee on census and population, held hearings on the subject. The first hearing was held in Oakland in March 1977, even before the pretest there had been finished. Local officials and representatives of ethnic organizations—Latino, Filipino, African-American and Chinese-American took the opportunity to criticize the census plans. They said the bureau's method for testing and hiring field workers was biased, that it had worded the question on Hispanic ethnicity poorly, and that it had failed to develop publicity materials in any language but English. Because of this, the Californians anticipated a low-quality pretest to be followed by a census in which minority groups would be badly undercounted.

The second hearing was held in Camden after the pretest there was completed, in response to a complaint from the city's mayor, who rejected the population total reported by the bureau. The mayor claimed that the city's population was undercounted in the pretest, which counted 87,305—down from 102,551 enumerated in 1970. The city's mayor assembled data from school enrollments, income tax returns, births and deaths, construction permits, and utility hookups, to support his claim. Camden's congressman advised the subcommittee, "If Camden is an example of what we can expect from the Census Bureau in 1980, then we had better prepare ourselves for a disaster of national proportions" (U.S. Congress 1977a:124). Apparently the mayor found a sympathetic audience in the committee; the representatives, especially Lehman and Patricia Schroeder, agreed with statements about how "defensive" and "recalcitrant" the bureau was. (Ultimately, the 1980 census confirmed that Camden's loss of population was just what the pretest had shown.)

In August 1977, Representative Lehman introduced the Census Reform Act (U.S. Congress 1977b). The act purported to solve two major problems of the census that arose around 1970; its supposed burden on the privacy of the citizenry, and the problem of resolving disputes between municipalities and the bureau. The act had two main provisions. The first proposed a "two-stage" census. Stage one would consist of a seven-question census of all households that everyone would be compelled to answer. Stage two would have more detailed questions (equivalent to the long-form) that would be distributed to a sample of households. Answering questions at stage two would be voluntary. This would solve the privacy problem by giving the individual the right not to answer all but the most basic questions. Likewise, it would reduce the burden on anyone who refused to answer. The second provision required the bureau to develop an internal evaluation unit that could challenge and even overrule census conclusions. This independent unit would resolve complaints from municipalities and other governmental units.

Census administrators rejected the Census Reform Act. They said that the two-stage census would be unwieldy and expensive. They claimed that it would not reduce the burden upon the public because everyone who fell into the second stage sample would have been bothered twice, whereas under the old system even if they had to fill out the long form they would have gotten it over with in one operation. Census administrators also rejected the idea of an independent evaluation unit. The bureau's director said that no administrator could be expected to house an antagonistic unit under his own roof. He also objected to a provision of the act that gave local governmental officials access to census records for their communities so that they could check them. This proposal threatened to undermine the confidentiality provisions of Title 13. The Census Reform Act would probably have been unwelcome to census officials at any time, but as it happened, it arrived at a particularly inopportune moment. Congressman Lehman introduced it in 1977, a little over two years before the census, a time when officials at the bureau should have been working on the census itself. Instead their attention was on fighting the act.

The subcommittee on census and population held a hearing on the proposed act at which a number of statisticians and data users testified. They all advised the subcommittee not to enact the Census Reform Act and ultimately it was defeated.

While the census administrators succeeded in quashing the act, the hearing revealed a poor relationship between the subcommittee and the bureau; there was an unpleasant flavor to the representative's remarks at the hearing (U.S. Congress 1977b; Volner, 1981). For example, Representative Solarz asked why census surveys could not be taken as quickly as public opinion polls and Representative Schroeder suggested that by resisting the proposed new evaluation unit, the census officials were simply guarding their turf. Representatives delivered gratuitous insults during the hearings. Representative Leach described his perception of the "exasperation of Congress with the Census Bureau" and the bureau's "inbreeding." Later, subcommittee Chairman Lehman remarked, "I appreciate the professionalism of the Census Bureau. Also, I think that there is a limitation of professionalism, there is an ivory tower, holier-than-thou attitude that you can get in professionalism that somehow or another gets shut off from the real world" (U.S. Congress 1977a: 103). He went on to suggest that the census officials were "sitting up in their ivory-tower playpens juggling figures." Census officials were no kinder in their remarks about the members of Congress. One official claimed that Schroeder, who had previously chaired the subcommittee, had absolutely no interest in the census. Another referred to Lehman as a former used-car salesman (which he was) who had once said that he had no interest in statistics except about baseball. Both sets of 1977 hearing transcripts validate Martha W. Volner's (1981:33) assertion that "the relationship between the House of

Representatives and the Census Bureau was acrimonious during most of the decade."

In late 1978, according to Courtenay Slater, who was then chief economist at the Department of Commerce, officials at the department asked whether the Census Bureau was set up to do the job of the forthcoming census. Their answer was yes, they had done a careful job of planning, but they concluded that "Manny Plotkin was not up to the job" (Slater 1983). The Carter administration then made an inspired, move. It asked Barabba, a Republican, to return to the directorship of the bureau to take charge of the forthcoming census, which he did.

At the same time, the secretary of commerce asked the Committee on National Statistics of the National Research Council (NRC) to undertake an independent evaluation of the technical and procedural designs for the 1980 census (Panel on Decennial Census Plans 1978:vii). Eight years earlier, the bureau had asked the NRC for advice on ways to improve the completeness and accuracy of information collected in censuses and surveys. A special committee was formed which issued a report three years later, entitled, *America's Uncounted People* (National Academy of Sciences 1972). The thrust of its message was that the bureau should do more research on the undercount, asking, how do people respond to the census?; who is missed? why are they missed? The committee advised the bureau to use new research methods such as urban ethnography and to get more involved with the other social sciences in order to get new insights into the undercount problem.

In December 1977 the NRC responded to the second request by establishing a 14-member Panel on Decennial Census Plans under the aegis of the Committee on National Statistics. The panel must have done its work rapidly, because it published its report entitled *Counting the People in 1980: An Appraisal of Census Plans* in less than a year. The report reflects intensive scrutiny of the plans for the forthcoming census. Although the panel questioned and criticized many of the plans' particulars, they approved of the overall package. "These plans are well considered, reflect the concerns expressed by advisory and other groups . . . and can be expected to be generally effective," they wrote. "Several innovations have the potential for considerably improving the enumeration" Panel on Decennial Census Plans, 1978:126). The panel did not hesitate to question specific aspects of the plans and to make suggestions. They were particularly critical of the format and wording of the census questionnaire, especially the long form. They advised census administrators to conduct research to discover if respondents adequately understood it and whether it could be made easier to use. They advised the bureau to study the costs and benefits of coverage improvement procedures. They asked census administrators to improve their methods of training temporary staff members. However, the panel's main conclusion was that the census plans for 1980 were sufficient to get the job done.

The political environment of the census shifted dramatically in the 1960s and 1970s. During this period the Census Bureau experienced political challenges from the Nixon administration and from the House Subcommittee on Census and Population. But more importantly statistics became more valuable in new ways, especially to minority groups and municipalities. In conjunction with the rules established by the Voting Rights Act, the one person one vote principle established new ways of drawing political maps, such as congressional districts. Likewise a proliferation of federal grant-in-aid programs that distributed dollars through formulas also relied upon census statistics and made them valuable. Across the country communities and minorities began to examine closely their population numbers. Each one had the same goal: to maximize its own numbers. Many were willing to complain to Congress, to the administration, or to the Census Bureau itself. Thus, the bureau had to conduct censuses within an environment of increasing demands and heightened scrutiny.

4 Measuring and
Overcoming the Undercount

IF AN UNDERCOUNT refers to people who were not counted, how does anyone know that they exist, let alone their numbers? The United States had taken censuses for 150 years before demography developed methods with which to measure census coverage. George Washington suspected an undercount in the very first census taken. Even before the final results were in, the president wrote that he expected they would not reach four million, as they should. (The reported total was 3.9 million.) Washington said that the numbers would be undercounted because some people had "religious scruples" against a census, others feared the imposition of a tax, and some of the officers responsible for enumeration had been negligent (Pritzker and Rothwell 1968:56). While there were occasional squabbles over undercounts in the nineteenth century, early twentieth-century census officials assumed that censuses counted all the people. As Hauser (1981) has written, "Prior to the 1940 Census of Population, the officials of the U.S. Bureau of the Census, largely nonprofessionals, insisted that the census canvass counted everybody in the nation."

How to Measure an Undercount

After the 1940 census, however, the bureau acknowledged that there was an undercount and researchers began attempts to measure the extent of undercoverage. At first the question of census coverage was primarily a matter of academic interest. Demographers began to measure census coverage in the 1940s, and more intensively after the 1950 census. One of the first studies was by Daniel Price, who took advantage of the fact that in 1940, in addition to the decennial census, there was also a compulsory registration of all males for military conscription. Price compared the numbers of men counted in each enumeration. He discovered that the draft had registered more men than the census had enumerated; the census had counted 97 percent of the men, leaving a 3 percent net undercount. This first study also showed a racial differential with 13 percent of black males being undercounted (Price 1947).

The bureau conducted another early study in which results of the 1940 census were matched against birth records, indicating a "considerable underenumeration of infants" (Pritzker and Rothwell 1968:71). Census officials reasoned that perhaps people failed to report their infants because they did not think of them as household members or because they put them into another category. The bureau conducted a similar match in 1950, and then contacted households that had been identified in the birth records. These contacts revealed that 80 percent of the times that babies were missed in the count, their parents were missed also. So, the problem was not merely an underreporting of infants per se, but rather of entire families in which infants were present. Therefore, "improved questions about babies would have been no solution for the redefined problem. It called for more thorough canvassing techniques" (Pritzker and Rothwell 1968:71).

The next landmark appeared eight years later when Princeton University's Ansley Coale (1955) published the first of his studies of error patterns in censuses. Coale is considered to be the originator of the demographic method, which is one of the two major approaches to measuring census coverage. In order to use the demographic method, an analyst requires several sets of data: the results of previous censuses; data on births, by sex and race, since the last census; age-specific death rates for the years since the last census; and data on immigration and emigration. (Unfortunately, migration data are far less accurate than census, birth, and death statistics.) Using those materials, demographers can compute how many persons the population contains at any given time, by age, sex, and race. For example, assume that the census of 1960 counted a certain number of twenty-two-year-old white women. These women would be twenty-three years old in 1961, twenty-four years old in 1962, and so on. The number of women in that age cohort could shrink by emigration and by death and the number could expand by immigration. The National Center for Health Statistics keeps track of deaths by age, sex, and race. The statistical division of the Immigration and Naturalization Service keeps track of immigration. Given this information, it is possible to estimate the number of women in this age group from year to year. In a census year, that estimated number becomes a benchmark against which to evaluate census coverage. In order to estimate a national population total, demographers at the bureau make such calculations not just for twenty-three-year-old white women, but for every age-sex-race category. The only age group that cannot be computed in this way for a census year is children under 10 years of age, since they were not alive at the time of the previous census. Their numbers are estimated on the basis of the last 10 years' birth records, subjected to the appropriate death rates, along with measures of immigration and emigration in those age-sex-race categories. After an actual census is taken, demographers can compare the number counted in that age-sex category with the number calculated by demographic analysis. If the 1970 census failed to count the calculated number of thirty-two-year-old white females, the demographic method would suggest that an error had occurred (an under- or overcount.)

In developing the demographic method, Ansley Coale built upon studies of "age-heaping" in censuses, a form of error that had been recognized earlier (Myers 1940). In most censuses, more people report ages ending in 0 and 5 than any other number: apparently some people round their ages to the nearest multiple of 5 or 10 when they answer census questions. Demographers have developed techniques with which to reassign some of these cases to other age categories in order to make the census numbers conform with other known facts such as the numbers of persons born in past periods and the rates at which those birth cohorts have died off. Looking at past censuses, Coale applied these techniques, and he carefully examined sex ratios by age, which revealed error patterns in census data. Sex ratios are useful in analyzing census coverage because sex ratios at birth are known and, for any given age cohort, the death rates over its life period are also known. If the sex ratio of an age group in a census departs from what it should be, an error in the census is presumed. Coale utilized data from four sources external to the census: births in years prior to the census and deaths of young children; estimates of populations by age from recent censuses combined with estimates of deaths and internal migration in intercensal periods; draft registration of males of military age; and the 1950 postenumeration survey. Based upon these data and correcting for error patterns, he estimated population in 1950 by age, sex, and race. Coale concluded that the census must have missed approximately 5 million people in April 1950 when it counted about 151 million and that young black males were the most likely to be missed.

Continuing to examine the error patterns of censuses, Coale and Zelnik (1963) refined the demographic method and succeeded in estimating census undercounts by age for the white population in the years 1880 to 1960. They generated a series of successive approximations of the population at each point in time after adjusting for age-heaping and other sources of error. They estimated annual fertility (births) which they took into account along with estimates of mortality. Coale and Rives (1973) then applied demographic analysis to the censuses from 1880 to 1970, focusing on the black population. They took advantage of the fact that international migration had a negligible effect on the black population, so they could treat the population as closed. After constructing life tables and computing total fertility rates, they were able to reconstruct the black population in census years by means of successive approximations. According to Coale and Rives, the greatest net undercount occurred in 1920, when 16 percent of black females and 14.4 percent of black males were missed. In each census after 1920, the male undercount exceeded the female. Census coverage of females improved consistently, with the undercount falling to 5.4 percent by 1970. Black male coverage improved somewhat also, but by 1970 there was still a 10.4 percent undercount.

Since the time of its introduction, it was apparent that the demographic method had two major limitations. First, it was mainly applicable at the national level, not to smaller areas. Demographic analysis could not be used effectively for states, cities, and other subnational areas because internal migration, movement from place to place within the country, has powerful effects upon local populations. The American statistical system lacks a universal, accurate method of recording internal migration. At the national level, even though they were not of the highest quality, the statistics on immigration and emigration, at least until 1980, were adequate for demographic analysis. The method's second major limitation was that it applied to the total white and black populations, but not to Hispanics. This is because traditionally the birth and death certificates that are used to produce natality and mortality rates have not recorded whether mother, father, or child is Hispanic. Since 1978 the standard birth record recommended by the National Center for Health Statistics has had a Hispanic category, but only twenty-three states and the District of Columbia use it.

For 1950, demographic analysis showed a net undercount of 3.3 percent. The net undercount fell in 1960 to 2.7 percent and again in 1970 to 2.2 percent. As soon as demographic analyses were used, they showed a far greater undercount of blacks than of whites. In 1950 the census missed 9.7 percent of "Negroes and other nonwhites," a rate approximately four times that of whites. In 1960 the black undercount was 8.0 percent and in 1970, 7.6 percent. The black undercount rate in 1960 was four times as great as white, and in 1970 it was five times as great.

In 1950 the bureau introduced another way of measuring census coverage, the postenumeration survey. The idea of the postenumeration survey was to draw a sample of dwelling units and to send interviewers to the households soon after the census to re-interview them. Then, after the completion of the survey, clerks at the bureau would check the two sources of data (the post-census survey and the census) against each other; the results of this would help reveal the accuracy of the census. Post-enumeration surveys became the second fundamental tool with which to discover undercounts.

In the words of Ivan Fellegi, Chief Statistician of Statistics Canada, the strategy behind the postenumeration survey was to "do it again, but better" (Citro and Cohen 1985:123). Census enumerators are hired and trained quickly, but the postenumeration survey was to be done by experienced interviewers who had already worked for the Census Bureau on other surveys, and they were to be supervised by experienced supervisors. Presumably the work of experienced interviewers would be more complete and accurate than that of ordinary enumerators. Before the sample was drawn, these survey interviewers were to list the dwellings in certain areas, presumably preparing more complete lists than the census had. If the survey's lists were really superior to the census's lists, then entire households that had been missed by the census could fall into the sample.

After the survey, clerks compared individual survey and census protocols for the same areas and dwellings in an attempt to "match" them. The clerks took each housing unit in the survey's address list and looked into the census files to see if a household was found there. The clerks also took each person in the survey and looked in the census files to find the person's census return. The objective was to discover whether there were persons in the census who were not found in the survey and likewise whether there were persons in the survey who were not found in the census. Assuming that the survey fieldwork was done more accurately than the census, the extent to which the survey found people that the census missed was a good representation of census undercount. The postenumeration survey looked for persons or households that had been erroneously enumerated at a particular location and ones that had been missed, and ones that had been correctly enumerated by the census. The first category represented a gross overcount, the second category represented a gross undercount, and the third category was ok. The difference between the first two categories would reveal the net undercount. The problem remained, however, that there may have been some persons or households that were missed by both the census and the survey.

In executing this first postenumeration survey, researchers encountered the problem of "correlation bias," which was to persist for decades. The census and the survey represent two separate systems of data collection. In order to use their results together, analysts must make the assumption of independence, meaning that an individual's probability of being "captured" in the survey is independent of his or her probability of being captured in the census. Unfortunately, however, it appears that this assumption is not completely valid insofar as there are some categories of individuals who are unlikely to be captured by either data collection system.

In 1960 census officials conducted another postenumeration

survey with a larger sample. They also tested a new technique, the record check, in an attempt to overcome correlation bias. The plan was to find administrative lists that contained names and addresses of large numbers of persons that might include persons in those groups that were likely to be missed by the census and the postenumeration survey. Names on these lists could be matched against census returns to see if any individuals had been missed. Two lists were chosen, elderly recipients of social security benefits in March 1960, and samples of students enrolled in college in spring 1960 (Citro and Cohen 1985:128). These matches yielded an estimated undercount of between 2.5 and 2.7 percent of college students and between 5.1 and 5.7 percent of the elderly.

In a separate project, census officials tried to conduct a "reverse record check." This procedure takes a sample of individuals from the previous census, augmented by a sample of immigrants and children who had been born in the previous ten years, and tries to determine whether they had been counted in the new census. The bureau drew a sample of about 7,200 names from four sources: the 1950 census, the 1950 post-enumeration survey, birth records, and alien registrations supplied by the Immigration and Naturalization Service. Then they attempted to find these same individuals in the 1960 census. Unfortunately, this project was fruitless because of another persistent problem; it is inherently difficult to match records from one list to another. In nearly 1,200 cases, or 16.5 percent of the total, it was impossible to tell definitively whether a person had or had not been counted in the census (Ibid.:120). With such a high proportion of unmatched cases they were unable to estimate the undercount with this method.

After the 1970 census, there was another coverage study, but census officials decided not to conduct a special survey. They chose instead to match the census to the March 1970 Current Population Survey. They also conducted record check studies of specific population groups such as persons age 65 and over, based on a sample of approximately 8,000 names from Medicare files.

For 1980, census administrators designed a postenumeration program (PEP) on a far larger scale than ever before. Its purpose "was to provide estimates of net undercoverage, with considerable geographic detail, possibly down to the level of states and large cities" (Ibid.:139).[1] The 1980 PEP was basically a pair of very large survey-based matching projects. Unlike previous postenumeration studies, the 1980 program required two samples. The first, known as *P-sample*, consisted of all the households in the Current Population Surveys (CPS) for April and August 1980, each totalling about 70,000 households and 185,000 individuals. After the P-sample survey field work was completed, the survey record of each household and individual that lived at their designated abode on Census Day was matched, if possible, to its particular census protocol. The matching task was to discover whether each household and person in the CPS had been counted in the census. A second sample, the *E-sample*, was drawn from 100,000 completed census questionnaires. Its purpose was to discover the extent of erroneous enumerations and incorrect geocoding. After questionnaires were selected, follow-up enumerators were sent out to find the households they represented and to conduct an interview in order to verify the original census data (Ibid.:143).

Census officials brought forward a statistical theory known as *capture-recapture* to help measure coverage in 1980. Capture-recapture originated in entomological field studies when scientists wanted to determine the number of moths in a particular habitat but were unable to catch them all. They caught a sample of moths, marked the ones they had captured, and released them. Later they caught another sample. Some of the moths in the second sample carried marks from their earlier capture. The proportion of marked moths in the second sample represented the ratio of the first sample to the whole population. Ecologists have used this method to estimate the numbers of various populations such as fish, birds, and deer. Demographers have also used capture-recapture techniques to estimate human populations in countries where neither the censuses nor the vital statistics are highly accurate (Marks 1978).[2] In measuring census coverage, the census itself represents the capture and the post-enumeration survey represents the recapture. After analyzing the capture and the recapture, an analyst can estimate the size of the total population. The difference between the number counted and the estimate would represent the number missed by the census.

In this form, however, the capture-recapture technique fails to overcome the problem of correlation bias, which is the likelihood that there are types of persons that are missed by the census and the survey. In order to solve it, census officials decided to apply the logic of capture-recapture within designated strata of the population. The strata were defined by age, race, sex, ethnicity, and area of residence. Statisticians introduced two new assumptions at this point, "that the individuals *within these strata* had equal probabilities of capture and that the capturing mechanisms operated independently *within strata*" (Ibid.:141).

Another major problem in coverage studies has been the inherent difficulty of matching a census and a survey. Matching problems proved to be particularly severe in the 1980 postenumeration survey as they were described by census officials in the context of a lawsuit known as the "New York case." In a court affidavit, Charles Cowan (1983), who was responsible for the operation, described matching: once a P-sample questionnaire was received in the office, a clerk attempted to find its address in the census master address register. If the address was found, the census serial number for that location was transcribed and the clerks looked for the corresponding census questionnaire.

If the census questionnaire was found, and all persons on the P-sample form exactly matched the census questionnaire as to name, age, sex, and race, they were all deemed to be matched and the form was sent to be [keypunched]. If the address was not found, the case was sent to "professional review." Professional review was performed by traveling squads of specialists trained to deal with problems in the matching. . . . For cases for which a census questionnaire could be found, the professional reviewers adjudicated unusual situations, such as name inversions, transpositions of digits in ages, and other comparable problems. . . . Approximately 20% of the P-sample households were sent back to the field for a personal follow-up visit with the respondent. (Cowan 1983:19)

It is not hard to imagine all the ways in which survey and census records might fail to match. A person's given name might appear in different forms in the census and survey, perhaps a nickname or foreign-language version appears in one protocol but not in the other. A surname might be misspelled. Age, race, or sex might have been written incorrectly on one protocol, and the errors might give the matching clerk reason to wonder if the information refers to the same person in both records.

There is no problem if the clerk simply cannot match the cases. For example, if the census return for a particular apartment shows five persons and only four of them appear on the P-sample survey form, then the fifth person simply represents an unmatched case, counted in the census but not in the survey. The problem arises when a definite match status, either counted or missed, cannot be determined. This can happen, for example, if facts about a person (year of birth, spelling of name) are recorded differently on the two forms, or if the person refused to answer the follow-up survey. For cases in which unknown match statuses are wrongly assumed to be nonmatches, the estimate of the undercount will be too high; if they are wrongly assumed to be matches, then the estimate of the undercount will be too low. Simply stated, in a clear situation the matching clerk can evaluate whether or not a person was counted in the census. In an unclear situation, the clerk cannot tell and the result is a case of unknown match status. Ultimately a considerable proportion of the cases could not be matched. In fact, "in approximately 8 percent of the [E-] sample cases, match status could not be determined because sufficient data were unavailable" (Bailar affidavit 1983:35).

A historical review of census undercounts reveals two patterns, that the coverage of the black population has always been inferior to that of whites and that the extent of undercounting has diminished consistently (Robinson 1988). Relying upon Coale and Rives' analyses of coverage from 1880 through 1940, Gregory Robinson, chief of the bureau's section on population analysis and evaluation, compiled estimates of undercounts. His compilation shows that the censuses of 1880 through 1920 missed approximately 7 percent of the people. The record began to improve in 1930 when the overall undercount fell to 5.3 percent; it continued to fall in 1950 and in every census thereafter, dropping to 1.4 percent in 1980.

Within the black population, certain age-sex categories are especially likely to be undercounted. Black children of both sexes under age five were undercounted in every census. Black males in the twenty to forty-four age group were always the most undercounted. In the past four censuses, there have also been substantial undercounts of black males between ages forty-five and sixty-four. The greatest undercount of blacks occurred in the 1890 and 1920 censuses, when approximately 15 percent were missed. The black undercount began to fall in 1930 and reached its lowest point, 5.9 percent, in 1980. However, since the white undercount in 1980 was estimated to be only 0.9 percent, the differential was still evident. Although the black undercount has been declining since 1920, it is still far greater than the white undercount.

Demographic analysis and postenumeration surveys represent sophisticated ways to measure the undercount, but they cannot reveal individuals' personal situations and the reasons they might have for avoiding the census. In the spring of 1969, an Advisory Committee on Problems of Census Enumeration was formed in the National Academy of Sciences to advise the bureau on ways to improve the completeness and accuracy of information collected in the decennial censuses of population and in other surveys. That committee advised the bureau to conduct a wide-ranging behavioral study, including ethnographic research, of the reasons for underenumeration (Advisory Committee on Problems of Census Enumeration 1972:38–9). Actually, some research in that direction had already begun in the late 1960s.

The 1960 postenumeration survey suggested that some individuals were not counted because they were not staying in "conventionally enumerated places." The bureau explored this problem in 1967 and 1968 in test censuses conducted in New Haven, Connecticut, and Trenton, New Jersey. Researchers devised a procedure called the "casual setting interview." Field workers were sent to such places as bars, poolrooms, and street corners to interview men. Afterward, the test census records were checked to see if those men had been enumerated at home. In most cases they had not. In comparison with men who had been enumerated, the ones found in the casual settings had less education, fewer family ties, and they moved more frequently (Advisory Committee on Problems of Census Enumeration 1972:30–31). The panel of experts speculated that these men may not have had one place that they considered to be their "usual residence."

A closer study was done in conjunction with the 1970 census (Valentine and Valentine 1971). Anthropologists Charles and Betty Lou Valentine were living in a big-city slum neighborhood, collecting ethnographic data on very poor black and Hispanic people. The Census Bureau contracted with the Valentines to count the people on one city block at the same time as the census. As skilled ethnographers, they had gained the residents' confidence and were able get personal information from them. Indeed, the anthropologists already knew who lived in most of the households. The Valentines enumerated the households, and then their data were compared with data collected in the regular census. Both counts found twenty-five households, but the Valentines counted more people than the census, 153 versus 127. According to the anthropologists, the census' main error was that it missed seventeen males age nineteen and above. The census also missed seven children under age eighteen and two females age nineteen and above. The Valentines said that respondents had deliberately withheld information about certain individuals. The respondents were not confused by the census questions and they did not lack the required knowledge. "The overwhelming weight of the evidence indicates that the respondents simply chose to omit certain key individuals from their answers" (Ibid.:14). Four-fifths of the respondents were women and most of the omissions were made by "adult females who had some reason for neglecting to mention productive men residing in their domiciles" (Ibid).

In slum neighborhoods, people often get income from some combination of three sources: low-wage employment, public assistance, and "numerous types of extra-legal enterprise" (Ibid.:15). Ninety-four percent of the households were supported by conventionally earned income and 81 percent received some form of public assistance. The rules of public assistance required that there be no earned income above a specified low level. Most forms of welfare required, in effect, that there be no significant wage earner in the household. For these reasons, "most people are strongly motivated to withhold information about their personal affairs because such knowledge might well be used against them by the authorities" (Ibid.:16). According to the anthropologists this potential trap was the reason most of the men had been omitted from the official count. "In all 15 households where male heads and other adult men were not reported, the domestic unit receives significant support from both employment and welfare" (Ibid.). Violations of welfare rules also explained why the census missed two females in the neighborhood. Both women live with their parents even though they receive public assistance that is supposed to support them in separate quarters. They could not report themselves and their children as members of their parents' households.

This would seem to imply that the respondents were unaware of the confidentiality guarantees provided by the census or that assurances of confidentiality would not be believed even if they were aware. "Many of the queries on census forms are too much like the questions asked by policemen, social workers, landlords, creditors, and tax agents not to arouse threatening suspicions" (Ibid.:18).

The Valentines' study contradicted two major points in the conventional image of black men who are missed by the census. First, the missed men were not young, only two being under age 30, with a majority over 40. Second, they did not belong to floating or transient groups, since they were all "reasonably settled household members and residents" (Ibid.).

More recently, two young demographers at the bureau, David Fein and Kirstin West, reported the results of an intensive study of the social and behavioral aspects of the undercount. In 1986 the bureau conducted a test census in part of Los Angeles, followed by a postenumeration survey. Fein and West's survey came after that and it was designed to learn more about households and persons who had been missed in the test census and subsequently found in the post-enumeration survey.

Their study showed that certain kinds of housing and households were prone to being missed. Attached single family dwellings, such as duplexes, and "unusual units," especially abandoned-looking buildings, converted garages, and secondary units on a lot, were likely to be missed. Small households, composed of one or two persons, were likely to be missed as were renters and households that had moved within four months of the test census. Households were also likely to be missed if they included recent immigrants, if they received welfare, or they were crowded (with more than one person per room).

Some individuals were missed within enumerated households. Such persons were likely to fall into the twenty to twenty-nine age group, to be males, and to have had no formal education. They were unlikely to be citizens or to be close relatives of the head of household. The test census missed more persons through partial enumeration of found households than by missing entire households. "Partial omission . . . accounted for twice as many missed persons, reflected more intractable sources of error, and biased more individual-level census characteristics" (Fein and West 1988:237).

All of this demographic and behavioral research into coverage problems was a means to a more complete enumeration. Census administrators wanted to overcome the undercount and every ten years they modified their enumeration techniques with "coverage improvement" plans.

How to Improve Census Coverage

Census administrators anticipated unprecedented difficulties in carrying out the 1970 census. They noted that people were less likely to be at home during the daytime and evening hours when census interviews had traditionally been conducted. The officials acknowledged "reports of increasing resistance on the part of the public to being interviewed, and growing hostility toward government" that might make people unwilling to cooperate with the census (U.S. Bureau of the Census 1976:7-1). They were also concerned about "a decline in the proportion of . . . well-educated women, ordinarily not in the labor force, who were willing to take enumerator assignments" (Ibid.). In previous censuses, such educated housewives had served as enumerators and their unavailability might make it hard for the bureau to recruit a large team of competent workers.

Census officials decided to do the 1970 census by mail, at least in major metropolitan areas. The potential shortage of enumerators would be handled by not relying on them so heavily. People would fill out their own questionnaires, so most of the census would be done by mail instead of face to face. The new "mailout-mailback" system was used for approximately three-fifths of the households in the nation, in the larger metropolitan areas and adjacent counties (Ibid.:1-6). To facilitate the mailing and checking-in of questionnaires, the census would develop address registers. The Census Bureau purchased commercial mailing lists containing about 34 million residential addresses. The lists were checked by the post office, which produced about 8 million corrections. These corrected lists were used for addressing questionnaires and for building address registers (Ibid.:1-7).

One coverage improvement procedure in 1970 was designed to improve the address lists. Enumerators conducted a "precanvass" in urban neighborhoods where houses and apartments were occupied by more households than the number for which they were designed. Enumerators were told to search for housing units that were not shown in the address registers (Ibid.:7-2). Neighborhood residents were hired as enumerators in their own areas. Post office change-of-address cards were used to find persons who moved at census time. The 1970 program also introduced the National Vacancy Check (NVC), which required an extra visit to housing units that were classified as vacant (Citro and Cohen 1985:99). The NVC examined a sample of 15,000 housing units that had been identified as "year-round vacant" and then imputed persons into a fraction of such housing units across the country (U.S. Census 1976:7-6).

In anticipation of the 1980 census, the bureau developed another coverage improvement program (Herriott 1979; Littman 1979). For 1980, census officials had decided to enumerate 95.5 percent of the nation by mailout-mailback and 5.5 percent by a "conventional" method (U. S. Bureau of the Census 1986:1-12). The conventional method, essentially a door-to-door census, was used in sparsely settled areas, mostly in the western states. In conventionally enumerated areas, postal carriers delivered short-form questionnaires to all households on their routes. Then census enumerators went to pick up the completed questionnaires. If a household fell into the sample for the long form, the enumerator then asked the long-form questions. Most of the coverage improvement procedures applied to mailout-mailback, but there were special procedures for the conventional areas as well.

As outlined by Peter Bounpane, Assistant Director for Demographic Censuses, the coverage improvement program had several parts (Bounpane and Jordan 1978). For mailout-mailback areas there were (1) procedures to improve the mailing list; (2) questionnaire edit; (3) tracking down transient persons; (4) checking on vacant housing units; (5) local review; and (6) "Were You Counted?" Each of these procedures attempted to locate and count households and individuals that might have been missed.

Improving the mailing lists. The census planned to acquire mailing lists with approximately 40 million addresses and to geocode them to census geography. Calling upon the post office for assistance again, the bureau printed a card for each address, which they forwarded to the post office for checking. When postal carriers discovered addresses on their routes for which there were no cards, they notified the Census Bureau, which added those places to the lists. As in 1970, there was a precanvass, designed to follow the postal check. This time, however, all mailout-mailback areas were to be precanvassed. Before questionnaires were mailed, a census enumerator systematically canvassed an assigned area, identified all housing units and added to the list any units not already listed (Ibid.). The postal checks and the precanvass were designed to overcome the known deficiencies of commercial mailing lists.

Questionnaire edit. This was a procedure designed to use completed mailback questionnaires in order to find households and persons that were missed. In 1980 the bureau inserted the question: "How many living quarters are there in the building in which you live?" The office procedure required clerks to compare the answer to this question with the mailout count for addresses with 10 or fewer units. If the clerk found that a questionnaire reported more units in the building than questionnaires mailed, an enumerator went out to check whether every housing unit in the building had been enumerated.

To determine whether the person who filled out the questionnaire had included all individuals who lived in the household, census planners also employed questions and edits to verify the completeness of each questionnaire's roster. On the cover of the questionnaire there was a place for a list of the names of all persons living in the household on Census Day and for those who were staying or visiting there and had no other home. In editing, the clerk looked to see if the body of the questionnaire included information about each of the listed individuals.

Tracking down transient persons. Different procedures were employed to locate different classes of transients. The postal service notified the census offices of persons who had filed change of address orders around Census Day so that they could be pursued. Another procedure was designed to count people who were away from their usual residence on Census Day. They were asked to fill out questionnaires where they were found, and then the district office that received them forwarded their questionnaires to the census offices in their home areas. A third procedure was designed to improve the enumeration of individuals who lacked conventional homes. As in the past, such persons were counted on a designated night called M-Night, at places such as missions, shelters, and railroad stations. Based upon the casual-settings visits in

1967 and 1968, the new casual count operation required enumerators to go out to visit places where transient persons might congregate, such as employment offices and street corners, to look for persons who had not been counted.

Checking on vacant housing units. As had been learned in the survey for the 1970 national vacancy check, this was an important area for improvement. As the 1980 census approached, the planners were concerned that there might actually be people living in dwellings thought vacant. Census planners decided to require a field recheck of all housing units designated as vacant or nonexistent (a dwelling that existed on the address register that the enumerator was not able to find). The recheck, known as unit status review, was conducted by someone other than the original enumerator. The 1980 unit status review was the same procedure as the 1970 vacancy check, except that in 1970 it was done on a sample of housing units and in 1980 it was done everywhere.

Local review. This called for the Census Bureau to prepare preliminary counts for review by local officials. Before the census, local officials were to see counts of addresses on the mailing list for every block in the community. (Unfortunately, the bureau cancelled this procedure at the last minute and was widely criticized by local officials for this omission.) After the census but before the field offices were closed, local officials received preliminary population and housing counts. The local officials could then question the data and add information which might help the census officials to count missed housing units.

"Were You Counted?" This procedure was introduced in the 1970 census, and continued in 1980. It was a small campaign, timed for the end of the fieldwork period, in which newspapers printed forms with which individuals could notify the census office they had been missed. Most persons who submitted such forms were found to have been counted already, but this effort did add approximately 25,000 persons to the 1970 census (Bounpane and Jordan 1978).

For those rural districts enumerated by the conventional method, coverage improvements fell under two headings: changes in field procedures and the resumption of a postenumeration post office check. Hoping to minimize the potential for an enumerator to miss a housing unit, census planners developed instructions for enumerators to canvass their enumeration districts in a more systematic fashion. Presumably rural enumerators missed housing units in 1970 because they did not all travel through their districts according to a prescribed routine. The planners also devised improved techniques for maintaining quality control over enumerators' work, and they required that post offices conduct a postenumeration check similar to the one done ten years earlier in PEPOC. The planners reasoned that this check was equivalent to the precensus checks done by post offices in mailout-mailback areas.

While all of these new procedures together might add relatively few individuals to the census count, it is important to remember that the 1970 undercount was approximately 2.9 percent. The purpose of coverage improvements was to find those individuals who were not counted by ordinary procedures. Coverage improvement was working at the margin, trying to move closer to 100 percent enumeration. Note also that all of the coverage improvement procedures were expensive because they were labor-intensive. For example, consider the labor costs involved in sending enumerators to dwelling units from which mailed forms were not received. According to the enumerators' manual the two rounds of "followups" could involve as many as seven return visits to a single dwelling in an attempt to obtain a complete form. "Unit status review" was also labor-intensive. Enumerators had to go to addresses of listed dwelling units that had been deleted "nonexistent" to determine the validity of this classification. In all, 8.4 million listings were checked in this way, and the review showed that approximately 10 percent of them had been misclassified. After the errors were discovered, enumerators collected information on the persons who lived in those dwellings; nationally, this procedure added 1.7 million persons to the 1980 census count (U.S. Bureau of the Census 1986:5-29). In terms of cost per additional person counted, repeated callbacks and unit status review were expensive procedures.

In addition to technical refinements, coverage improvement meant dealing with minority groups in new ways. If low income blacks and Hispanics were reluctant to participate in the census, ways had to be developed to gain their cooperation. The broad strategy was to persuade people that they should be counted. Census officials wanted to convince people that providing information about themselves would benefit their ethnic groups and communities and that this information would not be used against them. It wanted to persuade them that governments at all levels use data to help people in various ways including political representation, distribution of benefits, and planning facilities. The difficulty was in making this case without promising any specific benefit from participating in the census, and in sending this message to people who distrust government and expect nothing but inferior services and facilities from it.

In an attempt to remedy this perception, the Census Bureau turned to the Advertising Council, which coordinates the advertising industry's public service contributions. The Council assigned one of the biggest New York agencies, Olgilvy and Mather, to the census. The agency developed slick advertisements for billboards, periodicals, and television, using animation and celebrity endorsements. Advertisements were also placed in media directed specifically at black and Spanish-speaking audiences.[3] The project was so successful in getting free space in magazines and free time on television that for a time the Census Bureau was the country's single largest advertiser.

In addition to advertising, the bureau expanded its outreach program, hiring hundreds of community relations officers to work with groups in minority areas. These officers themselves were members of the same minority groups with which they were assigned to work. The bureau also established a set of minority advisory committees, consisting of officers of large minority associations and professional people from the same minorities. Starting in 1975, these committees met about twice a year with top-level census officials to discuss plans for the census. Technical staff members at the bureau reported to the committees on various aspects of census planning. Committee members and census officials discussed and debated those matters which pertained to the enumeration of their group. As Vincent Barabba said in his introductory statement to the Hispanic committee, census officials were hoping that the new minority advisory committees would stimulate cooperation at the grass roots level (Levine 1983b). No one spelled out an exact mechanism through which this might take place, but presumably the committee members were well connected within the leadership networks of their groups and would be able to sway public opinion toward the census. If these minority leaders could be persuaded that the census was valuable and trustworthy, perhaps they could influence their groups to cooperate. Furthermore, perhaps they could be instrumental in getting other influential persons, such as editors and broadcasters, leaders of local groups, and church leaders to promote the census.

Despite the bureau's outreach campaign and coverage improvement program, the undercount issue persisted through the 1980 census, when it was met with demands for a new solution: adjustment. In lawsuits filed in 1980, lawyers representing the mayors of Detroit and New York argued that undercounts are inevitable and that statistical adjustment of census counts is the only answer; they asserted that there should be a statistical adjustment to the census counts to "correct" for undercounting.

While the 1980 lawsuits represented an explosion of the issue, the first major discussion of methods of adjustment had taken place two years earlier within a panel of social scientists. Appointed by the National Research Council's Committee on National Statistics at the request of the secretary of commerce, the Panel on Decennial Census Plans was asked "to undertake an independent evaluation of the technical and procedural designs for the 1980 census" (Panel on Decennial Census Plans 1978:vii). While the panel considered a wide range of technical issues, they assumed that no matter how well it was executed, there would still be an undercount. By then a bill had already been proposed that would require the secretary to establish procedures for correcting census counts for persons missed. It was within this context then that the panel looked directly at the question of adjustment and discussed three methodological approaches, one based upon demographic analysis, one based on postenumeration surveys and matching, and a third called the synthetic method. They concluded that all three were feasible, but that the synthetic method was inferior to the others for certain purposes (Ibid.:102–104). They also concluded that "on balance an improvement in equality would be achieved" [by adjustment] (Ibid.:112). They stopped short of making a direct recommendation on the grounds that their original mandate did not call for such an action; nonetheless, they advised the secretary to consider adjustment. They said that adjusted numbers could be used for all purposes except legislative apportionment.

A year later, as demands for adjustment continued, Director Barabba convened a pair of meetings. Like the 1967 MIT-Harvard conference, these two events signified another turning point by highlighting adjustment as a possible solution to the undercount. The first meeting, held in September 1979, brought together nineteen of the bureau's senior staff, plus six "outsiders." They conducted their discussions in a highly structured discussion format devised by Ian Mitroff and Richard Mason, two business school professors. The workshop's main goal was to define the key issues and assumptions regarding undercounting and adjustment (Mitroff, Mason, and Barabba 1983). The second meeting, held in February 1980, drew in more individuals from universities and other nongovernmental organizations. Reports from both meetings demonstrate that adjustment was almost a new concept in 1979–1980. Papers presented at the February conference refer frequently to previous writings on census coverage and underenumeration, but rarely to publications about methods of adjustment. At the conference, statisticians and demographers presented and debated original papers that outlined methods of adjustment (U.S. Bureau of the Census 1980). Senator Moynihan, who had already introduced a bill to require adjustment, spoke at the conference. Like the panel on decennial census plans, the conference considered the main methods that might be used for adjustment. All three methods of adjustment—demographic, survey/matching, and synthetic—grow out of the methods used to measure undercounts.

Adjusting by means of the demographic method requires an analyst to estimate the undercount for each age, sex, and race category and then to add the number of missed individuals in the appropriate places. (If some categories were overcounted, the adjustment subtracts from them.) This procedure will yield new counts, including a new total. To some extent, the demographic method may be useful for adjusting white and black populations for the nation as a whole, but for the purposes of adjustment, the demographic method has the same limitations it has for measuring coverage. It cannot be used to adjust the populations of Hispanic or other minority groups other than blacks, or to adjust subnational areas.

Since the demographic method cannot be used for the Hispanic population or even with complete confidence for the total national population because of the lack of information on illegal immigrants, the bureau must rely upon surveys combined with matching techniques to estimate undercounts. Adjusting by means of surveys and matching requires an application of those same techniques that were used to estimate census coverage. One major problem in adjusting the census is how to adjust the counts for counties, cities, and even smaller areas such as census tracts and city blocks. Depending on how the sample for a post-enumeration survey was designed, this method could conceivably be used to generate undercount estimates for these smaller areas. If a large survey included a proper sample of each state, then it could support state-level undercount estimates that, in turn, might support state-level adjustments. This logic could be extended to smaller geographical areas, but each extension would make the sample larger and would eventually make the survey inordinately expensive.

The synthetic method offers a way of adjusting for subnational units. Its principal proponent, sociologist Robert Hill, who was then director of the National Urban League's research department, defined it as a statistical procedure for distributing the undercount of a larger geographical area among its subunits. Thus, the first requisite is an estimate of the undercount by age, sex, and race for a large area such as the nation, which can be generated by demographic analysis, perhaps in combination with a survey/matching method. The second requisite is the census itself for the smaller places, also grouped by age, sex, and race. Given this information, "the synthetic method can easily be used by nonstatisticians to derive the census undercount for any areas below the national level. One only needs to apply the appropriate percentage increases to the official 1970 census count for specific race/sex/age groups in specific localities" (Hill 1980:131). Hill recognizes that the synthetic method is based on the assumption that there is no difference among places in the extent to which these subgroups were undercounted. In his paper at the conference, Hill presented a set of adjusted population figures for the states in 1970 to demonstrate that the synthetic method could be applied to actual numbers. He advocated the use of this method on the grounds that it is internally consistent, simple, timely, and reliable and that it yields results that promote equity. In his summary of the February conference, Conrad Taeuber wrote that "there appeared to be general consensus that some form of adjustment for the undercount is needed" for the allocation of federal funds but not for reapportionment. (U.S. Bureau of the Census 1983:3). Otherwise, the conference opened many questions and closed almost none of them.

From the outset, the adjustment issue was bifurcated since census numbers are used for congressional apportionment as well as for other purposes including the distribution of federal grant monies. The Constitution calls for an "actual enumeration" of "the whole number of free persons" for purposes of apportionment. (The Constitution excludes "Indians not taxed" from the enumeration and also includes three-fifths of other persons, i.e., slaves.) Presumably, then, adjusted totals would not represent such an enumeration. Taking that as given, early advocates of adjustment recommended that adjusted numbers not be used for the purposes of reapportionment. This is evident in the statements by the panel as well as in the proceedings of the February conference; note that Taeuber's summary statement referred to the advisability of adjustment only for the purpose of allocating funds. Apparently advocates of adjustment assumed that it was somehow less risky to use adjusted numbers for that purpose. Around 1980 the only ones who advocated adjustment for all purposes were the plaintiffs in the major lawsuits who argued that this was required in the interest of equity.

In recounting the attempts made by demographers and statisticians to measure the undercount certain methods emerge as noteworthy. Demographers in the 1940s and 1950s recognized that the censuses routinely missed certain categories of persons, and they devised a demographic method with which to estimate census undercounts by age, sex, and race. In refining this method they succeeded in analyzing error patterns in censuses back to 1800. Unfortunately, the demographic method had one fundamental limitation: it could show census coverage for the entire national population for whites and blacks, but it was inherently incapable of showing undercounts for individual places, or for other racial or ethnic groups such as Hispanics. Thus the demographic method offered no way to satisfy recent political demands to correct for census undercounts. Starting in 1950, the Census Bureau also experimented with survey research and matching as a means for measuring census coverage. After each census, except in 1980, they conducted a postenumeration survey. By matching records between censuses and surveys and analyzing the results, they attempted to estimate the fraction of the population that had been included in the census, the fraction that had been missed, and the fraction that had perchance been counted twice. This approach had the potential for measuring and adjusting undercounts for subnational areas—states and cities—and for major ethnic groups. Beyond these improvements in measurement, census administrators have attempted to overcome the undercount. Each census has contained innovations designed to count people who might have been missed. Some innovations, like mailout-mailback, fundamentally changed the census. Some, like community outreach and local community review, yielded a new involvement between census and community. And some, like local status review, required more intensive field procedures. Many of these innovations proved to be quite costly. They may have succeeded in counting more people but they failed to overcome the differential undercount.

5 How They Did the Census: District Managers' Stories

ONE GOOD WAY to learn how the census works is to talk to the people who carry it out "in the field." This chapter is based upon first-hand stories of four census officials who directed big-city district offices in 1980, dealing with the nitty-gritty of enumeration. Such a close-up look at the process should provide a feel for how field work is actually done. In the political context, one source of tension between cities and the Census Bureau is revealed: the assignment of federal "outsiders" to count local populations. In the scientific-technical context, this study will observe how hard it is to count the entire population, how well the censustakers work at that task, how many error-detection procedures the census includes, and yet how many opportunities there are for the census to make errors.

These 1980 district office stories serve as a lead-in to the accounts of the 1980–1987 lawsuits. They also introduce the census of 1990, which incorporated many of the same operations at the district level. The only major operation described in this chapter that was not repeated ten years later was questionnaire check-in and editing. District offices in large cities in 1980 received mailback questionnaires directly from the postal service; in 1990 city mailbacks were sent to processing offices. Otherwise, though, 1990 district offices did all the same work developing address lists, interviewing in the field, and conducting local review. In 1990, the bureau continued to use the strategy of redundant procedures to catch errors.

Six themes emerge from the story of the 1980 district offices:

• The whole field operation, down to the smallest detail, was planned and set up in advance.
• The operation was done on a gargantuan scale.
• Everything happened very fast.
• District managers engaged in a large personnel operation, including testing and hiring, training, supervision, and payroll.
• There was a complex and difficult relationship between census officials and locals, especially journalists and municipal officials.
• Census plans called for a series of deliberately redundant procedures designed to catch omissions or errors. These procedures existed not only in the plans, but also in the actual field operations.

The four individuals I interviewed were Rich Takei, who managed a district in San Francisco; Marshall DeBarry, Detroit; Janet Tippett, Baltimore; and Tom Jones, Providence, Rhode Island. Rich, Marshall, and Tom were approximately thirty years old, and Janet was around fifty. They all became district managers in 1979, after the bureau circulated a memorandum inviting regular staff members to volunteer for temporary assignments in central cities. Census administrators wanted to use permanent employees as managers, rather than the temporaries who would run the other types of offices. For each of them, managing a district office had been an exciting experience.

District managers reported to their cities for training in December 1979. Tom Jones reported, "We started training in Boston in mid-December, 1979. Five days of training. In retrospect, most of us think it was inadequate. They taught us detailed operations of the district office. . . . They [the trainers] said, 'Here's what the census is; here's how to do it' " (Jones 1983). When asked about the training, Rich Takei said,

We didn't have five days in December. Part of that time was spent looking for housing, etc. We had three days, then two additional days of training in March. We also had . . . self-teaching training tapes to listen to before the training sessions. They included basics like the history of the census. The training included [instruction on] reporting and administrative tools like staff and calendar. (Takei 1983)

District offices were subordinate to regional offices. The Census

Bureau had twelve permanent regional offices which were augmented by temporary district offices every ten years for the enumeration. Each regional office had a regional census manager, an experienced administrator from the field division. Under the regional census manager was the assistant regional census manager for technical matters (sometimes called the regional technician or the ARCM-tech). According to one district manager, "This was the key person. You would be on the phone with him all the time." All of the district managers said that they had received very strong, competent support from their regional technicians. The district manager was controlled, in effect, by the regional technician, who visited the district office weekly with a checklist asking, "Did you do X?; did you do Y?; Did you do Z?" The district manager had to call the regional office weekly, at a specified time, to report on 'Cost and Progress,' giving the payroll situation.

Although I spoke with the former managers three years after the census, they recalled vividly how they established their offices. They remembered arriving at the large, empty offices that had been rented for them by the regional offices and varied in quality. For example, recalling Providence, Tom Jones said, "When I got there I found the place they rented for us. Each district office needed about 13,000 square feet of space. Ours was in the fourth floor of an abandoned warehouse in a warehouse district. It was very well laid out for our purposes. But it had no air conditioning, and they never cleaned up [or] emptied our waste baskets" (Jones 1983). Likewise, Marshall DeBarry recalled, "Our office was in an old building in Highland Park [Michigan]. Three floors. The owners were gutting and reconstructing it. There was unfinished wiring and we had to talk to the landlord about it. The places for testing and supplies were not finished" (DeBarry 1983).

The four managers recalled the arrival of the telephone installation crews. The phone company had received plans and specifications well in advance of the manager's arrival including the assignment of the office's phone number, which had to conform with the number that was printed on labels affixed to the questionnaires for that area. The managers' most vivid recollection however was of the arrival of two fully-packed semi-trailer trucks.

In their December training sessions, the new managers had received detailed operations manuals. One manual told how to unload the trucks and set up the office. All of the boxes were to be formed into a large rectangle on the floor in a certain order. Then, they were to be unpacked in a prescribed order. The shipment contained different types of cartons. Some contained enumerators' kits, which in turn contained questionnaires, long and short, in English and Spanish, instructions, envelopes, a portfolio, and two sharpened # $2\frac{1}{2}$ black-lead pencils with erasers. Other cartons contained training manuals, and still others contained file boxes. The shipment included heavy cardboard desks for the office workers. "Everybody thought it was all clever," according to DeBarry, the way the whole office had been set up like a kit. "The first two days are a numbing sensation; the pile of boxes is so big. There is a kit for 'telephone follow-up,' a kit for 'follow-up one' training, a kit for 'pre-canvass corrections,' and many others" (DeBarry 1983).

The *Handbook for Opening the District Office* showed how to build a sort of honeycomb—the central bin file—for sorting and filing completed census forms as they arrived. The bins were made of cardboard boxes, stacked four or five high, according to instructions in the manual. Each bin was for one Enumeration District (ED). An ED is, presumably, an area that can be covered by a single enumerator, approximately 350 housing units. These filing bins became the center of operations in the months which followed. In addition to a master manual, each district manager had been given a calendar-chart, showing dates for all operations along with deadlines. The calendar-chart showed when the manager would be called and visited by the regional technician; when reports and payrolls were to be submitted; when new batches of employees were to be hired and trained; when ongoing employees were to be retrained for new tasks; and when each follow-up operation was to begin.

Staffing of district offices was partly political. Traditionally, temporary census employees have been appointed by the party in power. As the 1980 census' procedural history recounts, "The President [a Democrat] waived the requirements of the 1978 Civil Service Reform Act to enable the Census Bureau to develop a system for recruiting temporary census employees through Federal political referral, State agencies, national and local civic organizations, minority and women's groups, and other appropriate sources. . . . As in previous censuses, the recruitment process gave preference in most instances to persons recommended by the political party of the incumbent administration" (Census 1986:5-12). In addition, applicants for census jobs had to pass a written test. Appointments for managerial jobs were made by regional census offices, so the district managers could not name their own assistant managers.

Each district office had an assistant district manager and four supervisors: for office, fieldwork, administration, and "special places." The office supervisor was in charge of bins, office procedure, matching forms, counts, and registers. The administrative operations supervisor was in charge of payroll, forms, and ordering things. The special places supervisor was in charge of enumerating places such as group quarters, trailer parks, hospitals, dormitories, and nursing homes.[1] The special places supervisor was also responsible for T-Night and M-Night, during which transients were counted. In most cases, the political parties and regional offices got competent persons for these appointments, and they worked well with the district managers. There were stories, however, about mismatches and conflicts. According to the district managers, some of the political nominees did not realize that the census would require a great deal of hard, precise work. There were occasions when assistant district managers had to be fired, sometimes after acrimonious struggles.

District managers observed that local employees, especially those affiliated with city hall, seemed to resent their presence. The locals treated them as "the guys from Washington who don't know anything." As Rich Takei recalled, "The people with political referral were locals; they knew the area which some of us did not. . . . The local political officials trusted them in a way which they did not trust us. We were outsiders sent in by Washington. They thought they could trust the locals to get a good count (Takei 1983). The implication was that local residents could obviously count the inhabitants better than these outsiders could. Indeed, given our tradition of federalism and local self-government, it is odd that we send people from Washington to conduct the census.

Every district office ran a large-scale employment operation, in order to recruit hundreds of employees, mostly enumerators, crew leaders, and clerks. The district office administered a test to each applicant in 1980; in the aggregate, the bureau was operating an enormous testing operation. Over 1 million applicants took the nonsupervisory test; 79.7 percent passed (Census 1986: 5-14). Across the country, districts varied in the quality of the temporary workers who were available. "Districts differed in the exam pass rate. If yours had lots of people passing with high scores, you could hire at that level. But in others the pass rate was so low that you had to hire people who had just [barely] passed. You wanted people with high scores." Takei said, "San Francisco had a 70 percent pass rate [so] we could take people with high scores. There are lots of people out there looking for temporary employment." Baltimore, where Tippett worked, had much lower scores (Takei 1983).

District managers were told precisely how many people to hire for each operation. Those numbers had been determined by formula, based upon the number of housing units in the district. Week by week, the managers kept adjusting the staffing figures. If the plan for a district had an erroneous estimate of the number of workers needed for a particular procedure, there would be a crisis in that office. For example, many offices received more mailed-in questionnaires than had been projected, and they had not hired enough clerks to check them in. Jones recounted that problem as it applied to his office: "We had an authorized number of employees for 'check-in.' That number was woefully insufficient. In a day we saw that. Had to double or triple the number to 100 people. . . . Evidently the planners had overestimated the number of forms one person could do in one day" (Jones 1983).

Having hired new employees, district managers had to train them. Training began at employees' swearing-in, when managers explained the idea of confidentiality. They told the new workers that they could not divulge the personal information they would encounter, not even to their husbands and children. Managers explained the penalties attendant upon the violation of confidentiality. After the swearing-in ceremonies, the training system was "pyramidal." Each field operations supervisor, who had been trained at the regional census office, trained four field operations assistants. Then each field operations assistant selected and trained ten to thirteen crew leaders. Each crew leader selected and trained nine enumerators. Enumerators' training took two or three days. At times, Tom Jones had training in progress at forty different sites around his district, including schools and community centers.

Every job had a manual that was used in the training sessions. The teaching method was to read the manual aloud, supplementing it with film strips or slides. One district manager reported that the bureau failed to send out all the training manuals on time, so he sometimes had to get quick copies made.

From January through March 1980, the main job was to improve the master address register. To explain this I must explain "census geography." When the census is published, its volumes indicate how many persons live in each state, county, and municipality. The books also show smaller areas within metropolitan areas, giving the number of persons—and many details about them—in each "census tract" and on every city block. A census tract is an area in which approximately 3,000 persons live. Every fact collected in the census must be assigned to a location. In order to accomplish this, the bureau needs to designate every location, down to the city block, by a unique number. Between censuses, the Census Map Office, in Jeffersonville, Indiana, produced detailed maps, assigning numbers to all the tiny sections of the nation.

For the 1970 and 1980 censuses, the bureau developed computer programs for matching individual addresses to census geography. These programs, known as GBF-DIME files, along with their associated programs, represent years of development.[2] DIME files were produced locally by organizations such as city planning departments and as a result they vary in quality. Under the best of circumstances, the Census Bureau could purchase a mailing list of the households in an area, process it with the local DIME file, and end up with the census geographical identifiers attached to each address. That process is known as geocoding. For the 1980 census, the geocoded version of my address was State 17, County 019, Place 0990 (in Minor Civil Division 022), Tract 5, and Block 408.

Geocoding a large list of addresses never works perfectly. First, commercial mailing lists tend to list households in prosperous neighborhoods more carefully than those in poor neighborhoods, since advertisers target the former. Second, it is difficult and expensive to keep DIME files up to date. New subdivisions may be built, old streets may be ripped up, and these changes must all be entered into the files.

How does this affect the district manager's task of improving the district's master address register? Each district manager received a master address register (MAR) from a processing center.

The registers arrived as wirebound volumes of computer printout, one for each enumeration district. Each page in the register had a column showing a street address and a place where a field worker could write in a person's name for dwellings in multi-unit buildings. In a sense, the master address register was at the center of the census because, ultimately, the job was to get a census return from every household in the register. As Tom Jones put it, "The completed address list is a major element of the census. You use the list as a control, check returns against it. . . . [and] use it also to direct the follow-up" (Jones 1983). But, before going for the returns, they had to determine that all the dwellings were listed in the register.

When the bureau geocoded the commercial mailing lists, they found addresses that could not be assigned place numbers. They printed a yellow card to represent every place (address) that would not computer-match. District offices tried to geocode each of those addresses manually and enter them in the registers. After processing the yellow cards, the district office conducted a precanvass. Enumerators were instructed to walk through neighborhoods with address registers, look at each housing unit, and compare it to the register. If they found housing units that were not in the registers, they were to list them. Enumerators were also supposed to correct the census geography if a listed address had an incorrect block number, for example.

The postal service was also supposed to check the district office's address list. Local post offices received questionnaires in early March to be held for delivery later in the month. In the intervening period, mail sorters were to conduct a "casing check," sorting all questionnaires to their address boxes in the post office. If they found an address or household for which there was no questionnaire, they were to fill out a card for the census district office. After the casing check, they were to pull the questionnaires and hold them for delivery on March 28. Concurrently, staff members at the district office addressed questionnaires to households that had not been included in the first master address register.

Maps posed real problems for the conduct of the census. "District managers also had difficulties with small area maps." Jones said, "A big problem came from the map delays. . . . We didn't have the maps at the right point. It didn't go according to plan" (Jones 1983). DeBarry corroborates this: "We received maps at the end of January. They came with a note, 'Don't use these maps.' We were told to wait for the second set. . . . A week later, the 'real maps' came." To further complicate matters, DeBarry continued, "Between 1970 and 1980 they renumbered the census tracts in Detroit. The block numbers were not the same in a large portion of [my] district. But they still used the 1970 maps, with handwritten numbers over EDs and over block numbers. They sent us magnifying glasses" (DeBarry 1983).

Takei also complained about the maps: "They were hard to read. They had used orange markers to mark boundaries, and they might obliterate names of streets or other numbers. Then the lists. One list might show a block in ED 'x' while the other list might show the block in another ED. And on the map it might be designated otherwise altogether" (Takei 1983). The poor quality and untimely production of maps precipitated the bureau's nationwide cancellation of 1980s precensus local review.

One special task was to determine where to count a person found in a hotel. Also, the census had to find persons who did not reside in ordinary dwellings. To this end, the census conducted two special operations, "T-Night" (for transients in hotels) and "M-Night" (for people in places such as missions, shelters, and bus stations). Rich Takei told about those events in San Francisco:

On March 31 [T-Night], we left ICR forms, Individual Census Reports, at hotels, all those charging more than $4 per night. One was supposed to be left by each room's door or given to each occupant by the manager. The form asked [in effect] "where's your permanent residence?" After we got the completed ICR with this address we would forward it to that area.

Some hotel managers wouldn't let my women enter, thought they were hookers. The hotels called me at home. I had to explain that they had identification and I described the IDs so they could see if they were valid.

There was also "M-Night" [or] Mission Night . . . [which] covered all places that charged less than $4 per night. Flophouses, YMCAs, bus stations, pool halls, all-night movies. Each person was to fill out an ICR unless they said they had an address elsewhere, or that they were already enumerated.

The single great event in the history of a district office was the first arrival of mail returns. The mail delivery on April 1 was an amazing experience. Just as the district managers recall the arrival of the supply trucks they also remember that first shipment of mail. The 1980 mailback rate was higher than had been predicted. Jones said, "We got perhaps 50,000–70,000 pieces of mail on the first day. Lasted like that for 3 or 4 days. Then it continued to come in at a few hundred or a thousand a day. It came in bags and carts" (Jones 1983). The manual instructed the manager to count, sort, and serialize the envelopes. Jones continued, "We had to open each piece and sort them to EDs, to the central bin file, then put in serial number order. Each return should match a line in the master address register. Then we check the forms in. We had two weeks for this" (Ibid.).

Clerks checked the mail returns. Given a completed questionnaire, a clerk had to find its address in the master address register, mark the register to show that a questionnaire had been received, and write the number of persons who lived there. If the address referred to a multi-unit structure, such as an apartment building, the clerk had to write in the name of the householder, so that eventually the register would list a name for each apartment. After checking in the mail returns, clerks edited them to ascertain whether the questionnaire had been filled in completely and neatly. Neatness was important since the forms were to be optically scanned by a machine called FOSDIC. Clerks retranscribed messy forms as well as Spanish-language ones. If the return failed to meet the prescribed standard, it was given to a telephone enumerator, who called the household and asked for the missing information. Most problems could be resolved that way, although some questionnaires were sent out with field enumerators. In Tom Jones's Providence office, checking-in and editing occupied forty to fifty people for several weeks.

After editing mailed-in questionnaires, the district office began "followup 1." Its purpose was to get census information from all the addresses for which there were no mail-back questionnaires. Each blank in the master address register for number of persons meant the office lacked a mailed-in return from that housing unit, so they sent an enumerator to visit it. The enumerator had to determine whether each housing unit in his or her enumeration district was occupied or vacant. As Tom Jones emphasized, "The followup was the most crucial operation, and it had the most problems. It was hard work; some people refuse [to provide information to the enumerator] or are never at home" (Jones 1983). If an enumerator went to a dwelling four times (at different times of the day) and failed to get an interview, the enumerator was instructed to get "last-resort" information, which was information from a neighbor on how many persons live in the unit, their names, race, and ages.

Once district managers had enumerators in the field conducting followup 1, they had to guard against "curbstoning," which is when an enumerator fills in a questionnaire by fabricating the answers. Survey interviewers always have an incentive to curbstone because it is easier than contacting a household and conducting an interview. Census enumerators in 1980 had a particular incentive because they were paid for completed questionnaires on a piecework basis.

It was the crew leader's responsibility to prevent curbstoning. One of the census's many manuals told crew leaders, in detail, how to check enumerators' work (U.S. Bureau of the Census, D-554 Manual 1980). After an enumerator submitted a batch of completed questionnaires, a crew leader was supposed to take a sample of them and phone the households to verify that they had actually been visited. Takei explained that crew leaders had to be wary. We noticed "if the enumerators were turning in too many forms or too many which were incomplete. One enumerator turned in enough to be paid $1,000 in one pay period. [It was] impossible to do that many. We probably had to dismiss at least a couple of enumerators" (Takei 1983). The crew leaders' manual had explicit instructions on how to fire an enumerator who had fabricated data.

Another major concern for district managers was the enumeration of people in urban slums and the safety of employees who went into them to enumerate. Rich Takei said that the district adjacent to his had two "notorious" areas, Hunter's Point and Mission District. The district office could send enumerators who lived in the areas and would not be afraid to go there (however enumerators were not allowed to enumerate their own blocks). Takei said that he sometimes used a team method, sending a group of five enumerators together. In such areas the enumerators were to leave before dark. Janet Tippett described an episode in her Baltimore district.

Our biggest problem was in a public housing area. There had been a confrontation there between a welfare group and the city about the size of household: how many people could live in each apartment, who could live there. Usually we could ask the city for help—they had community relations workers—but in this case the city was the enemy. We sent an enumerator there, but people were throwing bottles at her. The enumerator lived there but she said, "I wouldn't go in."

I called the community services person [of the regional office]. We asked the mayor if there was anyone who had worked with these people that they trusted. We found a person who had worked with poor groups. She said, "I'll go in and see if it will help. I'll make some calls to certain figures. Certain contacts. Wait a couple of days." . . . After that, we sent in the enumerator and she did her work. (Tippett 1983)

There were other difficult fieldwork situations, of course, including dealing with people who would not answer. Takei said that aliens would not answer, nor would people who were beating the welfare system—for example, if they were collecting for five people but there were really only two in the household. An enumerator who found someone drunk would make a second visit. Takei related some adventure stories: "We had guns drawn on one person. Once one of our enumerators was knocking at the front door and someone poured a bucket of water on him. Other enumerators had their bicycles stolen" (Takei 1983).

After the completion of followup 1, which took about five weeks, the office proceeded to "merge and tally." The office staff did hand tallies, "lots of clerks with calculators, doing checks and re-checks," to generate preliminary population numbers (Jones 1983). "One big important operation was called *merge*. You take the crap out of the bins. Check to see if the questionnaires on hand are the same as what's in the register. This got rid of the problem stuff and assured that the population counts [tallies] were correct" (DeBarry 1983).

Stated somewhat more formally by Tippett, the story sounds like this:

After followup 1, we had to do merge and reconciliation. Reconciliation was for coverage improvement corrections. We had to compare the actual questionnaires, which were serialized in bins, with the master address register. We also had to compare two registers, the MAR and the field register. Had to see that deletions made in the field were transferred to the MAR; had to be sure that you *don't* have a questionnaire for some address which was deleted. (Tippett 1983)

Just to give you a feel for how census manuals were written and for how much detail there was in executing the census, following is a paragraph on "merge" from the *District Manager's Manual*:

An ED is "merged" after followup 1, edit, and telephone followup have been completed. During the merge operation, merge serialization clerks put the completed questionnaires (in the #6 carton) and the failed-edit question-naires (in the "personal visit" plastic bag) in serial number order. After an ED has been serialized, merge clerks obtain the master address register, the #6 carton of completed questionnaires, and the plastic bag of failed-edit questionnaires. They match the questionnaires against the listings in the master address register and identify missing and duplicate questionnaires. They list the serial number of each failed edit, missing, and duplicate case for followup 2 on Form D-384, Record of Questionnaire Followup, and put all questionnaires requiring followup (failed edits and duplicates) in a plastic bag labeled "Hold for FU 2." (U.S. Bureau of the Census 1980, D-507 Manual: 64–65)

After making the first population tallies, district offices pro-ceeded to followup 2, in which they had to perform three main tasks: to "clean up" the non-response cases; follow up on failed edits, those that were not finished by phone, and double-check every housing unit that had been designated vacant. This last task had to be executed by a different enumerator, not the one who had called it vacant in the first instance. This procedure was designed to catch errors made by enumerators, to find people in households that had been coded as vacant.

In suburban Detroit, according to Marshall DeBarry, followup 2 was underway in the middle of the summer. There was a lot of pressure at the district office, he said, because they had to resolve problems and move toward finishing. Furthermore, it was stress-ful to read what the local newspapers were saying about the census and to deal with municipal officials in the local review. It was hot and the office was not air conditioned. "You sweat," he said. "I'd go to an area and look for a building [one that municipal officials insisted was there]. I found a house in a factory area. That made me pleased. I thought, 'Gosh, it worked!' " (DeBarry 1983). It was hot in Baltimore, too. Janet Tippett said, "Later, in July, the work was harder. The temperature was getting up to 100, and we had to go after the tough cases" (Tippett 1983).

Given their other responsibilities in the offices, district manag-ers had little time for community relations work. Career census employees were not experienced at public relations activity, and the district manager's job did not necessarily call for it. The regional office took care of community and press relations and even handled contacts with municipal officials. One of the manag-ers I met struck me as a shy person who was disinclined to make public appearances. "We had publicity coordinators," he said, "their job was to get stuff into the media. I felt my job was to stay in the office" (Takei 1983). Another district manager said, "Our job was to take the census" (DeBarry 1983).

But Janet Tippett, an outgoing person, did get involved in community relations. She reveals a good deal about the problems of getting good data from lower-class households.

> For two weeks before the census I was doing a daily talk at schools. Let me tell you one episode that made a big impression on me.
>
> I went to a grammar school. The yard was covered by broken glass. The building was locked; they had to look at you through the window before they let you in. . . . But the inside was lovely. . . . I was supposed to meet with the sixth graders (all black). Before I met with them, the principal told me that *they* will be the ones who fill out the census forms in their families. They had already studied about the census in their social studies unit. They were already familiar with census forms.
>
> I showed them the envelope they would be getting. I went through the forms with them. Then they asked all sorts of questions I didn't expect: "What about my brother in jail, are we supposed to answer for him?" "What about the three cousins who are staying with us who don't have anyplace to live?"
>
> This is the reality. Being here in the Washington office, planning the census, how do we anticipate this, writing the questions and the manuals?

Tippett appeared on Baltimore television, including a call-in show, often enough that people came to recognize her in public. One day she was at lunch in a restaurant and a man came up to her and said, "Aren't you that census lady? You should get after my sister. She didn't send in her form" (Tippett 1983).

Actually, census confidentiality rules prevented district managers from talking with journalists in some situations. DeBarry mentioned that the Detroit papers frequently criticized the census. "It hurt us enormously when the newspaper would find an old man in a building who they said hadn't been counted. It was always on the 6 o'clock news. The journalists didn't know about followup 1 and 2. . . . In that case we checked and we did have a form on the guy. We couldn't refute the TV story, though. We could not say that we had him. That would violate the rules of confidentiality" (DeBarry 1983).

Shy or gregarious, all the managers had to have a great deal of outside contact during post-census local review. The bureau was to provide to municipal officials lists of all city blocks, showing how many housing units were on each block. This would give local administrators an opportunity to scrutinize the data and tell the census takers where they had missed housing or made other errors. Post-census local review was held in the summer, after followup 1, when the bureau provided preliminary tallies by city block to civic officials for them to check. This review precipitated a considerable amount of work for the district managers, who had to meet with city officials after they examined the tallies. Local officials were free to criticize the data, pointing out locations where they had reason to believe there were more people than were counted. In challenging the count for a particular location, local officials were supposed to provide evidence that the count was incorrect. District managers were then obliged to recanvass the areas in question. Local review necessitated numerous meetings between district managers and local officials. Jones recalled local review in his district:

Out of the five jurisdictions in the Providence district, two complained. The City of Providence lost 20,000 [persons, according to Jones' tallies]. They said, "We think we have 9,000 more than you show." We re-canvassed, despite the absence of hard data in their complaint. . . . In Providence the final count was upped by 3,500. (Jones 1983)

DeBarry had a substantially different experience. Metropolitan Detroit's three district offices released population and housing tallies in June and July. East Detroit showed a 20 percent drop. DeBarry's district had an 18 percent drop. He remembered how local journalists made use of the numbers:

It hits the papers; they have enormous headlines: "Detroit Loses 17%." The *Detroit News* printed each release, mapped by block with each block shaded to show change. I kept trying to tell people, this is just preliminary. There are still other operations. But the papers made it sound like "This is the end of the world; Detroit is doomed." Eventually we reduced it [our district's loss] by about 2 percent. (DeBarry 1983)

Local review was clearly the point at which the district managers had the most contact and the most friction with municipal officials and the press. Recalling his experiences in the middle of the summer when he and his staff were under a great deal of pressure, DeBarry said, "We were all tired. In the paper, the city is yelling how stupid you are. I had to go to meetings and they'd say, 'Here's where you are wrong' " (Ibid).

While local review was still underway, each district office embarked upon its last big job, to make "final population and housing counts" for the enumeration districts. Clerks with calculators made the counts, and entered them on summary forms, which were checked by senior clerks. The forms were taken to the regional census center to be keyed into a computer and relayed to the Census Bureau. At the bureau, the counts were checked against "limits" that had been predicted for each ED on the basis of the previous census and accepted or rejected. District managers could expect 24-hour turnaround on keying and checking. If a final count fell outside of the limits, the bureau rejected it and required the district office to verify it. Jones recalled that such a message might say,

"There used to be a group quarters in this ED, and you don't show it." . . . We would get printouts which would say that our tallies were "out of tolerance." We had to check. Usually found that most of the housing had been torn down. Then we would tally our changes. Sometimes we found an additional housing unit, or we had one in the wrong ED which had to be moved. (Jones 1983)

After checking the ED totals, the bureau ran the same sort of check against the totals for census tracts.

Marshall DeBarry said that making the final counts was "incredibly draining." It was August, and his offices had no air conditioning. Everyone was sweating. Their landlord provided fans. The staff was down to under fifty, including three supervisors, senior office clerks, clerks, and a few enumerators. "We seemed to be a month behind schedule, and it was time to close our office" (DeBarry 1983). Finally, after the final counts were accepted by the bureau, DeBarry's office was down to a skeleton crew of fifteen people. They were told to close by September 30. They packed all the questionnaires and registers in long, flat boxes in order of ED, with the lowest serial number on the bottom.

Friday, the truck came. I stood and watched every register and box. I shipped the master map. They loaded the truck and locked it. The boxes took just a fraction of the truck; it was pathetic [that so much work took up such a small amount of space]. . . .
The trucks were sealed with special numbered locks to prevent the truckers from opening the trucks to add another load, even though the trailer was mostly empty. The truck and its contents were sent to the appropriate

processing center. . . . I felt tired and happy. The clerks stood around. They gave me a party and some presents. (DeBarry 1983)

So the experience of running a district office was punctuated by three visits by trucks: when the supplies were delivered to an empty office, when the post office brought those heaps of returns, and when the manager shipped the results.

During that summer of 1980, while these four district managers were conducting followup 2, local review, and making final counts, the City and State of New York sued the government, alleging that census offices were in a state of wild disarray under incompetent management. Talking with DeBarry, Jones, Takei, and Tippett, I got a totally different picture of how a big city census office worked. I got the impression that new procedures were introduced quickly and according to plan. Eventually, though, the operation stretched monotonously into the summer—after all, checking forms in an office is just repetitive, meticulous work. I envisioned people working long hours in grungy environments to meet their deadlines.

Kits, tests, questionnaires, payroll forms, yellow cards, maps, bins, manuals, registers—I was amazed with the multiplicity of detailed elements that had to mesh. All of them were prepared in advance, made to fit each other, produced in precisely the correct numbers, and shipped to arrive at the right time. You will recall all the built-in checks and repetitions in the process, for example, in the development of address registers. First the bureau acquired commercial lists and geocoded them. Then clerks hand-processed the unmatched addresses. Next, the enumerators walked through their enumeration districts, reviewing and correcting the registers. The postal sorters also checked all the questionnaires against their delivery routes. There could be an error in any of these processes, but the redundancies were designed to make it difficult for a dwelling to slip through all of the procedures. Furthermore, if a household were missed in these various listing operations, it might still be contacted by an enumerator during a follow-up, or someone in the household might contact the census.

Nonetheless, a close look at the day-to-day execution of the census also revealed the multiplicity of points where errors could be made. Some of the original ingredients, such as address lists and maps, were deficient in quality. Respondents filling out their own questionnaires may fail to follow instructions correctly. Forms may be misdirected from one district to another (in the cases of persons in hotels or vacation homes and students in dormitories). Neighbors may provide incorrect information in last resort interviews. Clerks may incorrectly mark questionnaires or tally sheets. There are backup procedures to detect these and other possible sources of errors, but some mistakes must creep through. The controversies over undercounting refer to a small margin of error. These controversies usually refer to "difficult-to-enumerate" segments of the population. But a close look at the census process reveals that errors are inevitable, even under ordinary circumstances. The census was done extremely well, but there were undoubtedly errors.

To conclude on a personal note, it was easy to detect the district managers' sense of commitment and excitement. For them the 1980 census was an extremely engaging, yet stressful, experience. In speaking with me, DeBarry's first words were: "I started smoking three packs per day, working in the census." Later, he remarked, "Every night I thought what an enormous responsibility I had. I was terrified. You are responsible for the whole thing" (DeBarry 1983). On the other hand, when I asked Takei, "Was it fun?" he answered unhesitatingly, "I'd do it again; sure" (Takei 1983). As Tippett said, "It's a once-in-a-decade opportunity. . . . The census was a tremendous accomplishment. Imagine, covering the whole country!" (Tippett 1983).

6 The 1980 Detroit Case

EVEN BEFORE the 1980 census was taken, the city of Detroit sued Secretary of Commerce Philip Klutznick, and Director of the Census Bureau Vincent Barabba. Initiating *Young* v. *Klutznick*, the "Detroit Case," Mayor Coleman Young and the city of Detroit sued to compel the bureau to adjust the forthcoming census results to correct for an anticipated undercount. The Detroit case reveals the interplay of nonscientific and scientific issues. The case began with two nonscientific considerations: the decision by the judge as to whether or not the plaintiffs had legal standing to sue, and whether or not their complaint was based on constitutional considerations. But they also asked scientific questions: how likely was it that the census would yield an undercount?; and how capable was the bureau of adjusting statistically for that undercount? This question was followed by more nonscientific issues, such as whether the Constitution and federal census laws permitted the bureau to adjust the numbers.

Some of the lawsuit's main controversies were semantic. Was the census an enumeration, a headcount, or an estimate? Was the statistical procedure known as imputing the same as adjusting? What did it mean to say that only a statistically defensible adjustment would be acceptable to the Census Bureau? While the Detroit case reflects the tension between science and politics, ultimately the nonscientific concerns were of overriding importance. Scientific issues receded into a secondary role.

The Detroit case moved much faster than any of the other

major 1980 census undercount cases. Detroit filed its case on March 31, 1980. Judge Ralph Guy of the federal district court in Detroit ruled on May 29, 1980, that the plaintiffs had standing to sue. A trial took place from August 18 to August 27 before Judge Horace Gilmore. On September 25, 1980, he handed down his decision, ruling in favor of Mayor Young and the city. The defendants immediately appealed, and on June 15, 1981, in Cincinnati, the Court of Appeals for the Sixth Circuit reversed Judge Gilmore's decision. The plaintiffs petitioned the Supreme Court to review the case, and on February 22, 1982 the High Court rejected that appeal. By contrast, the New York case was not decided until December 1987, more than seven years after the suit had been filed! Across the country, cities, counties, states, and organizations filed suits resembling those of Detroit and New York. Thirty-nine of them were referred to one federal court, where they were treated as one multidistrict case "for coordinated or consolidated pretrial proceedings," which never came to trial (Mitroff, Mason, and Barabba 1983: 62).

In Detroit, two attorneys represented the city: James Tuck, an attorney in a small firm, and Robert Sedler, a professor at Wayne State University's law school. Tuck's firm, located in an old downtown office building, specialized in personal injury, but as Tuck said, "We also do civil rights cases, offbeat cases where lawyers are hard to get" (Tuck 1983). Explaining how he got involved in the case, Tuck said, "I was just intrigued. I have a mechanical engineering background. I am good at organizing the science aspects of a technical case. Sedler could organize the legal aspects. Bob had been active in busing litigation—in NAACP cases and Kentucky desegregation cases. He is a constitutional lawyer" (Ibid.). In the lawyers' division of labor, Tuck took the technical census issues and Sedler took the legal issues. Sedler began developing his approach in preparation for a hearing of the House Subcommittee on Census and Population, which was held in Detroit in November, 1979 (Sedler 1983).

The government was represented by Bill Elliot, the senior attorney on the case, and Shiela Lieber, a pair of young lawyers from the Justice Department's civil division in Washington, D.C. While Sedler had months to work on the city's brief, the government lawyers had only three weeks to prepare their defense (Lieber 1983).

Detroit's lawyers quickly won a crucial battle over the issue of legal standing. Standing was a fundamental issue in all of the legal challenges to the 1970 and 1980 censuses, since as a rule, in order to be accepted as a valid party to a lawsuit, a plaintiff must demonstrate that he or she has the legal right (standing) to sue. In lawsuits regarding the 1970 census, plaintiffs routinely failed this test, which prevented them from taking their cases to trial. At that time judges ruled against mayors and other complainants, because they believed there was no necessary connection between a city and the Census Bureau or that no injury to the mayor or the city's residents had been proven as a direct result of a census. In those unsuccessful 1970 cases, each plaintiff was treated by the court as a resident of a state. The rulings said that since the plaintiffs could not show that their state had lost a seat in Congress due to census procedures, the plaintiffs had not been injured by the census. Departing from that precedent, Sedler based the Detroit case on intrastate malapportionment of congressional and state legislative districts, which was easier to demonstrate.

Before *Young* v. *Klutznick* came to trial, the defendants (secretary of commerce, census director, and other federal officials) moved to have the case dismissed because the plaintiffs lacked standing to sue. The government's lawyers said that the plaintiffs' argument was merely speculative because it was impossible to demonstrate that they had suffered an injury before the census was taken. A hearing was held on the government's motion before Judge Ralph Guy, who rejected it, determining that the plaintiffs did have standing. Judge Guy wrote, "While the original concern of the 'capital framers' was with representation of one state vis-a-vis another, the reapportionment cases clearly extend the requirement to equal representation within the state" (Gilmore Opinion, 1980:1323). Sedler explained, "We satisfied the criterion for standing known as injury in fact" (Sedler 1983). This ruling marked Detroit's first victory. This struggle over the issue of standing, however, illustrates an important point about the undercount-adjustment controversy. Although the issues may appear initially to be scientific and political, when they enter a courtroom they become primarily legal. Like all lawsuits, the 1980 census cases were embedded in the trappings of the court where there were many nonscientific issues that only lawyers could handle.

In the Detroit case, the plaintiffs' attorneys were able to file suit before the census began because, they argued, based upon previous experience in 1960 and 1970, there was no doubt that the census would yield an undercount. This part of the argument was known as the "inevitable undercount." Since the city housed hundreds of thousands of blacks and poor people—the very categories most likely to be missed—the city would undoubtedly suffer from an undercount. In his opening statement, Bill Elliott, from the Justice Department, said the bureau did not know if there would be an undercount in the new census, but Barabba later testified that he expected one. The defendants then stopped disputing that there would be a differential undercount, and one major scientific point—the inevitability of a differential undercount—was accepted by both sides.

Detroit's attorneys defined the need to adjust as a constitutional question: "There are two fundamental issues in this case: (1) Does the Constitution require that an adjustment be made in the official population count of the decennial census for the anticipated differential undercount of blacks and Hispanics?" and (2) if so, how? (Plaintiffs 1980:1). The principle of "one person, one vote" guided Sedler's arguments:

Census data is used for various purposes, but the sole constitutional purpose is to apportion. . . . The Supreme Court has treated Article 1, Section 2, so that equal representation [in congressional districts and within states] requires equal numbers of persons in each district within a state. There must be strict mathematical equality. A judge in Michigan recently required a plan in which the districts would be off by no more than four persons! (Sedler 1983)

The Detroit lawyers noted that

an official population count based on the raw unadjusted census data does not accurately reflect the *actual* population of the states and of the cities and governmental sub-units in each state. This is because in every past decennial census, there has been a racial differential of completeness in coverage, with blacks being undercounted at a rate grossly and disproportionately higher than whites. Since the black population is concentrated in certain cities and in certain states, the black undercount differential produces a *constitutional distortion*. States with a relatively large state-wide black population are undercounted at a rate higher than the states having little or no black population, and the cities and other places where the black population is concentrated are undercounted at a much higher rate than the predominantly white suburbs and the areas having little or no black population. As a result, the residents of those states and cities have less representation and less weight of vote than the residents of the states and other areas having little or no black population. (Plaintiffs 1980:2–3)

Sedler's argument said that a black person who lives in a black district is underrepresented because the state, in effect, is counting that district at less than its true size. There are actually more people who live there too; they just were not counted. Sedler explained: assume that the census counts 600,000 blacks in Detroit and that there is a 7 percent black undercount. If all the districts in Michigan are exactly equal based on the census, there are actually more people in the black districts than there are in the white districts. "So the black citizen doesn't have equal representation with the white individual" (Sedler 1983).

Sedler continued his argument, "Because of the concentration of blacks and the differential undercount, failure to adjust will prevent equal representation" (Ibid. 1983). "The command of Art. I, Sec. 2, cl. 3, that there be equal representation for equal numbers of people is, in fact, violated" (Plaintiffs 1980:3). Detroit asserted that if the census were not adjusted, blacks would not receive the same proportionate representation in Congress as whites and that this would violate their rights guaranteed under the Fourteenth Amendment (Plaintiffs 1980:17). Three years after the trial, Sedler told me that he still considered his theory to be perfect. "Our case was that the Constitution *requires* adjustment. Otherwise congressional apportionment will violate equal representation for equal numbers of people" (Sedler 1983).

Responding directly to Sedler's constitutional argument, the government's lawyers contended that the census was not causing these injuries to the city's poor black residents; that if they had suffered such an injury, the Michigan state legislature was to blame. Neither the Constitution nor federal law required the legislature to use unadjusted census numbers for the purpose of districting. Perhaps the legislature could adjust the numbers themselves if they saw fit. (The defendants' lawyers did not deny that the Constitution required the Congress to use the census for apportioning congressional seats among the states, but the plaintiffs had not claimed that they would lose a seat because of the anticipated undercount.) The defense contended that there were many other reasons, as well, why they should not be compelled to adjust the numbers. They argued that if an adjustment were necessary, it should be mandated by the Congress. They maintained that since the bureau was an administrative agency the principles of administrative law should apply in this case. They insisted that the court should leave the adjustment decision to the census director of the bureau, and merely require him not to be arbitrary or capricious. In light of this they deemed the director's decision not to adjust as reasonable.

The government's lawyers claimed that they had demonstrated that it is impossible to devise an adjustment that would be both timely and accurate. They asserted that "there is no means by which the Census Bureau will be able to derive statistically defensible estimates of the undercount for national, state, and substate areas within the statutory deadlines prescribed by the Census Act" (Defendants 1980:36). The defense attorneys noted that the census act required the bureau's director to deliver census results to the president by the end of the year. They noted also that the plaintiff's purposes of apportioning and districting required accurate black and Hispanic data down to the city-block level. The lawyers explained that while demographic analysis would yield results for the nation as a whole and matching studies would yield results for whole states, neither system could produce statistics for smaller areas such as counties, towns, and city blocks, all of which would have to be adjusted in order to satisfy the plaintiffs.

The government's lawyers asserted that neither the Constitution nor the census laws permits the bureau to adjust the counts. The bureau is required to make an "enumeration" of the people, they said. They cited the Constitution, Article I, Section 2, which says that there shall be an "actual Enumeration" of the people every ten years. The defendants said that "The terms 'census' and 'enumeration' mean nothing more or less than a head count" (Defendants 1980:14). Since the bureau was not permitted to prepare an estimate, they could not use statistical procedures like adjusting to alter the results of the census. To do so would transform the result into something that is not an enumeration.

The Detroit lawyers rejected the bureau's definition of the census as a headcount. They explained the bureau's history of imputing households and persons into the census. "In past censuses and again in the 1980 census the Census Bureau will create large numbers of persons who were not 'headcounted,' and whose

individual existence the Census Bureau has no evidence of whatsoever" (Plaintiffs 1980:21). In their brief, Detroit's attorneys
referred to five "1970 imputation programs," including the national vacancy check and the postenumeration post office check.
They noted that the bureau imputed over one million persons by
means of the national vacancy check and another 500,000 through
PEPOC. They concluded that "the creation of close to 5 million
persons by 'imputation' in the 1970 decennial census and the use
of 'imputation' in past censuses completely destroys the defendants' purported 'headcount' argument" (Ibid.). The cases in Detroit and New York generated considerable debate over the issue
of imputation and its definition.

Another part of the government's defense was that the bureau
is specifically enjoined (in Section 195, Title 13 of the U.S. Code)
from the use of sampling in producing population numbers for the
purpose of apportionment and that adjustment could not be done
without sampling. Sampling has been used in every census since
1940, but only to gather data on people's occupations, incomes,
housing, and other characteristics, not for information that is used
for apportionment. James Tuck insisted that the bureau itself had
established a precedent for the use of sampling in producing
population counts when it conducted the national vacancy check
in 1970. The national vacancy check, which incorporated sampling, was conducted as an attempt to overcome a problem that
contributed to undercounting in 1960. "The Bureau discovered
that a significant factor in the [1960] undercount was caused by
the census enumerators' failure to determine which housing units
should be classified as vacant on the census reference day." Enumerators had classified some housing units as vacant when, in fact,
they were occupied. The national vacancy check, which was not a
part of the 1970 census plans, was deployed in order to overcome
this source of error. "The bureau used interviewers with long
experience in interviewing methods and with special training in
this problem to undertake a systematic review of a national sample
of 15,000 housing units that had been classified as vacant by the
original enumerators" (U.S.Bureau of the Census 1976:14-5).

Thus, the imputation resulting from the 1970 national vacancy
check was based upon the sampling of housing units originally
coded as vacant, contrary to the bureau's assertions in court and

contrary, as well, to the provisions of Title 13. The only way census officials "knew" that those housing units were "really occupied" was on the basis of a sample survey. The results of that intensive survey showed that a certain percent of housing units classified as vacant were actually occupied. The survey also showed the average number of persons living in such misclassified housing units in each major region. Based upon those two pieces of information, census officials changed a certain percent of the vacant housing units in every ED into occupied units and they added—imputed—persons into those dwellings. The 1970 national vacancy check was a fundamental piece of evidence in Detroit's case because it showed that the bureau had established a precedent for adding people and for using sampling to create numbers that were used for apportionment.

More generally, the Detroit lawyers advocated the use of a novel standard for decision: they asked the judge to determine which numbers would be "closer to the truth": those from the regular enumeration or those that had been adjusted. The plaintiffs also contended that it was technically possible to adjust for the purpose of overcoming the differential undercount. They recommended the use of a "synthetic adjustment" to bring the census numbers closer to the truth. Lawyers for Detroit called upon expert witnesses to convince Judge Gilmore that adjustment was technically feasible. Three such witnesses were sociologist Robert Hill, director of the National Urban League's research division, sociologist-demographer Karl Taeuber of the University of Wisconsin, and most notably, retired sociologist-demographer, Philip Hauser of the University of Chicago. All of them asserted that adjustment was feasible and that the adjusted numbers would be closer to the truth. Robert Hill recommended "synthetic adjustment," which he had already applied to 1970 census numbers.

The synthetic method is a statistical procedure for distributing the undercount of a larger geographical area (such as the nation, state, county, or city) among its subunits (such as a state, county, city, or congressional district, respectively). For example, this method permits one to distribute the total 5.3 million persons that the Census Bureau estimated had been left out of the 1970 census not only among all 50 states, but also among every subdivision . . . within each state. (Hill 1980:130)

Hill also explained how it could be applied to a real dataset.

The synthetic method can easily be used by nonstatisticians to derive the census undercount for any areas below the national level. One only needs to apply the appropriate percentage increase to the official 1970 census count for specific race/sex/age groups in specific localities. For example, an undercount rate of 14.4 percent for black males ages 30 to 34 requires that the official (or published) census count of black men 30 to 34 years old in a locality be increased (or inflated) by 16.8 percent (or, more appropriately, by 116.8 percent). Similarly, an undercount rate of 9.7 percent for black females under the age of 5 requires that the official census count of black females under 5 be increased by 10.7 percent (or by 110.7 percent). This step is repeated for each age category in each of the four key subgroups: black males, black females, white males, and white females. (Hill 1980:131)

Philip Hauser proved to be an extraordinarily effective witness. On the stand he recounted his illustrious career, referring to his professorship and his presidency of three scientific associations, the American Statistical Association, the American Sociological Association, and the Population Association of America. Hauser said that he had worked on no fewer than six decennial censuses, serving as acting director from 1949–1950. He explained several statistical concepts and census procedures to Judge Gilmore. Hauser asserted that the Census Bureau was capable of implementing an adjustment and that such an adjustment would bring the numbers closer to the truth. Attorney James Tuck said of Hauser, "You only meet someone like him once in a lifetime. He has an original, organized mind. He has a rare ability, a way to simplify and explain complex scientific issues at any level. . . . He could come in quickly, and tell the lawyers what is important" (Tuck 1983). One Justice Department lawyer said, "Phil Hauser was a powerful figure on the stand. He said how he had run the census and had introduced this and that and developed this and that technique. Once Hauser testified on the first day, the judge decided" (Lieber 1983).

The defendants did not agree that adjusting was feasible. They explained that it would be impossible to prepare a demographic analysis in time to permit the production of adjusted numbers by the end-of-the-year deadline. "The only estimate of the undercount that would be available by the end of this year would be a crude estimate of the national undercount as a whole, undifferentiated according to characteristics of the population (e.g., age, race, sex and ethnicity)" (Defendants 1980:38). Citing the testimony of two eminent social scientists, Nathan Keyfitz, a demographer, and

William Kruskal, a statistician, the government's lawyers asserted that there was, as yet, no accepted scientific solution to the problem of adjusting the census. They quoted Kruskal as having said that adjusting at or below the state level was "at the frontier of research" and Keyfitz had said that adjustment at the state level is "beyond the frontier of knowledge" (Defendants 1980:48).

Rejecting this argument, Judge Gilmore rendered his decision on September 25, 1980, ruling in favor of Mayor Young and Detroit. Basically, Judge Gilmore accepted all of the plaintiff's points. Early in his opinion he reiterated Sedler's theory, saying that the Constitution:

> requires that the official decennial population count reflect as accurately as is reasonably possible the true population of the states, cities, and other governmental sub-units within each state. Plaintiffs claim, and it is not seriously disputed, that an official population count, using only raw, unadjusted census data, does not accurately reflect the actual population of the states and governmental units within the states. (Gilmore Opinion 1980:1321)

Then, following the plaintiffs' argument, Judge Gilmore connected their complaint to the matter of apportionment. "The necessity for an accurate population count among and within states is inexorably tied to fair apportionment of congressional seats. That is what this case is all about. The issue is as simple as that" (Ibid.:1323). Judge Gilmore rejected the government's assertion that the census is and has been a headcount. Reviewing the bureau's record of imputing households and individuals into the census, he said that it is "clear that the decennial census is not, and has not been for at least the past decade, a simple, straightforward headcount." He said that the census is "a relatively accurate estimate of the population developed through the use of self-enumeration by questionnaire, statistical techniques, and computer-control devices" (Ibid.:1329–1330).

Judge Gilmore summarized the arguments regarding undercounting and adjusting. He noted that censuses routinely result in differential undercounts. He referred to the testimony of expert witnesses who said that the census could be adjusted in 1980 by means of a synthetic adjustment. He concluded that "there are proper and adequate methods for adjusting the raw census data to give a reasonably accurate and statistically adjusted count at the national, state, and sub-state levels" (Ibid.:1331).

Having determined the various scientific-technical points, Judge Gilmore considered the question of whether the law requires the bureau to implement an adjustment. He rejected the defendants' assertion that the whole question should be left to the discretion of administrators. He concluded that the bureau must adjust the census counts. He enjoined them from "certifying" unadjusted numbers to the president. He ordered the defendants "to adjust population figures for the 1980 census at the national, state, and sub-state level to reflect the undercount, and adjust the differential undercount." Finally, he gave the bureau thirty days in which to report "the precise nature of its plan to implement the holdings of this Opinion" (Ibid.:1339). The government's lawyers immediately appealed the decision in the United States Court of Appeals for the Sixth District.

A few days after Judge Gilmore's decision, the bureau announced that it had completed the national census count. Vincent Barabba appeared at a press conference to announce the results, stating that the census had counted 226.5 million persons. This number was approximately four million more than the bureau's analysts had expected to find, based on their earlier demographic predictions (*Wall Street Journal* 1980). Barabba said that this large number meant that there was in effect no net undercount, so there was nothing to adjust. The announced total appeared to be within one percent of the true total (i.e., the total predicted by demographic analysis). Census officials said that the existing methods for measuring and estimating undercounts were not sufficiently precise to be used for adjustment. Existing adjustment methods might help to correct an undercount of 2 or 3 percent, but with a 1 percent underenumeration, the adjustment methods might introduce more new errors than they would correct. Officials maintained that given this small margin of error in the overall census, adjusting would not and could not create new numbers that would be closer to the truth.

A month after the case was decided, the bureau delivered a report on adjusting, "in response to the order of Judge Horace W. Gilmore." The document consists of a thirty-seven-page report, signed by Vincent Barabba, plus his affidavit and thirteen technical appendices (U.S. Bureau of the Census, Report 1980). The document consists mostly of appendices. Appendix 1 is a two-page progress report on results of preliminary field population counts as of October 22. Appendix 2 refers to corrections to the bureau's estimates of the undercount from the previous census. Appendices 3–8 report on technical aspects of estimating undercounts in 1980, including "limitations of the postenumeration program," which are highlighted.

The volume concludes with four appendices on how to adjust. They represent the main item ordered by Judge Gilmore, a plan for adjustment. In a mere thirteen pages, the bureau offers two ways in which they can adjust the census counts. Appendix 10 says that "it would be possible to produce synthetic corrections [adjustments] for states shortly after the national undercount rates are available, i.e., mid- to late-February 1981." So even using this simplest of methods, the bureau says that it would miss its December 31 deadline. Also in Appendix 10, the bureau notes that they do not have a good estimate of the Hispanic undercount. In order to adjust the Hispanic numbers, they say they could assume that the Hispanic undercount equalled the black undercount. Employing this assumption, the bureau could use the estimate of a black undercount rate to apply as a Hispanic undercount rate, too. In the same appendix, however, the bureau says, "This is a completely arbitrary assumption and without any empirical support. Consequently, it cannot be deemed defensible, statistically or otherwise, for use in so important a process as congressional apportionment." (These two sentences capture the tone of the entire report to Judge Gilmore.) Appendices 11–13 develop a more complex approach to adjusting the census, based upon district-by-district results of the postenumeration program, entered into regression formulas.

The bureau uses the report as a vehicle in which to argue that adjusting is impossible. The agency's argument is based upon an unexpected foundation: preliminary census counts, "new information," show that "the bureau has succeeded in eliminating at least four-fifths and perhaps all of the expected undercount for the United States, as determined through the method of demographic analysis" (U.S. Bureau of the Census, Report 1980:2). Since the undercount will be either nonexistent or extremely small, there is no "statistically defensible" method by which the bureau can measure it. Given that impossibility, it follows that there is also no statistically defensible way in which to subdivide the undercount to states and smaller places to adjust for it.

The bureau then asked the judge to tell them how to perform a statistical adjustment: "The Bureau would use whichever method of estimating the national undercount is selected by the Court and would distribute the undercount as measured by that method through a uniform synthetic method using racial and ethnic factors only." In other words, if you are going to force us to adjust, you must tell us how to do it. The bureau hastened to note that the synthetic method is really not very good. "The synthetic method itself is not statistically defensible, but in light of the fact that the national undercount figure to be distributed will itself be unreliable, no method of distribution could be defensible." The report concludes by recommending that the court permit the bureau to deliver to the president the regular unadjusted census counts.

James Tuck accused the bureau of using the report in order to resist compliance with Judge Gilmore's order (Tuck 1983). First, the bureau had no business bringing an obfuscatory report to the judge when he had ordered a plan for implementation. Second, the whole matter of the "bumper crop" of 226 million and the fact that there might not have been a net undercount was used deceptively by Barabba to obscure the fact that there was clearly a differential undercount. It was likely that whites were overcounted, while blacks again were undercounted. Detroit's lawyers and expert witnesses said that this differential undercount was correctable.

Determined to allow the bureau to deliver the census results to the president by December 31, the government's lawyers applied to the Supreme Court for a stay of Judge Gilmore's order. They succeeded on December 24, when Associate Justice Potter Stewart ordered a stay pending the outcome of the defendants' appeal. That stay permitted the bureau to deliver unadjusted counts to the president (Mitroff, Mason, and Barabba 1983:74).

On June 15, 1981, in Cincinnati, the Sixth Circuit Court of Appeals overturned Judge Gilmore's decision, ruling that the Census Bureau would not be required to adjust. One judge agreed with Judge Gilmore and filed a dissenting opinion. In their decision, the appeals judges questioned whether a synthetic adjustment would be appropriate to rectify the plaintiff's alleged problem. The judges accepted the argument that the only method of adjustment that could be applied in a timely fashion would be synthetic adjustment (U.S. Court of Appeals, 6th Cir. 1981:622). Then they reasoned that most blacks who are undercounted are in poverty, but that most blacks overall are not in poverty. The judges asserted that the effect of a synthetic adjustment would be to add blacks to nonpoverty areas, where they do not belong, while simultaneously failing to add them to poverty areas, where they do belong. Thus, a synthetic adjustment would distort the voting rights situation even further.

The court of appeals' decision said that the plaintiffs lacked standing to sue, after all, ruling that Mayor Young and the City of Detroit "lacked standing to bring action" and the "issue was not ripe for judicial review." The new decision said that "Plaintiffs have shown no judicially cognizable injury and lack standing to sue. The claimed injury is based on a state of affairs not yet in existence, and it is so hypothetical in nature that it does not present a controversy capable of judicial resolution" (Ibid.:619). Rejecting Robert Sedler's theory, the court of appeals stated that there was nothing in the Constitution or in federal law that required the State of Michigan to use census numbers in apportioning legislative districts, so, if the state was dissatisfied with the census, it could use data produced by some other mechanism. Thus, even if an undercount exists, it cannot be shown that census numbers directly cause injury to the people of Detroit. The appeals court invoked three other principles applying to legitimate lawsuits in federal courts: there must be "a distinct and palpable injury" to the plaintiff, "a fairly traceable" causal connection between the claimed injury and the challenged conduct, and it must be shown that the court's action can redress the injury (Ibid.:623). The majority opinion stated that Detroit failed on all three counts. There was no causal connection between the defendants actions and the injury claimed by the plaintiffs: "Contrary to the assertions by plaintiffs, the state legislature is not required by the Constitution to accept in all respects the census data supplied by the bureau" (Ibid.:624). The opinion deemed the lawsuit "not ripe", or premature. "Because the Michigan state legislature has not yet expressed reaction to the census enumeration, the issue before this court has not become as 'specific' or as 'particularized' as it will become after the legislature acts. . . . The dilution of voting power on which they [plaintiffs] base their claim may not occur at all and cannot occur until the Michigan legislature acts" (Ibid.:626). The idea that the Michigan legislature was free to adjust census numbers itself seemed (to me and to other observers) to be a curious argument. After all, by longstanding tradition all states base their districts on census numbers. No state conducts its own census. However, the decision got the census director off the hook.

In sum, the main controversy embodied in *Young* v. *Klutznick* was whether the court would compel the bureau to adjust the counts. Mayor Young and the city won Round One when Judge Gilmore enjoined the bureau from delivering unadjusted numbers for apportionment and ordered it to produce a plan for adjustment. The government won the decisive round, however, when the court of appeals reversed Judge Gilmore's decision. The case included several scientific-technical questions. There was no dispute over whether Detroit would suffer a differential undercount. The main question was whether the bureau was capable of producing adjusted numbers and whether they would be closer to the truth. The plaintiffs recommended the synthetic method of adjustment. The defendants admitted that it would be possible to use that method to produce new numbers, but they did not agree that such numbers would be closer to the truth. One technical dispute had to do with the timetable for producing numbers to meet certain legal deadlines. The bureau said that if they adjusted the numbers by the synthetic method, they would have to wait for the calculation of the undercount estimate, which would require them to miss the major deadlines.

There was a major semantic dispute in the lawsuit over the meaning of the terms *enumeration, estimate,* and *adjustment.* Census officials insisted that the Constitution and census laws required the census be an enumeration, which is a headcount. They said that they were not permitted to produce and deliver a statistical estimate of the population. Plaintiffs, on the other hand, asserted that the Constitution required that the census generate the most accurate number possible. They asserted that the bureau's use of imputation techniques, particularly in 1970, showed that they had already departed from the tradition of producing a simple enumeration. They showed that at least one imputation routine in 1970 was equivalent to an adjustment.

Perhaps ironically, the issue was decided over a completely nonstatistical issue, the legal question of whether Mayor Young and the city had standing to sue. Initially, it was decided in the federal district court that they had met that precondition for a trial. At the court of appeals, however, that decision was overturned, when a majority of the judges ruled that the Plaintiffs could not demonstrate that they had suffered an injury at the hands of the Census Bureau. All of these issues resurfaced in the New York case.

7 The New York Case, 1980–1987

FIVE MONTHS AFTER the start of the Detroit case, New Yorkers also sued the secretary of commerce and the census director. Their case, *Cuomo* v. *Baldridge*, ran for seven years including trial, appeal, retrial, and a thirty-month wait for the judge's decision.[1] In 1979 there was no obvious sign that New York would sue. Anticipating the census, local politicians and administrators in Mayor Edward Koch's office had defined it as an important event. According to David Jones, who was then Special Advisor to the Mayor for Minority Affairs and who was responsible for the city's census effort, the numbers were going to have a special symbolic significance.

[Before the census] the projections showed a major population loss for New York City. The worst showed us below seven million. The city was still in the financial crisis then. [A major population loss would be taken as] a sign that the city was coming apart, becoming an urban wasteland. Would discourage investment. In those days the Sunbelt was gloating, saying that northern cities would be ghost towns. We had to have a good census to maintain our economic base. (Jones 1986)

In dealing with the Census Bureau, city administrators' basic assumption was that New York was uniquely different from the rest of the country in ways that would make a difference for the census. New Yorkers spoke more languages than people elsewhere. People in New York were more suspicious and less cooperative; slums were more dangerous; there were more people who would be disinclined to cooperate. The city had thousands of children in poverty whose lives were unlike those of other children. New York saw their city as bigger and tougher than anyplace else—and they assumed that census officials failed to appreciate that fact.

New York viewed the Census Bureau's plans as highly standardized for the entire nation. According to Evelyn Mann, head of the population statistics division in the city's Department of City Planning, the bureau was rigid on insisting that it would use only those procedures which it could apply nationally. This principle, which she said lies at the heart of all census operations, had detrimental consequences for enumerating New York City, given its unique size, density, and diversity (Mann 1980:31). There was an inevitable tension between these two points of view, the city's unique toughness versus the bureau's commitment to nationally applicable procedures. At first, the city of New York cooperated with the bureau. The city began several months in advance to prepare a promotional campaign. Following the bureau's national pattern, the mayor's office appointed a Complete Count Committee, which was supposed to help generate popular support, and city officials planned educational and publicity campaigns.

The city was also prepared to participate in the bureau's new local review program. Evelyn Mann's staff in the planning department had developed sophisticated computerized files to describe the city's housing stock in detail, and she was prepared to check the bureau's lists before the census, thereby contributing to a more complete enumeration. Then the bureau failed to supply maps and lists for verification, and cancelled precensus local review. This cancellation meant that the preparation of Mann's staff had been wasted and that the city had lost an opportunity to check the census's basic housing counts.

New Yorkers anticipated that many of the census field procedures would not work because the city was so big, tough, dangerous, and complicated. They contended that many of these procedures might be appropriate for midwestern suburbs, but they just would not work in New York. In the months before the census, David Jones made several suggestions to the bureau about staffing and payment for enumerators in New York, which were rejected. "One big issue was over paying minimum wage to enumerators [as the bureau had planned]. You can't get competent enumerators in poor areas for that kind of money. It's not like getting parttime housewives in Winnetka, Illinois. You need skillful people. In New York, people are leery about giving information about themselves. They never open the door, even law-abiding people" (Jones 1986).

New York asked the bureau for resources and modifications of standard procedures. "The bureau said, 'We can't help you much.' We asked for fliers in foreign languages. They said, 'We have no money.' We asked for special training and for early set-up of offices. They said 'We can't do this.' Our good relationship came apart completely" (Ibid.).

New Yorkers disparaged the bureau's educational products saying that they would not work in the city's schools. New York's streetsmart kids live in a special world; they could not be given cutesy little booklets about white families in the suburbs. They cannot relate to these innocent, suburban scenarios.

The Board of Education assigned people to rewrite the materials. You couldn't use their [the bureau's] stuff in New York City. For example, the materials included a map of the United States without Puerto Rico. One exercise asked a child to list his relatives—what about a child whose family is still in Colombia? There was no feeling that you had to explain this to your parents. They included a little play that simply could not be performed in Harlem. (Mann 1983)

New Yorkers complained also about the bureau's publicity materials, saying that they could not be used because of the many different languages spoken there. City hall organized its own publicity program. To explain the census and to encourage people to cooperate, the city administration prepared flyers in fifteen languages and posted them in ethnic grocery stores, churches, and community centers (Ibid.). The city hired sound trucks to cruise certain neighborhoods, broadcasting tapes in twenty different languages to promote the census. The city translated the census questionnaire into twenty-six languages and sent them to ethnic media.

Despite the city's attempts to promote the census, David Jones was convinced by midsummer that many of the city's residents were not being counted and that they would never be counted if the bureau was allowed to close district offices in August, as planned. One of his sources of information was a twenty-four hour phone-in line at city hall. According to Evelyn Mann, people could phone in if they hadn't received a questionnaire and the operator would tell them where to call to get one. Mann said that the service had received thousands of calls like that. Furthermore Jones reported that he had heard from many persons who had called the bureau, several times in some cases, and still got no response—no form in the mail and no visit from an enumerator.

Jones complained about the disposition of the coverage improvement program's Were You Counted? forms. Printed in newspapers and on individual sheets, they offered a person an opportunity to notify the census that he or she had not been counted.[2] Toward the end of followup two, the forms were supposed to be distributed widely in places such as convenience stores and laundromats, welfare offices and public clinics. If a person sent in a Were You Counted? form, the district office that received it was obliged to check its records to see if that person or household had been enumerated and, if not, to make appropriate additions.[3] Jones alleged that at least some of the district offices were failing to examine the Were You Counted? forms. By late July the district offices were preparing to close, which meant that they would not be able to find and count the rest of the people. Jones and his colleagues strongly suspected that the census had stopped enumerating. They decided to sue the government in an effort to keep the offices open and also to press for a statistical adjustment.

Before joining the city administration, David Jones had been an associate in the famous law firm of Cravath, Swaine, and Moore. In the summer of 1980, as the mayor's envoy, Jones approached Frederick A. O. Schwarz, Jr., a Cravath senior partner, to see if the firm would be willing to represent the city, *pro bono publico*, and they agreed to do so. In August, they filed suit in federal district court for the southern district of New York on behalf of the governor of New York, the mayor, and several citizens, asking the court to enjoin the bureau from closing its field offices. The plaintiffs demanded that the census continue its fieldwork, utilize the Were You Counted? forms, and follow up on certain allegedly missed places that the city had reported during postcensus local review. The plaintiffs quickly won their first objective when the presiding judge, Henry F. Werker, enjoined the bureau from closing district offices in New York City for several weeks, ordered them to process the Were You Counted? forms and to follow up on the allegedly missed places.

Robert Rifkind, another senior partner at Cravath, joined Schwarz on the case. In 1981, Schwarz left Cravath to become the city's Corporate Counsel and Rifkind took responsibility for the case. He was assisted by several junior associates, including Alan Glickman, a fresh law school graduate with an inclination toward public-interest law.[4] Glickman, stayed with the case for more than six years, gaining increasing responsibility. He said that Cravath contributed resources to the case unstintingly, donating for extended periods the services of two major partners and eight to ten associates. If the firm had been billing a client for all of this time, it would have amounted to millions of dollars.

The lawyers prepared a two-part case. One main argument paralleled that of Detroit, that a differential undercount was inevitable and that justice required a statistical adjustment. This "inevitable undercount" argument said that even if the census had been conducted according to the bureau's plans, there would still be a differential undercount because the procedures were not adequate to the task of counting everybody in New York. Furthermore, New York was quantitatively different from other places, having many more people in the difficult-to-enumerate categories. Therefore, the city's undercount would be disproportionately great and, in consequence, the city would suffer inordinately. While other cities might have tens of thousands of poor, black, and Hispanic persons, New York had hundreds of thousands of them.

The lawyers also alleged that the bureau's effort in New York City was incompetent, that they were bungling the census. This argument was designed to support the plaintiffs' request for an injunction to prevent the bureau from closing its New York district offices so that they could continue their fieldwork. The plaintiffs asserted that the bureau had made an enormous error in basing the enumeration on commercial address lists that had been designed for advertisers. The city contended that since advertisers are not interested in poor people, the makers of commercial lists tend not to cover poor neighborhoods. Furthermore, according to the plaintiffs, the bureau had purchased a particularly bad list for New York which covered only 59 percent of the city's dwellings (Plaintiffs-Appellees, 1981:16–17). Evelyn Mann explained that despite the fact that they had such low-quality lists, the bureau failed to carry out a crucial part of its list improvement plan, which was to have the post office check the lists ten months in advance of the census. Mann said that the check was not begun until February and may never have been completed (Mann 1980:15).

According to the plaintiffs, another reason the census worked badly was because of the city's many large apartment buildings where forms were delivered incorrectly. Every envelope addressed to a multi-unit building was supposed to be addressed to a specific apartment number. Apartment numbers were distinctive because census address registers, against which the returns were checked, also listed apartment numbers. Unfortunately, some letter carriers treated the envelopes like ordinary junk mail, stuffing one into each mailbox, regardless of apartment number. Or the letter carrier might have left the envelopes in a heap near the mailboxes for people to pick up. Then, even if a person diligently filled out a form, it was probably the wrong one. After it was received at the census office, it would be checked in to the address register, because the office clerks could not know that it represented the wrong household. Eventually, this sort of mix-up created a good deal of difficulty for the staff during followup procedures.

The *pièce de résistance* in Cravath's case was the testimony of former temporary census workers who told about the incompetence and shoddy practices they had seen in the local district offices. As one census official put it, these former workers recited a list of "horribles." One witness claimed that he had seen other employees engaging in "curbstoning," thus introducing the judge to that concept. To *curbstone* is to fill in a questionnaire with fictitious information without conducting an interview. One witness reported that supervisors sent untrained persons to perform difficult procedures like counting transient persons on T-Night and M-Night. One witness said that when he was an enumerator, he had discovered a building that was listed as vacant but which was actually occupied by drug addicts who used it as a "shooting gallery." This former census employee testified that his supervisor told him not to try to contact the people in the building. Another presumably vacant building housed illegal aliens, one of whom told him that they would cut his face if he tried to enter. Other census employees testified they had seen census forms left on the floors in district offices. (U.S. Court of Appeals for the Second Circuit 1980: vols. VI, VII, and VIII)

Responding to these allegations, census administrators had to explain to the judge their overall strategy of field operations, which was designed to correct for errors such as these. But the plaintiffs' attorneys attempted to undermine their explanations. Interrogating these bureau representatives, the plaintiffs' attorneys often took advantage of the fact that administrators' were in Washington where they were out of touch with the events in New York City. Attorney Frederick Schwarz insisted that when one witness, George Hall, referred to census procedures, he was to talk about them only as they existed on paper, thus implying that the paper version may not have depicted what really happened. For example, Schwarz questioned Hall about training for M-Night.

Q. [Mr. Schwarz] Was special training required for that job because it is one of the several, but nonetheless difficult, activities that the Census Bureau undertakes?
A. [Mr. Hall] No, I wouldn't characterize it that way. There was special training for every procedure that we had.
Q. You mean there was meant to be special training for every procedure that you had?
A. There was special training for every procedure we had. I cannot testify that training was carried out in every instance, of course. (U.S. Court of Appeals Sec. Cir. 1980:A3220)

Thus Schwarz had gotten Hall to admit that he did not know if all the procedures had been executed according to plans.

The lawyers for the city of Detroit had never called the census takers incompetent. They had said, in effect, we grant that the census officials have great expertise and that they are doing their best in a complex and difficult project, nonetheless, there will undoubtedly be an undercount, and we insist that it be corrected. The lawyers for New York were not so respectful. They said, in effect: This is a big project being done in a slapdash fashion. These bureaucrats in Washington wrote a bunch of plans and procedures. They may claim to be classy scientists and administrators, but down here in the real world, nothing is working according to their plan. The situation has overwhelmed their plans and they have made a mess.

The bureau's defense was that they had anticipated all kinds of problems and had designed the census so that problems would be caught and rectified in due course. From experience, census administrators knew that errors could likely come from two sources. Census employees, hastily recruited and trained, might make mistakes. Also, unforeseen problems could arise in the field to introduce errors. Errors could occur in any phase of the census: in the creation of the address lists, mailing and collecting questionnaires, identifying vacant housing units, or conducting interviews. Given the kind of workforce the census could develop and the inherent difficulty of the task of counting people in the United States, it would not make sense to design a procedure to make a perfect count in one fell swoop. Recognizing the pitfalls, census planners designed an operational strategy built upon redundancy and this redundancy was the census's main strategy to insure completeness and to eliminate error. Census officials resented allegations of sloppiness, particularly at early points in the census, because they were certain critics did not realize their operation was designed to catch errors and omissions and to correct them. The census was to be implemented in stages; each stage was designed to catch and correct errors that occurred previously.

Following the strategy of redundancy, address lists were to be developed in phases. After the commercial mailing lists were converted into census address lists, two followups were supposed to find housing units that were not listed, to add them, and to catch and correct other errors. The first followup was based upon an agreement between the Census Bureau and the postal service. In post offices across the country, every letter carrier who served a residential area was given a census list of all the households on the route. The letter carrier was supposed to see if the list was complete and to notify the census of missed addresses or other errors. In response, the census was to add the new addresses and to make other corrections to its list, as needed. The second followup was to be done by the temporary census district offices as soon as they had hired and trained their first set of employees. Enumerators were to walk through the enumeration districts and to check the address lists again.

Likewise, there were checks against all sorts of other errors in the 1980 census. Supervisors were to verify a certain number of each enumerator's forms, especially new enumerators, looking for evidence of curbstoning. The master address lists were checked repeatedly to see if the office had a completed form for every listing. This was done twice, once during followup one and again during followup two. Given this strategy, the government's defense against allegations that census employees had performed badly (a point that the defense rejected) was that census plans anticipated that such events might occur, but there was always a followup procedure that would catch and correct errors. The government's lawyers never got to present this argument in court because the case hit a major snag.

The New York case foundered on a dispute over address lists. The plaintiffs' attorneys asserted that the bureau's lists were so deficient that even if every residence on the lists were enumerated, the census would still miss a substantial number of dwellings. The plaintiffs demanded copies of the census' master address registers and lists of all vacant housing units for New York City and for every other municipality in New York State. They wanted to be able to check the lists, presumably to show how many dwellings they had missed (Defendants 1981:13–14). The bureau countered that its list-checking procedures were adequate. Judge Werker ordered the Census Bureau to deliver the lists of names and addresses to the court. Census director Vincent Barabba refused to comply, on the grounds that the amount of work necessary to copy all those lists would be so great that it would cripple the census offices, which were then hard at work on other urgent tasks. More importantly, the names and addresses were personal information which he was required, by law, to keep confidential. Barabba said that he was not permitted to disclose them under the provisions of Title 13 of the U.S. Code. This dispute went all the way to the Supreme Court, which eventually supported Barabba's position.

To punish the defendants for refusing to supply the lists, Judge Werker issued a "preclusion order" that prevented them from presenting those witnesses who were to have demonstrated that the bureau's conduct was competent. This preclusion, which had been requested by the plaintiff's lawyers, substantially weakened the government's ability to make its case. On December 23, 1980 Judge Werker handed down his decision. He ruled in favor of New York, ordering the bureau to adjust the census results.

The government quickly appealed that ruling. They contended that Judge Werker's preclusion order was impermissible. They also asked Supreme Court Justice Thurgood Marshall to stay Judge Werker's order so that the secretary of commerce could deliver unadjusted state census results to the president on the traditional date, December 31. After consulting with the full court, Justice Marshall granted the stay, thereby permitting the timely delivery of census results to the president for the purpose of congressional reapportionment, which proceeded apace (Barabba 1984; *New York Times* 1980).

Pending the outcome of the government's appeal, the Census Bureau had a great deal of work to do back at their headquarters in order to comply with one of Judge Werker's orders. In the trial, the plaintiffs had asserted that New York's Medicaid Eligibility List was a good list of poor people in New York and that it included many persons who were missed but should have been counted. With 1.2 million names, the list included low-income persons known to several of the area's public service agencies. New York asserted that the Medicaid Eligibility List could be used as a standard against which to judge the census. Census coverage could be evaluated by matching the list of people counted in the census against the administrative list. The judge required the bureau to check the results of the census enumeration against this list to discover the extent to which they had missed low income people. In compliance with this order, the bureau instituted a large-scale matching operation. Instead of requiring the bureau to match all 1.2 million entries, though, the plaintiffs drew a sample of 16,536 to be matched. This was a major project that cost the bureau $440,000 (Bounpane 1983).

Also, the bureau proceeded as planned with their postenumeration program (PEP) to measure census coverage. They used expanded versions of the current population surveys taken in April and August 1980, to match against the census. The census also conducted demographic analyses of the growth of the white and black populations and they conducted special studies in order to estimate the number of illegal aliens.

The appeals court accepted the government's assertion that Judge Werker's order was impermissible and declared that there had been a mistrial. In so ruling, the appeals court also invalidated Judge Werker's order to adjust. And finally, the appeals court ordered the district court to re-try the case. Before the new trial was held, the two parties disputed its scope. In pretrial conferences with Judge John E. Sprizzo, who had been newly assigned to the case, lawyers from Cravath asked that the trial consider the injury of a census undercount to New York City and State and how it could be remedied. Government lawyers said that New York could not be considered in isolation from the other states, both in terms of adjusting the census numbers and of considering apportionment of congressional seats and allocation of federal dollars, since a set of adjusted numbers might send benefits to New York which would have to be taken from some other parts of the country. The court accepted this latter argument, saying that the new trial would consider a possible statistical adjustment for New York in the context of a possible adjustment of the numbers for all the states.

A second New York trial commenced on January 3, 1984. This trial had three parts: presentation of the case, rebuttal, and surrebuttal. When New York presented their main argument, they dropped the mismanagement component of their earlier case. That argument had served its purpose, gaining them a temporary injunction to prevent the bureau from closing its field offices in August 1980. In the retrial New York had one goal—to get an adjustment. Since the census was already finished and most of the PEP was done, New York could refer to the census results, point out the actual undercount, and demand a solution. New York sought to establish the fact that their city had suffered a greater undercount than the country as a whole. Their attorneys continued to press their case for adjustment on the grounds of disproportionate injury to their clients.

In defense, the government said that census and PEP results did not show that the undercount in New York City was greater than the undercount elsewhere, particularly in other large cities. The bureau admitted that its procedures failed to count some persons and that, to the extent that the census procedures are inadequate, they were inadequate all across the country, not just in New York City. In August 1984, the government's lawyers said, "Even assuming that there were some deficiencies in the conduct of the census in New York, there is absolutely no basis for any inference that the census was conducted any less efficiently in New York than elsewhere" (Defendants 1984:91). New York's lawyers noted that Judge Werker said earlier that census officials' defense appeared to be that "the management of the census was 'uniformly bad' " (Plaintiffs 1984:18). Census officials must have been embarrassed by their own lawyers' argument.

The bureau continued to pursue an argument it had introduced in its appeal to the Detroit decision, that the net undercount in 1980 was so small that it would be technically impossible to make a good adjustment. When they made that earlier appeal, they were armed only with national estimates of the undercount, but three years later, in the retrial, they were fortified with results of postenumeration coverage studies. They claimed to have discovered that it was impossible to make estimates of the undercount that would be strong enough to support adjustments. By the time of the retrial the bureau had completed most of the coverage studies, so the ensuing arguments in court swirled about their results. There were results from administrative records matching projects using the Medicaid eligibility list and another composite list, conducted in compliance with Judge Werker's orders. The coverage evaluation program included a regular demographic analysis, an examination of the size of the population of illegals, and the PEP. The most intense disputes were based on the results of the PEP.

The defendants brought results from these coverage studies as evidence. Most witnesses for the government were current employees of the bureau, along with some former staff members. The defense also used statisticians and demographers from the private sector, mostly from universities, as expert witnesses. Census staff members based their testimony on results from the coverage studies. Likewise, plaintiffs' witnesses used those same results, but they did not hesitate to reanalyze the bureau's data in ways that pointed toward radically different conclusions.

Testifying for the government, census demographer Jeffrey Passel presented the results of demographic analysis. After subtracting illegal aliens from national census totals, Passel reported that the undercount of the legal population was 0.5 percent. The undercount of blacks was "about 5.3 percent." Passel reported that legally resident whites and "other races" had been *overcounted* by 0.2 percent (Passel affidavit 1983). His testimony was consistent with the bureau's assertion that the overall count was higher than had been anticipated and that, in consequence, the undercount was too slim to correct. The unexpectedly "high" census count for 1980 gave rise to the question, why had the earlier estimates failed to anticipate this total number of persons? One principal answer was that the precensus demographic estimates had not accounted for illegal immigrants. There had been a great influx of immigrants during the 1970s, including illegals. Obviously, there were no immigration records for them, but apparently the 1980 census managed to count some substantial number of them.

In partnership with Robert Warren, a demographer at the Immigration and Naturalization Service (INS), Passel devised a procedure with which to discover how many persons were actually illegal aliens (Warren and Passel 1987). The two demographers tabulated data on aliens from the Immigration and Naturalization Service's files and compared their results with tabulations on aliens from the 1980 census. They used the INS data to determine the numbers of legally resident aliens in each state on Census Day. Then, using census data on country of birth, citizenship, and year of immigration, they determined the number of aliens counted in the census. Finally, they subtracted the number of legal aliens (the INS number) from the total number of aliens counted (the census number) and the difference represented the number of illegal aliens in the census. In their analysis, the two demographers had to adjust both sets of data in order to eliminate known forms of error such as too many foreign-born persons telling the census that they were naturalized. Ultimately, Warren and Passel estimated that the 1980 census had counted about 2 million illegal aliens.

The bureau also studied census coverage by means of matching studies. The postenumeration program represented a continuation of the practice of postenumeration surveys using current population surveys, as had been done in 1970. In 1980, the bureau also conducted matching studies with lists of administrative records as ordered by Judge Werker. In the retrial, the major scientific dispute was over the PEP results and whether they could be used to adjust 1980 census counts. After the 1970 census, the bureau matched the March 1970 CPS to the census and derived a single estimate of the undercount at 2.3 percent. Departing from that precedent in 1983, census analysts generated no fewer than twenty-seven sets of estimates of the undercount from the PEP, which they later cut to twelve sets. (A set of estimates included an undercount rate for each of the twenty-five largest cities, for the remainder of each state that had such a city, and for the whole population of every other state.) Stating that there was no scientifically defensible justification for preferring one set of numbers over another, census administrators refused to choose among them.

Two witnesses, Charles Cowan and Barbara Bailar, testified for the bureau regarding the PEP results. Cowan stated, "As Chief of the Survey Design Branch, I was among those responsible for the design, implementation, and analysis of the matching studies conducted to evaluate the under- and overcoverage in the 1980 census" (Cowan affidavit 1983:1). He explained the designs and procedures of the surveys and matching operations as well as the capture-recapture theory. As he began his testimony, though, he asserted that "the imprecision and uncertainties in the PEP data call into serious question any reliance on it at the present time to alter the census figures for such practical purposes as congressional re-apportionment or the distribution of federal population-based funding to the states and the 39,000 revenue sharing areas" (Ibid.:2).

Cowan explained that his staff had encountered many problems in carrying out the PEP studies, the most serious being "a lack of information in too many cases and . . . incorrect information in an unknown number of cases" (Ibid.:25). There were CPS interviews that lacked sufficient information for matching and there were addresses in the CPS sample where enumerators had been unable to conduct interviews. Bailar supported Cowan's assertions, saying that "in approximately 8 percent of the sample cases, match status could not be determined because sufficient data were unavailable" (Ibid.:35). These gaps in the data made it impossible to categorize numerous persons and households (Bailar affidavit 1983:37). The staff had been able to generate dozens of different sets of estimates by making different assumptions about the characteristics of those missing data cases. If they assumed that missed households were like their nearest neighbors, that resulted in one set of estimates. If they assumed that missed persons were like the average known person, that resulted in another set of estimates. "Each of the sets of PEP estimates is so riddled with inconsistencies that it is difficult to make a good case for any one of them" (Ibid.:59). Cowan concluded, "We assume the [PEP] data are incorrect (just as we assume that the census counts are not exact), but we do not know and cannot yet reliably estimate the degree of error or the extent to which the error varies" (Cowan affidavit 1983:27).

Cowan and other census officials asserted that the margin of error in the PEP appeared to be greater than the undercount itself. That meant that if the PEP results were used as the foundation for an adjustment, the adjusted numbers would become more erroneous, and even further from the truth, than the original census counts. The thrust of Cowan's testimony was that the court could not accept PEP results as a basis upon which to adjust the census. Barbara Bailar said this in different words: "When prorating adjustments from large areas to small areas, the resulting errors are not only unmeasurable, there is no clear way to guess their effect. Many small numbers may be moved further from truth by adjustment, even if that adjustment increased accuracy at larger levels of aggregated data" (Bailar affidavit 1983:75). More generally she said "the Census Bureau . . . continues to believe that we do not yet have sufficiently accurate estimates of undercount or methods of estimating undercount to permit an adjustment of the census figures for revenue sharing or apportionment purposes" (Ibid.:3).

Two of New York City's expert witnesses, Eugene Ericksen and Jay Kadane, rejected Cowan and Bailar's argument, asserting that it did not matter which set of estimates was chosen because they all indicated the same situation. Ericksen and Kadane had conducted their own statistical analyses of the PEP results. They subjected the bureau's various sets of undercount estimates to a regression analysis that showed that they were so highly intercorrelated that they could be seen as different measurements of the same phenomenon. The bureau's statisticians had conducted a similar analysis which failed to reach this conclusion. Earlier, Ericksen and Kadane had conducted another regression analysis designed to show that it is possible to estimate undercounts for small geographical areas such as census tracts. They also contended that it is possible to adjust census numbers for small areas.

The government strongly resisted this regression-based argument. They brought in mathematical statistician David Freedman, chairman of the nation's leading statistics department at the University of California at Berkeley, who criticized Ericksen and Kadane's analysis. Freedman argued that the analysis rested upon seven assumptions, none of which were made explicit by Ericksen and Kadane, and all of which were questionable (Freedman and Navidi 1986).[5] For example, Freedman said that their regression model incorporated two equations, the first saying that the PEP estimate for any given area equalled the true undercount in that area plus a "disturbance term." To use PEP results in that way is to assume that PEP is unbiased and that the errors in PEP are unrelated from area to area. But Freedman contended that neither of these statements is true: The PEP was known to be biased, and the errors were related from area to area. Freedman advised Judge Sprizzo to beware of these and other unstated assumptions in the statistical solution proposed by the plaintiffs. Freedman said that the use of statistical models based upon unsupportable assumptions represents a grave error in science and in practice.

A year after the final hearing and thirty months after the last witness appeared, Judge Sprizzo handed down his decision, ruling in favor of the government. He decided that "arbitrary and capricious" was the appropriate standard of review and it could not be demonstrated that the census administrators had been arbitrary and capricious. Stating that there were scientific experts who considered adjustment to be feasible and advisable and that there were other scientific experts who held the opposite opinion, the judge's ruling incorporated much of the government's argument. Census administrators had listened to both sets of experts and had chosen not to adjust, he wrote. Whether or not the census officials made the correct choice or the best choice, they had not been arbitrary and capricious.

Reviewing the 1980 Detroit and New York lawsuits, what can we say about the situation of scientists in this politically inspired maelstrom? For ten years, census statisticians, demographers, and administrators planned and prepared in the "normal" way for the 1980 census. They analyzed the operations and results of the 1970 census and decided to run the 1980 census like the previous one, with some fine tuning in the form of another coverage improvement program. They also decided to get into the public relations, community relations, and advertising games in order to cajole members of the difficult-to-count groups to allow themselves to be counted. They formed minority advisory committees and expanded the community relations staff. Census administrators also tried to obtain cooperation from outside agencies such as the Catholic church and the Immigration and Naturalization Service to facilitate the cooperation of members of poor minority groups. Together, these efforts toward publicity and community relations may be seen as a form of protective action to allow the "real" census work to occur. The results of these efforts were mixed. On the one hand, the census apparently counted a large number of illegal aliens, possibly as a result of coverage improvements and community outreach. On the other hand, the bureau's own survey showed that a large proportion of the poor, urban, minority population was ignorant of the census, even after all the promotional activities. Finally, there was undeniably a differential undercount once again, and most of the people missed were members of poor, urban minority groups.

Census Director Barabba drew the scientific community into the census decisionmaking process to some extent when he promoted a series of conferences on undercounting and adjusting. If you assume that he approached the adjustment decision with an open mind, these conferences can be seen as a way to get advice from talented, knowledgeable colleagues outside the Census Bureau. The conference also provided an opportunity for the bureau's leading statisticians and demographers to write papers in which they articulated their best thinking on problems of coverage and adjustment and to expose it to the scrutiny of outside colleagues. The conferences can be seen as probing exercises conducted in an attempt to make a good decision. Alternatively, if you assume that Barabba knew that adjustment was out of the question—that for several reasons he was not going to decide to implement an adjustment—then these conferences were a scientific charade, bringing outside scientists into the bureau to discuss a procedure that was never a real option. This second assumption is consistent with the director's need to establish a record of an intelligent and reasonable process of decision making for a possible legal defense against the predictable charge that he had been arbitrary and capricious. Participants in the process disagree on the merits of these two points of view (Mitroff, Mason, and Barabba 1983; Kadane 1984). In either case, the conferences can be seen as occasions to further the scientific-technical understanding of adjustment. Published proceedings of the conferences represent valuable parts of the literature on undercounting and adjustment. One clear effect of the political hubbub on census scientists was that they frequently had to state certain results in public forums. Furthermore, they had to frame them in ways that would help the bureau and the Department of Commerce in their conflicts with the mayors.

When the first count of the national population was ready in August 1980, Vincent Barabba announced it at a news conference. The announced count was merely a national total, but it became instantly useful in the government's legal defense against Detroit's Mayor Young. Census officials and their attorneys said that since the gross number exceeded prior demographic expectations, the consequence was that the undercount was slight. This meant that it could not be statistically corrected because existing techniques were inadequate to that task. Likewise, when the "results" of the PEP were presented in court they were brought in a form that would presumably support the government's legal defense. Without precedent, the bureau's statisticians delivered twenty-seven different sets of results, saying that they were unable to choose a preferred set. This multiplicity of estimates supported the defendants' contention that there was no technical way to make an adjustment. Could the bureau's statisticians have chosen one or more sets of results that represented their best estimate of the undercount? New York's statisticians said that such a choice was possible. It is not unreasonable to surmise that, under other circumstances, social scientists at the bureau might have found a way to choose a small number of preferred estimates, or even a single set of undercount estimates.

The New York case, then, highlighted the major issues of the undercount adjustment issue. New York alleged that their city suffered disproportionately because it housed extraordinary numbers of the hard-to-enumerate groups. The city insisted that, because of New York's housing conditions, diverse nationalities, and general toughness, the Census Bureau was incapable of counting all the people there. New York's undercount would then be inordinately large, therefore producing major inequities in political representation and grants allocation.

The retrial of the New York case in 1983–1984 brought some technical statistical issues to the fore. New York's expert statistical witnesses offered statistical techniques with which to make census adjustments, even for small geographical areas. The Census Bureau's statisticians rejected those claims, insisting that the 1980 data were flawed and that the plaintiff's statistical techniques were insufficient to the task of adjustment. New York's expert statistical witnesses insisted that the use of their techniques would undoubt-edly bring 1980 census numbers closer to the truth. The case dragged on until 1987 when Judge Sprizzo ruled against New York. He denied their demand for adjustment, leaving the 1980 census counts as they were.

8 Research toward Adjustment, 1980–1987

IN THE YEARS 1980 to 1985 the bureau's leadership insisted vehemently in Judge Sprizzo's courtroom that the results of the 1980 census could not be adjusted. At the same time, though, they were working at their Suitland, Maryland, headquarters, to lay the scientific groundwork for a possible adjustment in 1990. Census Bureau staff members Barbara Bailar, Associate Director for Standards and Methodology, and Kirk Wolter, Chief, Statistical Research Division, had begun to solve those technical problems that made it impossible to adjust the 1980 census. They wanted to discover whether they could develop a scientifically defensible technique for adjusting the 1990 census.

A summary of the deficiencies of the 1980 postenumeration program will provide a background to what they needed to accomplish. The 1980 PEP was based on the March and August 1980 current population surveys, which were used in lieu of a separate postenumeration survey. Those two CPSs were less than ideal for the purposes at hand.

Matching. Perhaps the biggest problem in the 1980 PEP was matching. PEP called for matching between CPS and census records. In practice it was extraordinarily difficult to match household records from the survey (P-sample) to the census and from the census to the sample as the scheme required. In part, this difficulty arose from the CPS sample design. Drawn in geographical clusters of households in every state, the CPS sample design also made it hard to search for matches. Starting with a CPS survey questionnaire, a matching clerk who failed to make a match in the census questionnaires from the most obvious enumeration district might have to search through a number of other possibly relevant enumeration districts. This procedure was clumsy and inefficient. CPS forms and census forms identified addresses differently, which also made it hard to match records. In the survey and the census, each household was identified by its street address. But the census identified each household by its "census geography," starting with an enumeration district number, then a tract number. Addresses on CPS interviews lacked such identifiers. This inconsistency made it hard for a clerk, given a survey questionnaire, to look for a matching census questionnaire. Another problem was that matching was done entirely by hand, a repetitive and tedious process. Human judgment was applied to easy matches, where it was not needed, as well as to hard ones, where it was.

Question wording. Some basic questions, such as street address and year of birth, were asked differently in the census and in the CPS. The CPS included college students in their parents' households while the census did not. Such differences exacerbated the difficulties of matching cases.

Statistical approaches to the problem of small areas. The 1980 PEP yielded coverage estimates for each of the states, the District of Columbia, and twenty-five large metropolitan areas. But the census provides counts for thousands of counties and municipalities and even smaller geographical units. If adjustment was to become useful, it would have to be capable of adjusting small-area statistics. But, as they testified in *Cuomo* v. *Baldridge*, census officials were dubious about the ability of current statistical approaches to bring coverage estimates down to the level of small areas in 1980.

Given these problems, Bailar and Wolter sought a method that would accomplish all the objectives that were impossible in 1980: to adjust numbers for small areas, not just for the total national population, and to overcome correlation bias, or at least to minimize its pernicious effects. Developing such a method would have to be based upon an improved postenumeration survey.

Bailar and Wolter used a talented group of statisticians within their section as well as elsewhere in the bureau to try to solve the problems of coverage evaluation and adjustment. Planning began by May 1980, quickly generating a "research proposal for a study of methods for 1990 decennial census coverage evaluation" (Mulry et al. 1981, cited in Hogan 1989). At first these statisticians could not work full time on the new research because much of their time was taken up with measuring and analyzing coverage in the 1980 census; they had to complete the analysis of PEP. Simultaneously, demographers in the bureau's population division had to conduct a demographic analysis of 1980 census coverage. Bailar and Wolter's group also had to conduct two large record matching studies that had been ordered by Judge Werker. Those studies, demanded by New York City, were to provide a "better" measurement of an undercount there. Thus, in the years 1980–1983, many social scientists at the bureau were working simultaneously on 1980 coverage evaluation (which they considered to be fundamentally flawed) and on studies that they hoped would lead by 1990 to a new solution to the problems of coverage evaluation and adjustment.

Wolter focused his own work on solving theoretical problems in the possible use of the results of a postenumeration survey (PES) for the purposes of making an adjustment. He began this work in 1980, and in 1983 brought Greg Diffendal into the project. By then Wolter had made sufficient progress on the problem to present seminars for colleagues at the bureau (Wolter 1990). Recalling the beginnings of the new research and development, Kirk Wolter said,

Around 1980 I formed an internal task force. The objective was to make a means of evaluating the PES. . . . No one had ever thought of that, how to evaluate the PES. The PES itself was supposed to evaluate the census, but how would you evaluate a PES? It was a struggle. After his group evaluated the 1980 PEP, . . . Barbara Bailar and I [Wolter] came to a realization: we needed a much different approach for 1990. We decided to consider a variety of alternative methods of measuring coverage. These included the *reverse record check* method and the use of *administrative records*. (Ibid.)

Both of these methods were carefully scrutinized.

In conducting a reverse record check, a statistical agency asks the question, how long can we trace a person by means of existing records? A reverse record check held the promise of overcoming correlation bias. This method "traces the current location of a representative sample of newborns, immigrants, and persons counted in the previous census or coverage evaluation program [survey]" (Citro and Cohen 1985:34). Canada had successfully used reverse record checks to evaluate census coverage. Wolter and Bailar's group conducted two large-scale tests of reverse record checks. In one study they drew a sample of persons listed in a 1977 current population survey to see if they could be matched to their own records in the 1980 census and reinterviewed. In 1981, the bureau initiated another inquiry, called the *forward trace study* (Wolter 1990). This project was designed to test methods for tracing people from their 1980 census address to their current address (Hogan 1983). The study tested three methods for keeping track of people: periodic tracing with periodic personal contact; periodic tracing with only initial personal contact; and tracing only at the end of the period. Internal Revenue Service lists featured prominently in the bureau's tests of administrative records. In the "IRS-Census Match" the bureau matched a sample of about 11,000 filers of 1979 tax returns to 1980 census records.[1] Although this study yielded some interesting results—it showed, for example, that persons who file single tax returns are less likely to be counted in the census than those who file joint returns—Hogan (1989) concluded that the method was not adequate for the purpose of coverage evaluation: "we decided that the IRS files excluded too many types of people to be used by themselves."

Results of reverse record checks and administrative records studies were unsatisfactory. As Hogan stated, "given the mobility of our population and the ten years between sample, we lost too many sample cases" (Ibid.). Since Canada conducts a census every five years, they can keep track of the records and individuals more accurately. Around 1984 the Census Bureau created a special unit, the Undercount Research Staff. The agency chose mathematical statistician Howard Hogan to head the new unit, reporting to Wolter. Hogan had previously directed the reverse record check and the forward trace study.

Hogan's mandate was twofold: to decide upon a method and to test and prepare it (Bailar 1990). So, after the creation of the Undercount Research Staff, much of the work in undercount estimation was consolidated. There was major work in other offices as well, particularly that of Jeff Passel in the population division, other individuals in Kirk Wolter's division, working on small area estimates (Cary Isaki) and quality assurance activities (Carol Corby). Quality assurance refers to such problems as detecting and avoiding fabricated interviews, assuring the quality of geographical information in the survey, and monitoring the quality of keying (data entry). They also created a separate unit, headed by Matt Jaro, to work on the problem of matching records between the census and a survey.

Starting in the early 1980s among the bureau's scientific administrators, the most important objective was to solve the coverage measurement/postenumeration survey problem. Scientists in the bureau perceived it as interesting and challenging. The bureau's administrators assumed that, if they could solve the coverage measurement/postenumeration survey problem, they would simultaneously have solved the adjustment problem. Building on Wolter's theoretical work along with the results of the studies of the 1980 PES and other research, Howard Hogan's Undercount Research Staff designed a new PES. The unit on record matching designed a computerized matching technique. "We conducted the first test in 1985 in Tampa, Florida. Immediately thereafter we planned a 1986 test to be conducted in Los Angeles and in rural East Central Mississippi. That was the peak of our work. The 1987 test was smaller" (Wolter 1990).

Hogan recalls that the 1985 test incorporated at least three basic features of the newly redesigned PES. It had an unusual kind of sample. In an ordinary survey the bureau draws a sample of areas and then draws a sample of individual households within those areas. In the new PES, they drew a sample of city blocks and included *all* the households within them. They introduced this procedure in order to maximize the efficiency in looking for matches in the census. In conjunction with the new sample design, they introduced a computerized matching system. With the new system, in order to look for a census record that corresponded to a particular survey record, a computer could search first through the census records of that block and certain adjacent blocks. This restricted search was much more efficient and would lead to a much higher probability of finding the appropriate census record. The 1985 Tampa survey was also designed to try out a new questionnaire. Hogan concluded that the 1985 test in Tampa showed that all three features worked.

The newly designed PES also had another major feature designed to overcome correlation bias: a set of *poststrata*. This feature was based on theoretical foundations for adjustment that the bureau's statisticians had constructed using capture–recapture techniques. The logic of capture-recapture had been developed for ecological field studies that attempt to estimate the size of a population of animals in the wild. With appropriate modifications, demographers and survey researchers have used related techniques to study human populations (Marks, Seltzer, and Krotki 1974; Cowan, Breakey, and Fischer 1986; Sudman, Sirken, and Cowan 1988).

PEP's designers attempted to overcome the problem of correlation bias by stratifying their survey's samples along dimensions that might account for the bias.

The Census Bureau stratified the population into subpopulations and used dual system estimation separately in each stratum. Thus the two assumptions used were that the individuals *within these strata* had equal probabilities of capture and that the capturing mechanisms operated independently *within strata*. The strata were defined using the variables age, race, sex, ethnicity, and area of residence. (Citro and Cohen 1985:141)

These strata would form the basis for adjusting census counts. Specifically, estimates of undercounting rates in each poststratum would be used in order to adjust census counts.

Imagine, for example, that PES had defined one poststratum as black male homeowners, aged 30 to 44, in New England suburbs. After completion of the PES, statisticians would estimate the extent to which this particular category had been under- or overcounted. Perhaps the analysis would indicate that 99.8 percent of the persons in this category had been counted in the census. Thus, the necessary adjustment would be to add 0.2 percent to this category. Computers would scan all the blocks in New England suburbs, looking for blocks with black male homeowners in that age category. In randomly selected blocks, it would add "phantom persons," so that the category would be boosted to 100 percent of what it should be. Thus the census counts are adjusted.

After the successful test in Tampa of the new PES (not including adjustment), Bailar, Wolter, Keane, (and perhaps other high census administrators) must have been sufficiently encouraged by the possibilities of adjustment that they established for themselves a decision deadline: May 1987. Bailar later recalled their attitude, "By 1986, the URS [Undercount Research Staff] was well on its way to eliminating or substantially reducing each of the problems that had beset the 1980 PEP. We in the bureau leadership . . . felt that the next step was to set a definite schedule for deciding whether to correct in 1990 . . . we defined a two-stage decision making process" (Bailar affidavit 1988:17).

In July, 1986, Barbara Bailar testified for the bureau before the House oversight subcommittee. She said, "In early 1987, we will decide on the statistical and operational feasibility of adjustment. This is not a decision about whether the adjusted numbers will be the official 1990 census counts. What appears feasible in 1987 may or may not be feasible in 1990" (U.S. Congress 1986:4). Thus, the bureau set May 1987 as a deadline for the first stage of their decision process. At that point the census director would have to decide and announce whether adjustment was feasible. "If the director decided that it was feasible, the bureau would go forward with the implementation of a full-scale postenumeration survey and, after the survey was taken, with the production of corrected census data" (Bailar affidavit 1988:17).

Then the second stage of the decision making process would have to wait for three and a half years. The second stage decision would determine whether to use the corrected data as the official census figures. "This decision was to be made in December 1990, after the corrected data were produced" (Bailar affidavit 1988:18). The director would be assisted in this decision by the three outside advisory bodies, which would scrutinize the results of PES. One of the main tasks for the Undercount Research Staff in the years before the census would be to define statistical standards with which to evaluate PES. Those standards were seen to be crucial in making an unbiased (nonpolitical) evaluation of the results.

In July 1986, while Barbara Bailar was on Capital Hill testifying before the subcommittee, one of the most important tests of the new methods was in the field in Los Angeles County. It was called *TARO*, a test of adjustment-related operations. According to Bailar, TARO was a "test census," which "would . . . test to see if we had cleared up the main 1980 problems" (Bailar 1990). TARO was conducted in six sections of East Central Los Angeles County, neighborhoods that were populated largely by Hispanic households along with a large Asian immigrant population.[2] TARO tested the same PES innovations that had been tried in Tampa: a sample of whole blocks, the computer matcher and the new questionnaire. In addition, TARO included an actual census of the neighborhoods and, for the first time, an adjustment to the results of that census (Hogan 1989).

Census forms were mailed on March 14, 1986, and "Census Day" was March 16. TARO's adjustment-related operations began several weeks later, right after the test census fieldwork was finished (Diffendal 1987). The first step in the PES was to create and check a list of residential addresses of the sample blocks. Creation of the address list was followed by PES interviewing in order to collect information about current residents and about persons who lived at the address around Census Day. In July and August, three months after Census Day, PES interviewing was conducted. After interviewing, there was processing, followup, and further processing. Then the PES interviews were keyed and processed through the computer matcher. Difficult cases were given to clerks to match. Eventually, a number of dubious cases were sent back to the field for followup interviews. Those followup interviews ended the field operation. Then, after the census staff provided census results to the Undercount Research Staff, the statisticians had their first chance to apply their new statistical models. "Dual system estimation produced estimates of the population for the post strata by age and sex" (Ibid.:11). These estimates, in relation to the actual census counts for these poststrata, yielded adjustment factors. A regression model was fitted to these, based on indicator variables such as age group, ethnic group, and whether the person rented or owned. "The next step was smoothing the adjustment factors," another statistical procedure, which generated usable adjustment factors.

Finally, there was a computer run to adjust the census files. Adjustment factors were applied to the counts for the blocks in the test site. Adjusting the census files involved imputing (phantom) persons into the census files. A few persons were subtracted from the file in poststrata that were overcounted (Diffendal 1987:12). This was finished on February 25, 1987, a historic date for the bureau—the first time they had ever adjusted the results of a census.

Hogan concluded that the results of TARO were satisfactory, although there was some dispute over this point, both within the bureau and in the National Research Council's Panel on Decennial Census Methodology. One controversy concerned the amount of time needed to finish the PES estimates of undercounts for the poststrata. Although the bureau's plans called for PES results by December 31, 1986, the statistical estimates were not ready until February 1987 (Hogan 1989). Eventually this delay became a sharp point of controversy in debates over the feasibility of adjustment in a full-scale census. Those who opposed adjusting said that if there was a delay in a small-scale test like TARO, that meant that it was impossible to assure that the results of a full-scale PES could be prepared on time in a census year. Those who favored adjusting replied that the PES was successfully completed and that the censustakers should be blamed for the delay in Los Angeles. Certain files of census results were prepared behind schedule, thereby causing the PES staff to miss their deadline. There was nothing in PES that prevented a timely adjustment, they said.

TARO was crucial in the overall research and development effort toward 1990. As Bailar recalls, "by then we were ready to make a decision" (Bailar 1990). When they finished TARO, census officials recognized two things: that they had developed and tested the main features of a new coverage measurement and adjustment system and that it was time to make a decision about implementing this system in 1990. The lead time for budgeting and other planning was such that a plan for the 1990 PES had to be made in 1987. The Undercount Steering Committee, which had been created about two years earlier, was responsible for evaluating TARO. The committee was supposed to monitor progress of the Undercount Research Staff and to make recommendations (Ibid.). The committee "reviewed all studies pertaining to undercount, anything that touched on the feasibility of adjusting" (Passel 1989).

The Undercount Steering Committee adhered to one "ground rule," that the bureau could do nothing regarding undercounting and adjusting that could be construed later as having been arbitrary and capricious. Cognizant of their embattled situation—they were still waiting for a decision in *Cuomo* v. *Baldridge*—they knew that their decisionmaking process had to be defensible in court. Furthermore they were aware that the big-city mayors and other advocates of adjustment were likely to sue again if the bureau decided not to adjust. Anticipating such lawsuits, census administrators documented their various tests and projects voluminously. At their steering committee meetings, one or another discussant would occasionally state that in the future (in court) some particular decision might or might not appear to have been arbitrary or capricious.

By the time they were finishing TARO, when at least some census administrators allowed themselves to become optimistic about the possibility of adjustment, there arose the consideration of feasibility. Feasibility suggested a new question: assuming the scientific problems have been more or less solved, will it be possible simultaneously to conduct a census, a large-scale PES, and an adjustment quickly enough to meet the census's main deadlines? Census administrators tried to answer this question in two different ways.

Various units that would have to carry out the census, led by the Decennial Planning Division (DPLD), were called upon to generate new timetables for 1990, attempting to accommodate the new PES and adjustment operations. They were asked to design, at least hypothetically, a new plan in which the bureau, during a census year, would conduct a census and a vast survey, analyze the survey, apply its results to the census, and retabulate census counts in order to produce adjusted numbers. One approach to creating a new plan was called the dual strategy. This meant that the bureau would conduct the census and the PES, evaluate the survey's results, and then decide whether to adjust the census counts. Within the dual strategy, census and PES would be discrete, independent operations. The dual strategy did not lead inexorably toward adjustment. An alternative to the dual strategy was called the integrated plan, in which there would be an integrated set of operations, including the census and PES, which would lead inexorably toward the production of an adjusted set of numbers.

Much of the work of the Undercount Steering Committee in 1986–1987 was devoted to evaluating these new timetables. The committee also debated the merits of the dual strategy versus the integrated plan. A new issue arose; would the new PES and the other adjustment-related procedures demand so much time and so many resources in 1990 that they would detract from the quality of the basic census? Advocates and opponents of adjustment argued over the allocation of time during the mid- and late-summer months of 1990. Advocates of adjustment wanted the census field offices to finish their field followup operations as early as possible in order to get PES interviewers into the field. Since it was undesirable to have census enumerators and PES interviewers in the field at the same time, census field operations would have to conclude earlier than had been planned. That might force census planners to lop off some coverage improvement procedures. Advocates of adjustment contended that most coverage improvement procedures wasted time and money and produced erroneous enumerations, so it might actually help the census if they were cancelled. Opponents of adjustment, on the other hand, contended that the coverage improvement procedures were indispensable in order to minimize the undercount.

Along with the Undercount Steering Committee, three groups outside the bureau also scrutinized and evaluated the results of TARO. They were the National Research Council's Panel on Decennial Census Methodology, the Census Advisory Committee of the American Statistical Association, and the Census Advisory Committee on Population Statistics.

On April 9–10, 1987, at a joint meeting of the population and statistical advisory committees, census officials made an extended presentation of TARO results (U.S. Bureau of the Census 1987). They also provided the committees with a proposed schedule for a 1990 PES. The main question to be considered was whether the PES should be implemented full scale in 1990, but there was also a great deal of discussion of TARO itself. Diffendal, Wolter, Isaki, Passel, Hogan, and Harner spoke to the assembled committees on aspects of PES and adjustment. Gibson, Bailar, Keane, and Jones also answered questions and participated in discussions. Census officials were bombarded by questions from members of both advisory committees.

Discussion at the meeting was wide-ranging and penetrating, examining many aspects of the adjustment process: the use of poststrata; how the PES and adjustment would affect the distribution of the population across states and places; whether the lack of blacks in the TARO sample undermined the study's usefulness; whether the cost of a full-scale PES, at 300,000 households, with an overall price tag of $50 million, was warranted. Much of the discussion pertained to the timetable: Was it possible to conduct all of these operations in time for the two main deadlines, December 31, 1990, and April 1, 1991?

There was a vigorous discussion of a paper by Jeffrey Passel about the ways in which phantom persons would be added into blocks through adjustment. For example, if adjustment added one

Hispanic male, age 30, to a particular block, should he be added to one particular household or should he be isolated into a new category which might be called, "missed persons in missed housing units"? What characteristics should be assigned (imputed) to him: income, education? Most statisticians on the advisory committees endorsed a proposal to isolate the phantom persons into the new category, but Evelyn Mann, New York City's municipal statistician, said they should be adjusted into regular census categories because many data users will need fully adjusted numbers.

Morris Hansen, the most senior and eminent statistician present—a man who was almost revered by members of the census fraternity—was skeptical about adjustment. He observed that bureau representatives and committee members alike seemed to assume that there would be a better census after adjustment if the PES is carried out according to the new system. Hansen challenged this assumption (U.S. Bureau of the Census 1987:32–33). As a retired census official who had been a pioneer of survey research, he reminded his colleagues that the bureau had conducted postenumeration surveys in 1950, 1960, 1970, and 1980. None of those four surveys produced black age-sex profiles that were more accurate than the census. Thus, the surveys failed to provide a solid basis for adjustment. Furthermore, matching survey records to census records had always been an insuperable obstacle. Hansen said he was not yet persuaded that the 1990 PES would solve these fundamental problems. He offered other objections as well: December 31, 1990, which was the deadline under discussion, did not give enough time in which to evaluate census and PES results; concentrating on PES might detract from executing a high-quality census; adjusting might introduce too much error into block-level numbers; and, finally, there were too many unknowns in the process, major unanticipated obstacles might arise along the way (Ibid.:20–39). Hansen was not alone in expressing doubts. There were influential staff members at the bureau who were unconvinced by the results of TARO and who doubted that PES and adjustment were feasible, most notably, Associate Director Charles D. Jones, who was in charge of the 1990 census. He endorsed all of Morris Hansen's doubts and added that there were "overwhelming timing problems" in carrying out the census and PES by December 31, 1990.

Surprisingly, by the end of the day-and-a-half meeting, the two advisory committees made specific recommendations. Presumably they were aware of the bureau's forthcoming decision deadline and knew that if an advisory committee recommendation were to have any potential impact, it had to be made right then. The population committee concluded that "adjustment of the 1990 census cannot be carried out in a reasonable and defensible manner by December 31, 1990" and that the bureau should not attempt to do so by that date (Ibid.:104). Furthermore, the committee endorsed the principle that the bureau's topmost goal should be to obtain the best enumeration during the regular census and that the PES should not be allowed to interfere with attainment of that goal. Nonetheless, the committee encouraged the bureau to seek funding for the full scale PES and to execute it. (Six months later, when the committees met again, Evelyn Mann rose to clarify the meaning of the Population Committee's first recommendation, not to attempt to adjust prior to December 31, 1990. She did not want their recommendation to be misconstrued as antiadjustment. Their recommendation had said only that no adjustment would be feasible by the end of 1990.)

The American Statistical Association's advisory committee leaned in a different direction. Overall, they complimented the bureau "on the substantial progress that has been made on the understanding of census undercount issues," and they urged the bureau to continue its work (Ibid.:102). Like the Population Advisory Committee, they endorsed a large scale PES, but on the question of feasibility, they deferred to the bureau. Apparently assuming that the bureau would decide to adjust, though, the committee advised them to "view the adjusted estimates as generally superior to the census counts in planning its data release program" (Ibid.:100).

On May 7–8, 1987, the National Research Council's Panel on Decennial Census Methodology met in Washington at the National Academy of Sciences. Cognizant of the bureau's rapidly approaching decision deadline, the panel put two main items on the agenda: a review of TARO and a consideration of the possibility of adjustment in 1990. Many of the same census staffers who had spoken at the advisory committee meetings spoke again at the panel meeting.

On May 26, Benjamin King, chair of the panel, wrote to Census Director John Keane. On the panel's behalf, King praised the

Census Bureau "for its significant accomplishments in research on adjustment," acknowledging that TARO showed that census adjustment is technically feasible. The panel recommended "that work proceed at the bureau on the development procedures." It further recommended "that adequate funds be provided for the large-scale postenumeration survey (PES) and other activities necessary to prepare for an adjustment of the 1990 census" (King 1987).[3]

TARO was covered by copious documentation; the Undercount Research Staff, led by Howard Hogan, wrote dozens of reports to record TARO's progress, procedures, and results. Then Kirk Wolter took the responsibility for repackaging these reports for the Undercount Steering Committee and the director. As Wolter recalled, "I was writing for weeks, sometimes from 5 a.m. to 10 p.m. I developed an outline for a report. The staff wrote and I edited and put it together. . . . It was something of a hodgepodge. Later we consolidated it" (Wolter 1990). The report took the form of a book, more than an inch and a quarter thick. It was circulated to the Undercount Steering Committee on April 24, 1987, with a memorandum on the subject of "technical feasibility of adjustment."

Wolter's book (1987) is mostly about TARO's achievements. Eight chapters of the twelve cover the technical problems that had been crucial in 1980: missing data, matching error, and balancing gross overcounts and undercounts. Each chapter starts by reviewing the situation in 1980 and then shows what was learned from TARO and how TARO's results can be applied in 1990. Wolter revealed his conclusion on page one: "adjustment is technically feasible." Happily, Wolter wrote that three recent tests of the PES had been successful. "The Tampa, Los Angeles and Mississippi tests have demonstrated considerable improvement over earlier coverage error studies, such as the 1980 postenumeration program (PEP), and provide convincing evidence that a structurally sound system will evolve by 1990 through a program of careful refinement and testing (Wolter 1987:3). Wolter argued then that it was necessary to plan to be able to adjust in case 1990's undercount was greater than 1980's. And he argued that the recent successes in testing the new PEP established a solid, scientifically defensible basis upon which to build a system for 1990. With Wolter's book in hand, the committee conducted an all day meeting at one of the bureau's auxiliary buildings, away from their main offices. The director and deputy director attended that meeting, which took the form of a question and answer session. (Wolter 1990).

Discussions about adjustment continued through the spring and into the summer of 1987, during which time census planners were asked to reexamine the timetables they had built for 1990 to see how they could accommodate the PES and other adjustment-related procedures. The bureau's Decennial Planning Division produced a book-length report showing how to "redesign" the census (U.S. Bureau of the Census, *Framework* 1987). Finally on July 17, there was another long meeting on the feasibility of redesigning the 1990 census to incorporate such procedures. Twenty persons were present, including the director, associate director, and Harry Scarr, representing the undersecretary of commerce (Whitford Minutes 1987). The entire Undercount Steering Committee was present along with other individuals who had major responsibility for planning the census. The purpose of this meeting was to enable the bureau's executive staff and, ultimately, the director to make a decision: was the bureau going to recommend to the secretary of commerce that they should tool up for a full-scale PES along with adjustment-related procedures to be ready to use them in 1990?

In his opening remark at the July 17 meeting, Director Jack Keane defined the group's task (Whitford Minutes 1987).[4] Adjustment is feasible, he said; we are asking whether it is practical. As one of the first to speak, Barbara Bailar reasserted that adjustment is feasible. She listed five scientific-technical advances since 1980: using a block sample, developing a computer matcher, making theoretical statistical progress, developing a smoothing algorithm, and demonstrating that we can improve on the census counts down to the state and county levels.

Much of the group's discussion that day referred to specific census operations to be carried out in 1990, whether they could be done earlier or more quickly or even if some of them could be eliminated. How could they conduct all the regular census procedures along with all the PES and adjustment procedures? Could Census Day be advanced to March 1, thus yielding a longer work period? Could questionnaires be mailed a few days earlier than planned? Which followup procedures could be eliminated? Could the census devote less time to quality control over information it received on the long form? If so, would that undermine the quality of sample based census data? One main goal of the redesign was to truncate census fieldwork, especially those followup activities that would ordinarily be done in the summer, so that the PES interviewers could conduct interviews. It had been decided that the bureau could not have census enumerators and PES interviewers out on the streets simultaneously; they might interfere with each other's work.

At the July 17 meeting, the director called for a vote in which each committee member had to support either the original census plan or the redesign, including adjustment. The original plan won, 14 to 4. In subsequent discussions, committee members explained their concerns about the issue of adjustment. Those who opposed adjustment were mostly the individuals who had planned the census originally and who would have responsibility for taking it. They were led by Charlie Jones, who pointed out that the bureau had not conducted a full-blown test census and adjusted it. He implied that even though TARO worked, it was too small to prove that the process would work on a bigger scale. There was no way to know whether the census *and* the PES could both be done on time. He and others at the meeting said that it was too late and too risky to disturb the plans for 1990. It was too late, he said, because concrete decisions for the census had to be made momentarily. For example, it was time to purchase cameras with which to microfilm census forms and if the planning process were delayed to conform to the redesign, the bureau would be unable to purchase this essential equipment on time. Also, redesigning would upset plans for the dress rehearsal and delay its execution.

Others who spoke against adjustment at the July 17 meeting stressed the difficulties they would have in justifying the use of adjusted numbers to data users. Peter Bounpane said that it would be hard for him to "stand behind adjusted results" (Ibid.:5). After all, statistical judgments at the bureau would determine the pattern of adjustments introduced. Different stratification patterns and different match rules would yield different results. How then could census officials justify their choices of particular patterns and rules? Finally, how could census officials justify the population numbers they published?

The four in favor of adjusting, of course, included Bailar, Wolter, and Hogan. Going beyond the statistical virtues of PES, Wolter justified adjustment on the basis of equity: having a census with a differential undercount tends to undermine the principle of one person, one vote. Now that we know how to adjust the numbers we should do so to support that constitutional principle. The main proponents of adjustment were from the bureau's Statistical Research Division; they had all been centrally involved in the PES research and development projects; they all held Ph.D.s in mathematical statistics. The opponents were more likely to have planning and operational responsibilities for the decennial census. None of them held a Ph.D. in statistics.

Later in the day on July 17, Director Keane met with those members of the Undercount Steering Committee who belonged to his executive staff. There are differing accounts—told to lawyers in depositions for a subsequent lawsuit—of what transpired at that second meeting. Evidently Keane acknowledged that there would be operational difficulties in being ready to prepare adjusted numbers by December 31, 1990, but said that he wanted the bureau to overcome them. He wanted to be prepared to adjust. In order to be ready, he wanted the Undercount Research Staff to continue to push forward with its research and development, and he wanted the whole agency to go forward with the full scale PES.

To summarize, by mid-July 1987, census statisticians had developed and tested a new system with which to measure coverage and to adjust census counts in order to compensate for differential undercounting. The cornerstone of the new system was a very large postenumeration survey with a sample of 300,000 households, to be conducted during the summer of 1990. The statisticians had constructed a theoretical rationale for the new system.

After a major test of the new system, there was an intensive debate about its possible use in 1990. That debate was restricted to the Census Bureau plus its scientific advisory committees. Three kinds of issues were debated: (a) scientific-technical: did the new system work; did it produce credible, dependable numbers that were closer to the truth than unadjusted counts; was the system defensible in terms of statistical science? (b) salability: could census officials explain and justify the adjustment process to data users, including political officials? (c) feasibility: given the complexity of the census and the PES and evaluation and adjustment, was it possible to meet the Census Bureau's first legal deadline for data delivery, December 31, 1990?

The bureau's scientific advisory committees were enthusiastic about the new system; they encouraged the bureau to move forward toward a full-scale PES in 1990. Likewise, mathematical statisticians within the bureau advocated that course. Other census administrators were far more dubious, especially on the issue of feasibility. At the director's request, those administrators who had planned the 1990 census and who would be responsible for carrying it out, had "redesigned" their plans in order to accommodate the extensive new activities required by the new system. Within the bureau, a steering committee of statisticians and census administrators evaluated and debated the results of the new system, along with the redesigned plans for 1990.

Although a majority of the steering committee advised against using the redesigned plan, the director of the Bureau of the Census decided to implement the new system. His next step would be to submit a budget for 1990 that included funding for the large-scale PES. That budget would have to be approved by the Department of Commerce.

9 1987–1988, Three Attacks on the Census

NINETEEN HUNDRED AND EIGHTY-SEVEN was another crisis year for the bureau. The Office of Management and Budget (OMB) challenged major sections of the 1990 census plan. Then the Department of Commerce preemptively announced that there would be no adjustment of the 1990 census. The city of New York, along with a passel of co-complainants responded in 1988 by suing the department and the bureau. What follows is the story of these three episodes, starting with the OMB controversy and then returning to mid-July 1987, with the decision-making process toward adjustment.

OMB Challenges the Dress Rehearsal

While this book is about the interplay between politics and science in the census with particular reference to the undercount, one of the most powerful intrusions of politics into the census process had nothing to do directly with the undercount. In 1987, the Office of Management and Budget attempted to delete dozens of questions from the census and to truncate the sample size for long-form questionnaires. Being an arm of the White House, OMB was one of the principal agencies used by the Reagan administration to enforce its conservative principles which asserted that the government had grown far too big, that it intruded too frequently into the activities of businesses and individuals, and that it should be cut back whenever possible. Statistical agencies such as the Census Bureau were too large and were producing services (for "free") that belonged more appropriately in the private sector (for profit).

Furthermore, conservatives recognized that by documenting certain social conditions, statistics had often been used to support social welfare programs (Young 1990). In general, Reagan and his fellow conservatives were unfriendly toward social science and in this context, OMB's 1987 challenge to the census reveals how the Reagan administration's philosophy of government affected statistical agencies.

The OMB's authority over the Census Bureau derives from two different sources. As the executive branch's fiscal control agency, OMB reviews and decides upon every budget request from the bureau, as it does for all other agencies. Therefore, the bureau's annual budget request, after review and approval by the Department of Commerce, is scrutinized by OMB. Also, for decades the budget office had the responsibility for reviewing proposals for surveys. OMB's predecessor agency was authorized to conduct such reviews under the terms of the Federal Reports Act of 1942 (Melnick and Lurie 1987). More recently, the Paperwork Reduction Act of 1980 required OMB to coordinate the work of the federal government's statistical agencies and to maintain statistical standards. Within OMB, the Office of Information and Regulatory Affairs handles the statistical agencies.

In 1987 OMB's Office of Information and Regulatory Affairs was headed by Wendy L. Gramm, a Ph.D. economist. She delegated responsibility for the census to OMB's chief statistician, Dorothy Tella, who in turn assigned the project to two staff members, Francine Picoult and Don Arbuckle, who had no prior experience with the census. In doing so, the assignment was taken away from Maria Gonzales, a trained statistician and longtime OMB staffer who was well qualified to handle census matters; Gonzales had handled census clearances for years and according to Young "knew all about the census" (Young 1990).

As its title indicates, the Paperwork Reduction Act, passed in 1980, was designed to induce federal agencies to generate less paper and to reduce the "burden" they impose upon citizens and businesses. Businesses had complained that, in order to comply with various federal regulations, they were being required to fill out an inordinate number of forms. Although few, if any, of the complaints referred to forms required by statistical agencies, Congress lumped those agencies in with regular administrative ones when it developed the act. The act's goal was to reduce "respondent burden," the amount of time a given firm or individual was required to devote to filling in forms. The act created a fiction, the national total paperwork burden, the aggregate amount of time devoted by all persons and firms in filling in forms (Holden 1987). Reaganites who ran OMB used the act as a tool with which to control the statistical agencies and they were able to use the concept of burden as a device for minimizing data collection (Rockwell 1990).

Administrators of statistical agencies had to justify any data collection instrument that was going to be imposed upon the public. The Paperwork Reduction Act required administrators of statistical agencies to estimate the burden that any proposed data collection effort would entail. The Census Bureau estimated that the 1990 census "would impose a paperwork burden of approximately 32 million hours" on the public.[1] OMB also required administrators of statistical agencies to justify the need for the data. Typically, the strongest justification for a survey was that a piece of federal legislation specifically required the information. Another strong rationale was that a particular federal agency required the data in order to administer some program. A weaker justification might be that some constituency—bankers or homebuilders, perhaps—relied upon the data.

As required by the Paperwork Reduction Act, the bureau, on June 15, 1987, requested approval of a questionnaire to be used in a census dress rehearsal. Scheduled for March 20, 1988, the dress rehearsal was to culminate a series of surveys and tests of various parts of the census that had begun in Spring 1985, with census pretests in Jersey City and Tampa. A year later the bureau conducted a sample survey known as the national content test, in which they tried questions that might be used in 1990. This was followed in Spring 1986 by pretests in Meridian, Mississippi, and Los Angeles (TARO). Then, in Spring 1987, they conducted another pretest in North Dakota.

The dress rehearsal was intended to be the last test of all

operations before the actual census. As its name implied, it was to incorporate all planned census operations, conducted in an integrated manner under realistic conditions. District offices were to be opened and equipped; personnel were to be recruited and trained; address lists were to be compiled; community outreach and publicity programs were to be conducted; questionnaires were to be mailed; field followups were to be conducted; and computerized reporting of field operations was to be used. In addition, there was to be a postenumeration survey, conducted according to the new method. When they sent the questionnaires to OMB, census administrators anticipated no difficulties in getting approval because OMB had reviewed and cleared almost identical questionnaires for the previous pretests and surveys. From the bureau's point of view, the dress rehearsal questionnaire was the final census form to be used in 1990 for the whole country.

Given this history and given the urgency of preparing for the dress rehearsal—they had to give questionnaire copy to their printers by the end of September (Gramm testimony in U.S. Congress 1987:367)—census administrators were surprised and alarmed to get bad news on July 24, 1987. There was a meeting between OMB and census administrators to discuss OMB's concerns. At the meeting, Arbuckle, Picoult, and Gonzalez represented OMB while Butz, Kincannon, and Young represented the bureau. OMB was prepared to challenge the inclusion of thirty items in the questionnaires. OMB would have deleted population questions on where the person lived five years earlier, their fertility, number of hours worked in the week before April 1, questions on commuting and questions on labor force participation and employment in the year before the census. All of those questions were asked in previous censuses and are widely used and intensively analyzed for a variety of purposes, practical and academic. OMB would also have deleted housing questions on monthly rent, source of water, sewer connection, numbers of bedrooms, number of automobiles, real estate taxes, and others. Rumors of OMB's move soon reached Katherine Wallman, director of the Council of Professional Associations on Federal Statistics (COPAFS). Sponsored by the American Statistical Association and other professional groups, COPAFS, is a nodal point in the Washington and national networks of statisticians. As Wallman recalls, "It appeared that the bureau needed help from outside." When we got confirmed word of OMB's action, we sent out a special notice to 200 people. "We got it out within 24 hours." It was a one-page "emergency alert" saying that OMB had advised the bureau that questions should be dropped. The letter from COPAFS requested letters to the director of OMB "giving particular attention to the uses made of census data for policy and program management purposes." This was the beginning of a quick national campaign to mobilize support from census data users (Wallman 1990).

The bureau also mobilized support. Census officials directly contacted influential data users such as the National Association of Realtors, the National Association of Housing and Redevelopment Officials, the American Planning Association, and many others (Young 1990). Between 1984 and 1986, the bureau had conducted meetings in scores of cities with local officials, housing groups, and other knowledgeable data users about specific plans for the 1990 census. These knowledgeable data users represent the bureau's constituency, its supporters. After the OMB challenge, the bureau contacted persons who had participated in those user conferences. The bureau prepared a statement that was widely distributed. Also, directors of State Data Centers all around the country were alerted and many of them called data users, advising them to write to OMB. Before long the director of OMB received more than 600 letters, all opposing his office's proposed actions. Also, Senator Paul Sarbanes, chair of the Joint Economic Committee, convened a hearing, which was held only fourteen days after the first OMB-census meeting (Ibid.). Census data users were represented at the congressional committee hearing by representatives from the American Library Association, the National Association of Homebuilders, the AFL-CIO, the National League of Cities, and New York City's Department of City Planning. At the hearing, each speaker presented detailed explanations of the value of census questions proposed to be cut. One after another the speakers opposed OMB's proposed actions.

OMB's Wendy Gramm testified on behalf of her agency. Referring to the July 24 meeting, she said, "The reason we talked to the Census Bureau and raised questions, was that the Census Bureau had not provided enough—even a minimum—justification of the need for some particular questions. So we went back to ask them for it—to tell them to make sure that they justified their need for particular questions" (U.S. Congress 1987:354).

In fact, the bureau had prepared voluminous reports justifying all the questions. At the hearing, Gramm repeatedly denied that her agency had proposed cutting questions. Senator Sarbanes asked her, "When was the first time that OMB told the Census Bureau that OMB was considering eliminating a large number of the questions?" Wendy Gramm replied, "There was no time" (Ibid.:365). She minimized the import of the July 24 meeting, calling it just a staff-to-staff discussion. "We have not made proposals. . . . we have raised some questions," she said (Ibid.:366). After being badgered and hectored by Sarbanes and three congressmen (Scheuer, Hawkins, and Dymally) Gramm said, "I personally don't think there are any questions yet that need to be dropped from the census." Referring to her staff's response to the thirty questions she said, "we said they were inadequately justified for the record" (Ibid.:382).

Gramm was disingenuous at least twice in her testimony. She insisted that "this is the first time we've seen the whole form, the whole package" (Ibid.:369). She said that her group had reviewed the questionnaire for other purposes, but never before for its overall burden on the whole American people in 1990. In fact, OMB had seen, reviewed, and approved the whole form at least three times already. She was also disingenuous when she said that her staff had made no proposal to eliminate questions, but had merely raised questions in a discussion. She assured the Senator and Representatives that the OMB–Census Bureau discussion had been an unimportant event. Then, forty days later, she officially disapproved the bureau's proposal for the dress rehearsal.

At the congressional committee hearing, Gramm said repeatedly that the Census Bureau had overreacted to the July 24 meeting, along with the press, the Congress, and all the interest groups. Referring to the document circulated by the bureau, Gramm said, "I think that is irresponsible of the Census Bureau . . . in issuing the statement that OMB has suggested this" (Ibid.:377). Representative James Scheuer said to her that even though she claimed that OMB was merely raising questions, "the public is concerned." He told her that she may not have intended to elicit such a response, "but it may be that you're, you know, the 600-pound canary. When you chirp, everybody gets very concerned" (Ibid.:372). The congressman said, "when you send out waves that you want to have a drastic cutback or that is being contemplated," there is bound to be a reaction of concern, just because OMB is so powerful.

Scheuer expressed a broader concern about OMB's attitude toward statistics. "What we are concerned about and apparently what a lot of other sophisticated people in the leadership of labor, industry, academe and so forth, are also concerned about is that you are really trying to slash knowledge, and we would be very concerned about that" (Ibid.:372). Representative Dymally went on to chastise Ms. Gramm. "The Paperwork Reduction Act does not give you a hatchet to destroy history, tradition, and statistics in the Census Bureau" (Ibid.:378). She responded, "I am not planning to" (Ibid.:378).

After several weeks the controversy was resolved; seven housing questions were shifted from the short to the long form; three housing questions were deleted and three new ones were inserted. The seven questions were (in abbreviated form):

- How many rooms do you have in this house or apartment?
- Do you have complete plumbing facilities in this house or apartment?
- Is this house or apartment part of a condominium?
- Is there a business or medical office on this property?
- Do you have a telephone?
- (For homeowners) what is the value of this property?
- (For renters) does the rent include any meals?

OMB required the bureau to delete three questions:

- What kind of heating equipment is used to heat this house or apartment?
- Which fuel is used for heating water here?
- What is the yearly cost of utilities and fuels?

Three new questions were gained: condominium fee, mobile home fee, and meals included in rent. OMB also allowed the bureau to introduce a question on whether utility and fuel costs were included in rent.

There are two ways to interpret this outcome to the dispute: that OMB succeeded in truncating the form sufficiently to damage the quality of housing statistics; or that OMB challenged the bureau and, after encountering so much opposition from Congress and data users, OMB had to yield. Art Young, retired chief of the bureau's housing division, recalls that the bureau got back most of the items OMB wanted to delete (Young 1990). On the other hand he notes that the bureau lost an opportunity to improve their small-area housing statistics for rural areas. The census's new geographical information system permitted the bureau to define small statistical areas in rural America for the first time. If the housing questions had stayed on the short form, they could have been used for this purpose. By moving so many housing items from the short form to the long and by deleting three items, the census lost that opportunity. In a broader context, though, OMB failed in its challenge to the census; the bureau won the battle.

Besides questioning those items in the census forms, OMB also asked the bureau to truncate the long-form sample. OMB ordered the bureau to cut its sample size down from sixteen million to ten million (Jones 1988). Once again Gramm justified this request in the interest of reducing the public's overall burden. After lengthy discussions and correspondence with the bureau, OMB had to yield this point too; the sample size eventually agreed upon was 17.7 million (U.S. Bureau of the Census 1988). OMB succeeded in getting the bureau to transform the design of the sample, but it failed to get a smaller sample size. If OMB had set out to clip the bureau's wings, it had failed to do so.

Undersecretary Cancels Adjustment Efforts

By July 1987, census administrators had tested a complex new system with which to measure coverage and adjust census counts in order to correct for undercounting. During the spring and summer of 1987, census administrators were working on redesigning plans for 1990 so that they could carry out the census along with the new system and, if necessary, produce adjusted numbers. A series of intense meetings on the feasibility of implementing the new plans revealed a division of opinion within the senior staff but, nonetheless, Director Jack Keane decided to proceed with the innovative plan (Bailar affidavit 1988:22). His senior staff was trying to decide how to announce that decision.

My previous description of research and development featured individuals and groups within the Census Bureau along with its advisory committees and the National Research Council's panel. However, during the summer of 1987, another powerful character emerged, Undersecretary of Commerce for Economic Affairs Robert Ortner. The secretary had delegated responsibility for the Census Bureau to Undersecretary Ortner, to whom the bureau's director reported. Census officials prefer to say that the bureau's director reports to the secretary through the undersecretary. Ortner was appointed to that position in 1986, having served previously for almost five years as the department's chief economist.

Ortner's qualifications to make a decision about adjusting the census have been disputed. Some observers assert that he was well qualified to make such a decision, noting that prior to his government service he had taught statistics courses in the economics department of a major university. Ortner's detractors contend that he was over his head in the technicalities of the new PES and that, furthermore, prior to mid-July, 1987, he had paid little attention to the bureau and the census. Those detractors say that Ortner was rarely if ever seen at the bureau. Ortner, in a declaration for the court, mentions two dates in 1987 when he visited the census building in Suitland. "I maintained a 'hands on' management role in the planning of the 1990 census. . . . I have had ongoing, frequent and detailed meetings, conferences and telephone conversations with officials at all levels within the Census Bureau." Ortner lists six committee meetings he chaired over a two-year period, pertaining to the census (Ortner declaration 1988).

In his declaration, Ortner recalled that his first formal discussion of adjustment occurred on October 1, 1986 when Bailar, Jones, and Kincannon briefed him. Ortner chaired a meeting of the Commerce Committee on the 1990 Census, on October 6, 1986; "the entire meeting was devoted to the adjustment issue" (Ibid.:3). On March 4, 1987, the committee met again, at which time the NRC panel made a presentation on adjustment. Bailar also presented her views on that occasion. In his declaration, Ortner reported that he met with census officials on December 15, 1986 and again on January 24, 1987 at which time they discussed the size of the PES sample—whether it should be increased from 150,000 to 300,000—and the resources that would be required for the larger sample. Ortner reported that in February

1987 he was briefed by census officials on the subject of adjustment and that in that month he met with John Keane to discuss adjustment, among other topics. He itemized about a dozen occasions in the first five months of 1987 when he discussed adjustment with bureau personnel, although adjustment might have been a minor topic on some of those occasions.

June 16, 1987, represents a turning point in Ortner's account.

On that date Charles Jones and Barbara Bailar, among others, briefed me on specific census operations necessary to carry out an adjustment. This was the first time I became aware of, or census brought explicitly to my attention, the fact that the method of conducting the 1990 census was to be redesigned . . . [I learned that] in order to do an adjustment in time to meet the legal deadlines for apportionment and redistricting, some operations of the regular census itself would have to be curtailed or eliminated to accommodate the adjustment process. [Prior to that time] I had understood that the Postenumeration Survey would be done after the census regular enumeration was completed. . . . Under this process the traditional census was not curtailed in any way. (Ibid.:9–10)

Ortner concluded that the integrated census plan would undermine the quality of the actual census. The price for integrating PES/adjustment into the regular time frame would be the loss of essential field operations. "The regular census would be restricted to a limited contact with each household and limited followup for non-response . . . an integrated census would require disposing of and curtailing many census operations and census data checks" (Ibid.:11). Thus Ortner's position corresponded to Charles Jones' from inside the bureau.

More generally, Ortner was dubious about the theoretical and practical strength of the new PES. Eventually, he met with William Verity, the new Secretary of Commerce (who had not yet been confirmed by the Senate), and recommended against adjusting the 1990 census "because of the unreliability of the suggested procedures" (Ibid.:15). The secretary "accepted the recommendation" and asked Ortner to make an announcement. On October 30, 1987 Ortner issued a Department of Commerce press release that promised "to make the 1990 census the best ever." The press release said that "the department does not intend to adjust the 1990 census because such an adjustment may create more problems than it solves and would impair the accuracy of the 1990 census" (Ortner 1987; also Ortner declaration 1988:16). So the department had preempted the bureau. Thereafter, the department took the issue of adjustment away from the bureau, retaining and controlling it "downtown."

Barbara Bailar's version of these events differs considerably from Ortner's. Shifting sides from 1980, when, as she says, she was a "principal architect of the defense" against adjusting, she became an expert witness for the plaintiffs in *New York* v. *Department of Commerce* filed in 1988. In a forty-four page affidavit, she told a different story (Bailar affidavit 1988). Her version was built upon a premise that Ortner rejected, that by 1986 the Undercount Research Staff had solved the main problems in the PES and had succeeded in devising a workable technique for adjusting. Furthermore, she asserted that that the bureau's outside advisory groups were on record as endorsing that claim.

According to Bailar, the bureau developed in 1986 a "two-stage decision-making process." The first stage was to be a decision in spring 1987. "At that time, the bureau director would determine whether correction was feasible, drawing on the URS's [Undercount Research Staff's] research and on the professional response to it. If the director decided that it was feasible, the bureau would go forward with the implementation of a full-scale postenumeration survey and, after the survey was taken, with the production of corrected census data" (Ibid.:17). The second stage of the decisionmaking process would not take place until three and a half years later, in December 1990. The second stage would entail a decision whether to use the corrected data as the official census figures. "The decision would be based on whether the postenumeration survey met certain pre-established standards of reliability" (Ibid.:18).

Bailar said, in effect, that the department (i.e., Ortner) had no excuse for not knowing the bureau's strategy. She had explained it in her formal testimony to the House subcommittee in July 1986. Jack Keane had restated it in his testimony before the Senate subcommittee in September 1986. Furthermore, the strategy was incorporated explicitly in the bureau's "management by objectives" memorandum to the department, which had been transmitted through Ortner's office in October 1986. So, according to Bailar, the bureau had kept the department well informed.

Bailar recalled that the department began in April and May 1987, "to increase its scrutiny of the bureau's correction work"

(Ibid.:23). On April 13, Kincannon reported to Ortner that the American Statistical Association's Advisory Committee had recommended going forward with correction plans. Ortner and his superior, Deputy Secretary Clarence Brown, quickly revealed their aversion to adjustment. Ortner apparently instructed his assistant, Harry Scarr, to look for problems with adjustment and Scarr dutifully supplied him with a list of problems. Likewise, after a briefing by Keane on the bureau's decision, Brown's assistant, who had attended the briefing, wrote that Brown had said that he had "great problems" with doing an adjustment and the assistant observed that Brown was strongly averse to correction.

Bailar alleged that partisan politics entered the scene when Ortner began to look closely at adjustment and that Ortner, as a member of a Republican administration, brought the party into the decision. She said that on May 4, "Republican representatives" met with the Undercount Research Staff "on the 'advice' of the Commerce Department and the Republican National Committee, to state their opposition" (Ibid.:28). Bailar said that Thomas Hofeller, a Ph.D. political scientist with great expertise in redistricting, then director of the Republican National Committee's computer services division, met with the same group on July 1. Two weeks later, Hofeller testified before the House subcommittee, recommending against adjustment. Ortner's interest in political ramifications of adjustment was shown again in October. According to Bailar, he asked Charlie Jones to explain how adjustment would affect the process of congressional apportionment. In that same month Hofeller called Bailar and Scarr called Kirk Wolter, chief of the bureau's Statistical Research Division (and, in effect, Bailar's deputy), both asking the same question (Ibid.:38). Bailar implied that these calls all served Republican party interests.

Bailar's chronology of the final decision making also differs from Ortner's. She wrote that Deputy Secretary Brown had decided by August 7, 1987 not to adjust. On that date Brown sent a memorandum to Ortner saying "I have not approved the request for an enlarged postenumeration survey. The [Commerce Department] budget should give a clear signal that we do not intend to adjust the results of the 1990 census" (Ibid.:29). Less than a month later, Acting Secretary Bruce Smart reaffirmed that point in a letter to the director of OMB. Smart wrote "[T]he department is not requesting funds for an enlarged postenumeration survey because we do not intend to adjust the results of the 1990 Census" (Ibid.:33).

These departmental decisions forced top census officials into a terrible bind. Ortner ordered Keane and Kincannon not to proceed with their plans to announce publicly the director's decision to move forward toward adjustment. Ortner ordered them also not to inform the bureau's staff or anyone else that the department was squelching their plans for a full-scale PES. According to Bailar's affidavit, during the first week of August, Kincannon informed the bureau's executive staff of the department's decision. "He also said that the department was prohibiting us from disclosing the decision to anyone, inside or outside the bureau" (Ibid.:30). For almost three months, then, the executive staff knew that the department had vetoed the full-scale PES, but they had to pretend that no decision had been made.

During August, September, and October, the director of the bureau and his executive staff misinformed the advisory committees and the House subcommittee. They even misinformed their own staff. When Keane testified before the House subcommittee on August 17 he failed to tell them that the department was not going to allow the bureau to proceed with the full-scale PES or with adjustment. When he met with the advisory committees on October 8, 1987, the director told them that it was too early to tell if there would be funding for the full-scale PES (U.S. Bureau of the Census, 1987:7). But, perhaps worst of all, in light of the bureau's collegial scientific culture, the executive staff withheld its knowledge from their own staff. Bailar recalls: "Throughout the three months, bureau employees continued to devote themselves to 1990 correction research, unaware that there was no prospect of correction. Some were drafting the standards to test the quality of the PES. Others were refining the use of the PES at the block level" (Bailar affidavit, 1988:30). Thus, in these months the senior staff violated a major tenet of their culture—open information. According to their traditional rules, they had behaved wrongly toward Congress and toward their colleagues outside and inside the bureau.

Finally, Bailar's chronology reaches October 30, 1987, the date of Ortner's press release precluding adjustment. After Ortner revealed the department's decision in that press release, outsiders could begin to imagine what had transpired during the summer and fall months. Indeed, members of the advisory groups complained to the bureau about how they had been misinformed.[2]

Ortner's October 30 statement is a curious document (Ortner 1987). It is curious that a policy statement should be made in the form of a brief press release rather than in a letter to the director, a statement in the *Federal Register,* a position paper, or some other formal medium. It was issued under the name of an undersecretary rather than that of the secretary or the director. Neither Ortner nor the secretary ever issued a proper statement or a more detailed rationale for the department's decision.[3] The two-and-a-half page, single-spaced press release was distributed on a Friday, the day officials choose when they hope to minimize press coverage. The press release's title was vague: "Statement of Robert Ortner, Undersecretary for Economic Affairs on the 1990 census."

The beginning of Ortner's statement gives no hint of its thrust. The first paragraph affirms that census quality has been improving over the decades and that the 1990 "will be the best census ever." Then there are seven short paragraphs elaborating on this theme, explaining innovations in the forthcoming census that will count more of the people. Ortner asserts that "we expect the Census Bureau to count 99 percent—perhaps more—of the population." Presumably by then the reader has been convinced that the problem of undercount has been overcome by improved census taking.

Ortner's main point is buried in the middle of page two, in the middle of a paragraph: "the department does not intend to adjust the 1990 decennial population count for purported undercount and overcount of population subgroups." After that, the press release consists of a list of assertions to support the main point:

• Once a census has counted more than 99 percent, you can't improve much by adjusting.
• "Adjustment would be controversial, even among statisticians." There is no professional agreement on a uniquely best way to adjust.
• The PES would divert resources from the census and probably would not be accurate anyhow.
• The public would be suspicious of an artificial process like adjustment.
• Apportioning the Congress on the basis of regular census counts is traditional and legitimate. If the Census Bureau adjusted census counts, it might appear that politics had been introduced into the statistics.

None of these statements is well developed. Indeed, at some points Ortner concatenates disparate points in single short paragraphs. For example, the PES would interfere with the census; the survey's sample would be too small; and since it would be conducted in the summer, it would miss people who were away on vacation.

Bailar, in her affidavit, ripped apart Ortner's argument. She noted that no one knowledgeable about the census expected to eliminate the usual undercount. Thus, it was unrealistic for Ortner to predicate his argument on that basis. Furthermore, Bailar noted that the problem is not the overall undercount, but the differential undercount, about which Ortner said nothing. She brushed aside the argument that there is no agreement among statisticians on a unique best statistical model. She said that even if statistical analysis yielded a number of plausible models to reduce the undercount, the census would be "better off with any one of them than with none at all" (Bailar affidavit 1988:35). She rejected his criticism of the PES, noting that a sample size of 300,000 would be the largest that the bureau had ever planned and that no statisticians had ever doubted that its size was adequate. Bailar noted that Ortner's contention that adjustment would politicize the census implied that nonadjustment would not do so. She asserted that not adjusting can also be seen as a political decision.

Bailar introduced one more fundamental issue in her remarks about the press release: the department's arrogation of power over the adjustment decision. She notes that in rejecting John Keane's proposal to move forward with the full-scale PES, the department was countermanding the delegation of decision making that secretaries of commerce had made to census directors. Specifically, the new secretary, Calvin W. Verity, was countermanding the delegation that Secretary Philip Klutznick had made seven years earlier. In 1980, when adjustment was already a hotly contested issue, Klutznick wrote to Director Vincent Barabba, acknowledging that adjustment was a technical issue and instructing Barabba to make use of his staff and advisors in order to make the best decision possible (Klutznick 1980). In October 1987 the department nullified that order. From then on, the department exercised increasing control over the bureau.

Ironically, the department's decision failed to destroy the Undercount Research Staff's momentum. They continued to analyze results from TARO and to conduct a PES in connection with the dress rehearsal, which proceeded according to plan in spring 1988. Those operations were already scheduled and budgeted; no one decided to cancel them, so they just went forward normally. One important part of their work was disrupted, however—their effort to develop statistical standards.

After October 1987 the Undercount Research Staff lost its sponsors; Bailar resigned in protest. "I resigned because I was prevented from responsibly performing my duties by a 1987 order of the Commerce Department" (Bailar affidavit 1988). Furthermore, she did not leave quietly; she severely criticized Ortner's decision in the *Washington Post* (Rich 1988) and in testimony before the House subcommittee (Bailar 1988).[4] Several months later, Kirk Wolter also resigned.

New York Returns To Court

Two groups that immediately noticed Ortner's action were the New York attorneys who represented the plaintiffs in *Cuomo* v. *Baldridge* and the statisticians who worked with them. Some statisticians who had served as New York's expert witnesses had stayed involved in the adjustment issue. The National Research Council panel included Jay Kadane, who had been part of the statistical group in the earlier lawsuit and Stephen Fienberg, his colleague at Carnegie-Mellon. Also, the city's demographer, Evelyn Mann, served on the bureau's population advisory committee. Once again, attorney Robert Rifkind prepared to go to court in pursuit of adjusted census numbers for New York City.

In 1980 the plaintiffs were the state and city of New York, plus the governor, the mayor, and eight private citizens. Eight years later New York formed a truly national coalition of plaintiffs, including Dade County, Florida, the cities of Chicago and Los Angeles, the attorney general of the state of California, the NAACP, the League of United Latin American Citizens, and the U.S. Conference of Mayors. Also, while Rifkind and his firm, Cravath, Swaine, and Moore, participated actively in the new case, the city's

Corporation Counsel, Peter Zimroth, and his staff took a much larger part in the legal work than they had in the previous case.

On November 3, 1988 they sued the secretary of commerce, the Department of Commerce, the census director, the bureau, and several other federal officials, asserting that Robert Ortner's October 30, 1987, order was arbitrary and capricious (City of New York complaint, 1988). They demanded that the court enjoin the Department of Commerce from continuing to enforce Ortner's order. They demanded that the full-scale PES be reinstated—specifically to a sample size of 300,000 households—along with adjustment-related operations. They demanded, furthermore, that the Census Bureau adjust the 1990 census counts. Their case came to be known as *New York* v. *Department of Commerce*.

The cornerstone for their argument was constitutional (City of N.Y. memorandum 1988). The Constitution requires fairly distributed representation among the states and among the people and thus requires census numbers that are as accurate as possible. The plaintiffs asserted that a differential undercount in 1990 was inevitable and that the bureau's research and development efforts produced a workable statistical system with which to correct the counts. They attacked Ortner's claim that coverage improvement techniques in the forthcoming census would solve the problem of undercounting. They contended that members of minority groups, poor people, and residents of big cities, in particular, would be injured by a census that was not adjusted.

Returning to their contention that Ortner's order was arbitrary and capricious, the plaintiffs vilified the department's decision to rescind its earlier delegation to the bureau of the adjustment decision. Since the bureau had acted responsibly over a period of years in formulating a decision, taking into account well developed research results along with the opinions of qualified scientists, its judgment deserved priority. And for the department, which lacked technical expertise, simply to reject the bureau's recommendation was both arbitrary and capricious.

The defendants attempted to refute these arguments in a brief supporting their motion to dismiss the plaintiffs' motion (U.S. Department of Commerce et al. defendants' memorandum 1988). Their lawyers, supplied by the Department of Justice, relied upon the same ideas presented in Robert Ortner's press release, expounded at greater length and with greater clarity. They asserted that adjustment is not a good idea and that the PES methodology was not fully developed. Statisticians did not agree on the best way to adjust or even that the census should be adjusted; even the advisory groups were in disagreement. The attorneys also said that there was disagreement within the bureau itself, particularly over questions of feasibility and timing. Ortner's order was not arbitrary and capricious, according to the defendants' lawyers. By law the secretary of commerce is responsible for the census; delegating authority to the director of the bureau is a matter of the secretary's discretion. It is true that a previous secretary once delegated the decision over adjusting to a director, but that was not a continuing order; it did not carry over to the current situation. The secretary was responsible for such an important decision and it was right that he retain it in his office. Ortner and his associates gave the matter due consideration and came up with the right decision. It was not arbitrary or capricious and it deserved to stand.

On April 27, 1989, Judge John M. McLaughlin issued a "memorandum and order" in which he rejected the defendants' motion to dismiss (McLaughlin 1989). The judge's eighteen-page statement must have been devastating in its impact upon the department and the bureau; he rejected every one of their claims. He found that the plaintiffs had demonstrated that they would be injured by an unadjusted census and that they had standing to sue. "The alleged loss of political representation can fairly be traced to defendants' failure to employ a postenumeration adjustment," he opined. He criticized one of the defendants' arguments as "woefully incomplete." Beyond ruling that the plaintiffs had standing, he clobbered the government with two major points. He decided that he would review the secretary's decision not to adjust the census and that "the arbitrary and capricious standard . . . will guide [his] review of the secretary's determination" (Ibid.:16). He also decided, even before the case went to trial, that statistical adjustment was a reasonable procedure in the decennial census. In his memorandum and order, he referred to affidavits by Bailar and sociologist-demographer-statistician Eugene Ericksen, one of New York's principal experts, that persuaded him that adjustment was justifiable on scientific and practical grounds. "On this record, I conclude that plaintiffs have—at this juncture—sustained their burden of demonstrating that a substantial likelihood exists that a postenumeration adjustment will produce the most accurate 1990 census possible" (Ibid.:9).

Three months later, on the morning of the day when *New York v. Department of Commerce* was to go to trial, the court announced that the parties had come to a settlement. The court released a nine-page "stipulation and order," signed by attorneys for plaintiffs and defendants, outlining the terms of an agreement. At the outset, the Department of Commerce agreed to "vacate" its October 1987 decision. They also conceded that "the question of whether or not to carry out a statistical adjustment of the 1990 Decennial Census" would be reconsidered (U.S. District Court 1989:2). The defendants agreed also to conduct the PES "and such other procedures or tests as they deem appropriate . . . in a manner calculated to ensure the possibility of using the PES, not solely for evaluation purposes, but to produce corrected counts usable for congressional and legislative reapportionment, redistricting and all other purposes for which the Bureau of the Census publishes data" (Ibid.:3). In these two concessions, backing away from Robert Ortner's 1987 preclusion order and agreeing to conduct the PES in such a manner that would permit adjustment, the department yielded almost everything.

The Panel and the Guidelines

The one thing they failed to give was an agreement that they would adjust the census counts. The stipulation and order (the settlement) established a peculiar set of devices that would lead toward a decision. The plaintiffs agreed on a deadline of July 15, 1991, which was fifteen and a half months after Census Day, for the secretary to decide whether to adjust and if he decided affirmatively, when he would have to publish adjusted population data. The stipulation and order specified that prior to July 15, 1991, all publications that reported census results had to carry a two-sentence disclaimer "conspicuously on the first page": "The population counts set forth herein are subject to possible correction for undercount or overcount. The United States Department of Commerce is considering whether to correct these counts and will publish corrected counts, if any, not later than July 15, 1991 (U.S. District Court 1989:4). Another peculiar device established by the stipulation and order was the "panel." The settlement required the defendants to establish a Special Advisory Panel of qualified experts to advise the secretary of commerce on adjusting the census. The panel was to have eight members and two cochairs. All members as well as the cochairs were to be chosen and appointed by the secretary, but four members would have to come from a list prepared by the plaintiffs. The defendants were required to provide the panel with a fund of $500,000 to support its work along with "access to all necessary or appropriate information and the opportunity to consult with any employee of the Bureau." Rather than call for any sort of group recommendation from the panel, the stipulation and order says that "each member of the panel shall submit his or her recommendations to the Secretary"[5] (Ibid.).

The third peculiar device in the stipulation and order was the guidelines. The document said that "the department will promptly develop and adopt guidelines articulating what defendants believe are the relevant technical and nontechnical statistical and policy grounds for decision on whether to adjust" (Ibid.:3). The stipulation and order required the department to publish proposed guidelines in the *Federal Register* by December 10, 1989, for public comment, and then to publish final guidelines by March 10, 1990. Then the secretary would be obliged to base his adjustment decision on these guidelines.

What was peculiar about these arrangements? First, the July 15, 1991, date was bound to cause trouble for federal and state governments. After all, the bureau was required by law to deliver state-level counts to the president by the end of 1990 to be used for apportioning seats in the House of Representatives. Again, according to law, the Clerk of the House would inform each governor, early in January, of his state's number of seats. Thus, by January 1991, the census's main constitutional function, reapportionment, would be finished. So, the creation of a deadline six months later was anomalous. Likewise, the July deadline was incompatible with states' redistricting practices. According to Public Law 94–141, state governments were to receive block-level statistics by April 1 of the year following the census. Those statistics were to contain those variables, such as age and race, that pertained to redistricting. Most state governments begin immediately to utilize those statistics in order to produce new congressional and legislative districts. Many states had deadlines by which they had to finish their redistricting (Melnick and Huckabee, 1989:10). Some even had to submit their new districts to the Department of Justice for "preclearance" according to the requirements of the Voting Rights Act. Other states had their own legal or constitutional deadlines; still others had to have their districts ready for elections that would be held in the fall of 1991. So, it is clear that a July 1991 deadline was incompatible with the needs of the states.

The requirement to establish an advisory panel was peculiar in different ways. Imagine the procedure by which a panel of scientific experts is usually assembled, for example, a panel to evaluate proposals in one of the National Institutes of Health. As a first step, in order to assemble a list of names of candidates—of productive, respectable individuals in the field—staff members might utilize their networks and collect colleagues' recommendations. They might seek a distribution of members by region, race, gender, and type of institutional affiliation. They might try to achieve a balance among differing points of view, avoiding extremists. What I have described may not represent an ideal way of constructing a panel of experts (it relies heavily on old boys' networks) but it is the usual way of bringing together a group of individuals who, in conjunction with agency staff, can work together effectively.

In comparison, the stipulation and order created the secretary's Special Advisory Panel in an entirely different way. The plaintiffs nominated several individuals from whom the secretary chose four. The secretary also appointed four individuals, entirely of his own choosing. The four chosen from the plaintiffs' list were: Eugene R. Ericksen, sociologist-demographer, Temple University; Leobardo F. Estrada, sociologist, UCLA; John W. Tukey, statistician, Princeton University (emeritus); and Kirk M. Wolter, statistician, A. C. Nielsen Company (formerly of the census bureau). The plaintiffs' nominees were well qualified statisticians (Tukey is extremely eminent), but all of them were on record as strong advocates for adjustment. Ericksen and Tukey had worked closely with New York's lawyers in *Cuomo* v. *Baldridge*.

The secretary's nominees were different. One was an eminent

statistician, William Kruskal, University of Chicago (emeritus) who had already expressed his reservations about adjustment. Another was a respected mathematical demographer, Kenneth Wachter, University of California, Berkeley, who was also doubtful about adjustment. Neither of the other two had strong credentials in social science or statistics, but both were loyal Republicans. One was V. Lance Tarrance, Jr., president of his own political polling firm, and the other was Michael McGehee, president of a political consulting firm. Ericksen and Tarrance were the cochairs of the newly created panel. Erickson represented the New Yorkers' nominees and Tarrance represented the secretary's nominees. So, instead of creating a collegial panel of experts who might come into deliberations with open minds, the stipulation and order created a panel divided into two camps, one in favor of adjustment, and the other more or less opposed, or dubious.

Like the deadline, the disclaimer, and the panel, the guidelines also turned out to be peculiar. As mentioned above, the stipulation and order required the secretary to develop and adopt guidelines and eventually to make and justify his final decision in terms of those guidelines. Logically, there could have been four kinds of guidelines: technical statistical, nontechnical statistical, technical policy, and nontechnical policy. Statistical science could supply only one type: technical statistical. For example, Tukey, when he proposed his "yardstick" in *Cuomo* v. *Baldridge*, had begun the process of developing a technical statistical guideline, so possibly the bureau could develop an objective guideline in that category (Tukey affidavit 1983). The other three categories were extremely vague. Drafting a set of guidelines that would serve their stated purpose proved to be an insuperable task. Indeed, the guidelines were a Pandora's box.

The secretary of commerce published preliminary guidelines in the *Federal Register* on December 11, 1989 one day after the date specified in the stipulation and order (U.S. Department of Commerce 1989). The secretary also invited comments on the preliminary guidelines. The department never revealed the manner in which the guidelines were developed. One member of the panel recalled, "We received a preliminary draft of policy guidelines and a summary of draft technical guidelines on October 30, 1989 the very day of our first meeting. Subsequently, we received a second draft of policy guidelines and lengthy preliminary technical guide-

lines on November 16, 1989 two days before our second meeting"
(Wolter in U.S. Congress 1990:194).

The twelve guidelines were a mishmash of vague nontechnical
statistical and nontechnical policy considerations. Here are four
examples (U.S. Department of Commerce 1989):

Guideline 1. The census shall be considered the best count of the
population . . . unless an adjusted count is shown to be more accurate, within
acceptable margins of statistical error, at the national, state, local and census
block levels.

Guideline 2. The size of any undercount or overcount inferred from demographic analyses of population subgroups shall be carefully scrutinized and
fully described, and the degree to which the overcount or undercount is
potentially an artifact of the assumptions underlying the analysis shall be
clearly presented.

Guideline 8. The 1990 census may be adjusted only if the adjustment is fair
and reasonable and is not excessively disruptive to the orderly transfer of
political representation.

Guideline 10. Any decision whether or not to adjust the 1990 census must
take into account the effects such a decision might have on future census
efforts.

In fact, before the issuance of these preliminary guidelines, the
bureau had prepared a seventy-page document that "set out detailed plans for technical analyses to inform the evaluation of
coverage and the decision on adjustment" (Wachter in U.S. Congress 1990:323). These technical statistical guidelines were never
published.

It is hard to read the preliminary guidelines without inferring
that they were based on the presumption that the unadjusted
census would stand. Guideline 1 said as much in positing the
census as "the best count of the population." Other guidelines
erected insuperable obstacles to adjustment. Some guidelines were
vague and therefore incapable of being satisfied. Consider guideline 10, which sets forth a condition that is simply unknowable.
How could anyone discover in 1990 what the effect of adjusting
would be on future census efforts? Consider Guideline 6: The
"census may be adjusted only if the general rationale for the
adjustment can be clearly and simply stated in a way that is understandable to the general public." Who represents the general
public? How could the secretary discover whether the general

rationale is understandable? Guideline 8 sets forth a condition that lies outside the purview of the secretary of commerce, who has no authority over the transfer of governmental power. The secretary's responsibility is to produce the best possible census numbers for the use of the federal and state governments. In general the preliminary guidelines did not serve their main purpose as stated in the stipulation and order. There is no way they could have been used logically by the secretary in 1990–1991 to evaluate the evidence of the census and PES in order to make a decision about adjusting unless that decision was predetermined to be not to adjust. They were simply not useful for that purpose.

Approximately 170 individuals and organizations wrote to Undersecretary Michael Darby in response to the call for public comment.[6] Writers included members of the new panel, statisticians in universities and other organizations, senators, members of the House of Representatives, and governors. The single largest category of letter writers was Republican members of state legislatures. Every one of these legislators asserted that adjustment would be a bad idea. One such letter claimed that "Every person who wants a statistical adjustment to the census has an ax to grind." That letter also asserted that since "statisticians can prove almost anything they want to prove . . . it would be very dangerous and setting a bad precedent to allow any statistical correction." Another Republican state legislator said he was "pleased that the guidelines recognize the potentially disruptive nature of an adjustment." He went on to say that "the methods of adjustment proposed would make a mockery of the census and provide ample opportunity for gerrymandering." One legislator inadvertently revealed that he was writing in response to "the letter of December 18, 1989, that I received from Elsie Vartanian from the NRLA [National Republican Legislators Association], soliciting comments."

Another set of letters, which I take to represent the Republican party position, came from Republican heavyweights in Congress, including Robert Michel, the Republican leader, and Newt Gingrich, the party whip. Both of them argue against adjustment. Michel endorses Guideline 6, which requires the rationale to be understandable to the public. He says that "the decennial census is not an academic, statistical exercise, sponsored by the federal government, upon which statisticians may impose their own social agendas." Michel goes on to say that "a pro-adjustment decision might be more a result of pressure for a well-meaning political adjustment, than an unbiased search for increased accuracy." Gingrich also takes a pot shot at statisticians, saying that "this decision should not be made by either academics or bureaucrats at the Census Bureau." Benjamin Gilman, Republican of New York, wrote that "the proposed use of statistically adjusted populations in redistricting boils down to statistically weighing votes." John J. Duncan, Jr., Republican of Tennessee wrote: "I am troubled by the prospect that a statistical process could be used as a substitute for the enumeration figures. To subvert the census figures with those gathered in a sampling would open the door to great mistrust by the American people, and justly so . . . the American people . . . need to know that they are represented on the basis of real people counted, not fictitious people created by a statistical estimate." One point that runs through many of the letters from Republicans is that they endorse the proposed guidelines precisely because they appear to make it difficult or impossible to adjust.

Two letters from midwestern states allege that adjustment would be unfair because it would confer benefits on undeserving big cities. The issue here is citizenship and its responsibilities. Recognizing that adjustment is a zero-sum game, the letter-writers imply that their states are filled with law-abiding citizens who fill out their census forms; these good citizens would be penalized to benefit the people who don't return census forms. These letters came from Minnesota's senate counsel and South Dakota's governor. Urging the secretary of commerce not to adjust, the Minnesotan wrote: "To say that the census is being adjusted to add people to New York, Chicago, and Los Angeles that the census could not find but thinks are present is something that the general public can readily understand, but I am not so sure the general public would readily accept it."

The general public in Minnesota anyhow. South Dakota's governor expressed similar concerns: "The issue is fairness. The adjustments . . . will only further bias the figures in favor of states with vast numbers of 'undercounted population.' Midwestern states such as South Dakota do not have large numbers of . . . the 'undercounted population.' "

Not all the letter-writers opposed adjustment. Historian Margo Anderson wrote to Michael Darby, advising him to consider adjustment in a historical context. Having studied the history of the census, she explained that there have been innovations ever since the first census (Conk 1987; Anderson 1988). Some of the innovations seem simple and obvious, such as switching from counting households to counting persons and having the federal government print census forms and hire enumerators. "Each change was prompted because it would make the census more accurate. But each change was also attacked at the time as possibly undermining census accuracy. . . . The new methods were not foolproof . . . but census officials justified them by noting that the count would be better—not perfect—but better" (Anderson 1990).

Anderson proceeds to justify adjusting the 1990 census on the basis of these historical lessons. "The problems presented by adjusting . . . are not terribly different from those that prompted earlier innovations." Furthermore, she challenges one of the premises of the preliminary guidelines, that adjusting would call into question the adequacy of the census. Anderson suggests that developing adjustment methods affirms the tradition of improving the census, which validates its role as an integral part of our democratic process.

The letters to Michael Darby included several from statisticians, mostly former bureau employees (Wolter, Bailar, Hansen) and individuals who had served on advisory committees or the National Research Council panel. Indeed, they were so knowledgeable that they could perceive what had been left out of the preliminary guidelines and they could see its biases. A number of these writers told Mr. Darby that, since the guidelines set forth conditions that could never be met, they effectively blocked the road to adjustment. John E. Rolph, of the Rand Corporation, wrote that "Adoption of these proposed guidelines virtually eliminates the possibility of deciding to adjust." Thomas R. Belin, of Harvard's Department of Statistics, wrote, "No adjustment procedure could ever satisfy these guidelines because the guidelines demand evidence in favor of adjustment that is beyond the realm of science to obtain." Likewise, writing for the Committee on Population Statistics of the Population Association of America, Clifford Clogg asserted that the guidelines were not realistic and that they set forth tasks that could not be implemented by the deadline.

Two writers noted that each of the guidelines had the power to prevent an adjustment, so that if even one of them were not satisfied, there would be no adjustment. A number of writers, including Barbara Bailar, pointed out a series of erroneous statements in the preliminary guidelines based upon the way in which it referred to the PES. The preliminary guidelines said, in effect, that numbers generated from a survey (the PES) could not substitute for the census. But the guidelines failed to indicate that the PES was not designed to stand alone as an alternative to the regular census. The idea of adjustment was to use the results of the PES in order to modify the counts from the regular census, thereby generating a new set of numbers.

Statistician Michael Stoto suggested that a better set of guidelines would frame the issue differently. The correct way to frame the issue would be to say that, at the end, the secretary would have to choose between two sets of numbers, the original census counts and the adjusted counts. It was wrong to say that the original census counts would be taken as the standard and that the alternative would be scrutinized to see if it could be proven that they were superior. Stoto's prescription was to put the two sets of numbers on an equal footing, to evaluate both sets of numbers, and then to choose between them. He insisted that the census itself had to be evaluated, not just the PES. He listed several kinds of potential errors in a census: listing errors; processing errors; lost forms; nonresponse; proxy responses; race and ethnicity misclassifications; geocoding errors; and duplicate records.

Morris Hansen stood out among the few statisticians who wrote without endorsing adjustment. But, he too criticized the preliminary guidelines. He stated his reservations: "I have not been and am not currently an advocate of adjustment unless and until potential adjustments have been carried through and carefully evaluated."

Then he proceeded to criticize the preliminary guidelines. "In my judgment it is counterproductive to try to impose some of the extreme requirements stated in the guidelines. . . . I am especially concerned over the fact that the proposed guidelines appear to reflect a predetermination by the Department of Commerce that an adjustment will be disadvantageous and will not be made." Three months after the publication of the preliminary guidelines, the Department of Commerce issued a set of guidelines with the unwieldy title "Final Guidelines for Considering Whether or Not

a Statistical Adjustment of the 1990 Decennial Census of Population and Housing Should Be Made for Coverage Deficiencies
Resulting in an Overcount or Undercount of the Population."
Undersecretary of Commerce Michael Darby released these final
guidelines on March 12, 1990, at a press conference. The
department's written presentation of the guidelines included several paragraphs of commentary to accompany each of the eight
final guidelines. The statement was padded with fifty-three pages
of detailed summaries of the comments received pertaining to the
preliminary guidelines (U.S. Department of Commerce 1990).

Darby's remarks at the press conference were less than candid.
As usual, he began by saying that "the department's goal is to make
the 1990 census the best and most accurate census ever" (Darby
1990). This assertion consistently implied that the forthcoming
census would be so complete that it would obviate the need for an
adjustment. The census itself would eliminate the undercount.
The persistence of the differential undercount, decade after decade, despite the bureau's best efforts, shows that this was never
a realistic assumption. At the press conference Michael Darby
implied that the new set of guidelines was responsive to the comments he had received. The department received 156 letters, he
noted, representing among others three Senators, seventy-eight
members of the House, seven Governors, and seventy-four members of state legislatures. Then, as though those letters were
equivalent to a poll, he reported the results: "seventy-six expressions of general support for the proposed guidelines as a whole
and sixty-five expressions of general disapproval" (Ibid.). But,
since dozens of state legislators submitted essentially the same
letter (presumably drafted for them by the National Republican
Legislators Association) it was certainly misleading to tally them.

The final set consisted of eight guidelines, down from twelve.
All technical statistical concerns are encapsulated in guidelines 1,
2, and 3. Guideline 1 once again sets the census as the most
accurate count, "unless an adjusted count is shown to be more
accurate." This is followed by eighteen paragraphs of explanation,
which include comments on demographic analysis and the PES.
Guideline 2 once again requires adjusted counts to be "consistent
and complete across all jurisdictional levels," from the national to
the block. Guideline 3, in effect, reiterates guideline 1 in statistical

terms, saying that the estimates produced by an adjustment must be demonstrably better than estimates that would be produced by some alternative statistical model.

Guidelines 4 through 8 deal with nontechnical policy issues, all of which had been stated in the preliminary guidelines. Preliminary guideline 6, which required a rationale that would be understandable to the general public, was restated to "The ability to articulate clearly the basis and implications of the decision whether or not to adjust shall be a factor in the decision. The general rationale for the decision will be clearly stated" (Ibid.).

Although some critics of the Department of Commerce saw little difference between the preliminary and final guidelines, I detected some notable changes. For one thing, the final guidelines were written more carefully. Also, they no longer framed the decision as a choice between a census and a survey; they posited a choice between unadjusted census counts and adjusted census counts. Most importantly, the final guidelines no longer said, in effect, that we won't adjust for reason 1 or we won't adjust for reason 2. They constructed the adjustment decision in such a way that the secretary could choose between unadjusted census counts and adjusted census counts. On the other hand, the final guidelines also retained nontechnical policy statements that were not subject to scientific evaluation. In issuing the final guidelines, the department rejected statisticians' advice to publish technical statistical standards and guidelines for decision. Instead, at his press conference, Michael Darby promised to release such standards and guidelines when they became available.

The Stage Is Set   So, despite this sequence of conflicts—a fight in 1987 between the bureau and OMB over the census questionnaire, Undersecretary Ortner's announcement that there would be no adjustment, New York's 1988 lawsuit demanding adjustment, the 1989 stipulation and order arising from that lawsuit, the establishment of the panel and the publication of the guidelines—everything was in place for 1990. All plans for the census itself had been previewed in test censuses and the dress rehearsal—the census was ready to go. The PES had been tested; statisticians on the Undercount Research Staff continued to develop techniques for analyzing and evaluating its results and for translating them into adjusted numbers. The bureau's computer programmers were still working on programs that would create adjusted census numbers.

But the 1980s had created a heightened political atmosphere for the census. Once the Department of Commerce injected itself into the planning process in mid-1987, it took control of the adjustment decision. It retained tight control over that decision and, more broadly, over the census director's office. The effect of this power shift was to exaggerate one trait in census culture, the distinction between "us" in the bureau and "them" at the department. Moreover, that power shift made census officials fearful; they understood that the department wanted to control the information that was released about the census. They sensed that the undersecretary's staff was watching them carefully. Consequently, census officials feared that what they did or said, particularly in public, might get them into trouble with their superiors at the department. This fear had the effect of inhibiting census statisticians' valuable relationships with outside groups, especially their own advisory committees.

Another problem in those years was the looming threat of a lawsuit. When New York City sued again in 1988, the threat became a reality. New York's attorneys, aided by their scientific consultants, particularly Barbara Bailar and Eugene Ericksen, were consistently aggressive. They testified again and again at congressional hearings, expressing their displeasure with Ortner's decision, with the guidelines, with the department in general. They frequently aired their grievances in the pages of the *New York Times*.

From the department's point of view, New York was the enemy. New York accused the department of acting in bad faith, of trying to torpedo the PES, of substituting political for scientific control of the bureau, of issuing obstructive guidelines, and of promoting the unrealistic goal of overcoming the undercount by conducting "the best census ever".

The bureau's situation was more complicated. Like the department, the bureau did not want New York to push them around. After all, New York's lawyers were the same ones who had accused the bureau of incompetence in 1980. Census officials did not want city officials and lawyers to force them to make decisions. But at the same time, the New York was pushing for adjustment, and this time there was a sizeable faction at the bureau that wanted to adjust or at least to carry out the full-scale PES. Furthermore, Barbara Bailar, who formerly led that faction, had left the bureau, and she was working with the opposition. That faction was being thwarted by the department, so their cause was bolstered by the dreaded New Yorkers.

10 Census Year 1990

CENSUS OFFICIALS had to face their perennial challenge in 1990, to count the American people, and once again their special challenge was to count the "difficult to enumerate." I will attempt to show that the design of the 1990 census was reasonable and the execution was competent. The Census Bureau, along with its army of temporary workers, put forth a remarkable effort. I will develop this theme by telling the story of the census itself, how it was conducted as a series of well planned, often elaborate procedures. A second theme I will develop is that none of these procedures was perfect; they allowed for errors and sometimes even injected them into the data. My third theme is that the census was conducted under closer public scrutiny than ever before; it was pounded by criticism from journalists, politicians, and others who constantly found fault with it.

The bureau's basic approach to data collection was the same as it had been in 1980. An address list was the backbone: the census's main objective was to develop a complete address list of all the residences in the United States, to find out which ones were occupied on April 1, and to collect population information from the occupied units. As Director Barbara Bryant pointed out, the census consisted of two different types of data collection efforts spliced together. Mailout-mailback, was basically a mail question-naire survey. Field followup, was basically a door-to-door inter-view survey to pick up the people who failed to mail back their questionnaires the first time. There were community relations and advertising programs to elicit popular cooperation. And there was a set of coverage improvement programs to help count the "difficult to enumerate." Many of the particulars differed from 1980—some of the coverage improvement programs were new—but the overall strategy was to use the previous approach with enhancements.

Although the 1990 census followed the basic strategy of the 1980 census, it differed in important ways due to the introduction of two computer systems. One was an extremely expensive, state-of-the-art geography/mapping system known as *TIGER*; the other was a management information system. Both systems were excellent, but the management information system made the bigger impact on the census.

Outreach and Advertising

The census was supported by an unprecedentedly large and elaborate outreach and advertising program. Hundreds of full-time census community relations workers began to publicize the census two years before it began. The 1990 advertising program was targeted especially to poor, minority audiences. The outreach program, community awareness and products program (CAPP), consisted of several activities. Every district office had at least one fulltime CAPP staff member who was responsible for sponsoring an open house at the district office for local residents, government officials, and especially, the media. They were in charge of a census education project designed "to make teachers aware of the 1990 census and provide them with teaching materials that will expose students and their families to the census." Every municipality was encouraged to form a "complete count committee," composed of "highly visible and well-respected local figures" who might support and publicize the census. District offices were to operate "walk-in assistance centers" in urban minority neighborhoods to provide information and help people with their questionnaires (U.S. Bureau of the Census 1990g).

At the national level, the bureau attempted to make liaison with minority organizations, such as the National Association for the

Advancement of Colored People (NAACP) and the League of United Latin American Citizens (LULAC). Census officials sponsored displays and presentations at these organizations' conventions. Special promotional programs were aimed at historically black colleges and minority churches.

Once again, there was a large-scale advertising program, based upon donations of time on radio and television and of space in publications. Advertisements were prepared by a major New York agency, and, for the first time, there were ads prepared by three minority advertising agencies, directed toward black, Hispanic, and Asian-American audiences. Media research showed that, in the weeks around April 1, the airwaves were saturated with census messages. A national survey, conducted between April 9 and May 9, showed that more than 90 percent of the public had seen or heard something recently about the census (Bates and Whitford 1991).

Nonetheless, once again, the messages failed to penetrate the minority audiences, particularly blacks. That same survey showed that more than 20 percent of blacks said that they had not seen or heard anything about the census. Needless to say, many of the difficult to enumerate must have been among that 20 percent.

Field Organization

The organizational structure of the 1990 census was also an outgrowth of the previous census. Once again, national headquarters were at the bureau in Suitland. At the second echelon there were processing offices and regional census centers, scattered across the country. Finally, at the operational level there were hundreds of district offices. The role of processing offices was expanded from what it had been ten years earlier; in 1990 there were seven processing offices as compared with three in 1980, and they did more work. For the 1990 census the bureau divided the country into thirteen regions and set up a temporary regional census center (RCC) in each one. A regional census center was a very large office containing six divisions under the overall management of a regional director and an assistant regional census manager. The divisions were: geography, with a computerized unit to produce maps; census awareness and products, to handle publicity, education, and community relations; automation, to handle the management information system; administration, to handle space, phones, personnel, payroll, and audit; PES, to handle the postenumeration survey; and the "area manager," who was the direct supervisor of the district managers responsible for the district offices. The area manager was responsible for training the district managers, giving them feedback, giving them administrative support, and "providing guidance and advice with management decisions" (U.S. Bureau of the Census 1990:1–3).

The bureau once again divided the nation into districts, increasing to 487 from 409 in 1980.[1] As in 1980, district offices were directly responsible for conducting field operations. When field operations peaked in June 1990, each district office had a staff of hundreds. District offices were divided into types. Type 1 district offices were located in large central cities. They differed from other types of offices in two ways. Type 1 offices were assigned fewer housing units to enumerate, approximately 175,000, as compared with more than 200,000 assigned to other types of offices. They did not receive and check in mail questionnaires. All the mailed back questionnaires for housing units in Type 1 districts went directly to processing offices. Personnel was a major concern for all types of district offices. They had to recruit and screen applicants; then they had to train and supervise them. This was done in large numbers and in short order. District offices were also responsible for keeping on schedule, reporting field activities, monitoring "cost and progress," and controlling quality. Each district office manager had assistant managers for administration, office operations, electronic data processing, recruiting, and most importantly, field operations. In turn, the assistant manager for field operations had two field operations supervisors. Crew leaders, who managed enumerators in field interviewing and other followup activities, reported to field operations supervisors.

The division of labor between Type 1 district offices and processing offices derived from an unstated staffing strategy. The idea was to locate the processing offices in areas where there was likely to be an abundance of qualified workers and to have them do as much of the in-office clerical work as possible. This was to divert that work from district offices in large central cities which presumably offered inferior clerical personnel. Bounpane and Jones (1988) stated the problem discreetly, referring to "more hard-to-enumerate urban cores where recruiting enough temporary census workers can be difficult." Census planners wanted central city district offices to concentrate on followup field work. Knowing that most temporary workers would prefer to stay in the office rather than go into the field, census planners designed the tasks of central city district offices in order to minimize their clerical work. Several processes that consumed a great deal of time and attention in district offices in 1980 included checking in mailed-in questionnaires, editing them, checking and rechecking the address lists to see if there were completed questionnaires to conform to them. The new scheme removed this work entirely from big city district offices.

Innovations: Computers

Computer systems had been used in previous censuses for data processing, to create tables for publications, and for accounting (such as payroll) at the central office. So, the bureau's main systems at Suitland were ready for 1990, along with another well-tested technology from recent censuses: FOSDIC and its associated microfilming machines. In planning for 1990, census administrators had considered alternatives to FOSDIC for data entry, but after consulting with several vendors, they decided to stay with an updated version of FOSDIC as the most efficient way to get data off of the original questionnaires. This "old" technology was used at processing offices in conjunction with two new technologies: barcoding and the management information system.

Barcoding of addresses was an innovation in 1990. As address lists were compiled, every housing unit address was assigned a unique number and that number was given a barcode. Then, when mailing packets containing questionnaires were prepared, every return envelope was imprinted with a barcode corresponding to the dwelling it represented. That meant that when a completed census form arrived at a district or processing office, the barcode on its envelope was "read" and, simultaneously, a computer recorded the fact that that address's form had been received. Laser sorters were used to read barcodes at processing offices. These great machines could handle up to 400 envelopes per minute. At a processing office, the laser sorter was located near the receiving dock, where the post office delivered truckloads of census returns. Census workers unloaded them from the trays into the laser sorter's hopper. The laser sorter slit the envelopes and sorted the packets into bins, read their barcodes and recorded their associated address list numbers. Every time the computer in the laser sorter reached a tally of 9,500 addresses, the information from its disk was "dumped" and sent to the computer system. In turn, the main computer system recorded, on the address list, that forms were received from those addresses. The laser sorter replaced thousands of clerks in district offices.

Nineteen hundred and ninety was the first year in which computers were dispersed to all offices and connected by means of a network. The new national computer network permitted census administrators to change certain ways of handling data and administering procedures. In 1987 the bureau let an $80 million contract to purchase computers from Digital Equipment Corporation (DEC). (The contract was later revised so that the bureau leased some of the computers.) These computers were ideally suited to the tasks of administration, data capture, and communications. I never spoke with a census staff member who had anything but praise for the system.

Overall, the computer system consisted of 555 minicomputers of varying sizes, dispersed throughout the processing offices, regional census centers, and district offices. The different-sized computers were all compatible insofar as their software was, in effect, interchangeable, and they could be connected for communications and data transfer. The census headquarters in Suitland had the largest machine, which represented the center of the system. District offices and processing offices also had terminals wired to their minicomputers for the purpose of data entry. Thus, at both types of offices, employees could key in data or administrative information. Data entry clerks at district offices keyed facts from job applications, personnel records, and wage and hour forms. These clerks also keyed information from field operations. These records went into the personnel file, the payroll file, and the ARA (Address Register Area) tracking file, and other components of the management information system.

So, how did this computer system change the census? It rationalized the operation of district offices. At the outset, district managers used the systems to build on-line personnel files. All data from applications and tests from applicants was held on line. Managers used applicant files to choose and call new employees. Then, as managers needed additional staff, they could continually search the files for new hires. Also, once an individual was hired, his or her data was transferred from the applicant file to personnel files. As the census proceeded, district managers used the information system to keep track of production. During every operation, the computer kept track of work, by area, by employee, and by work unit. Managers at every level could see where the work was getting done, at what rate, and by whom. District managers could see progress and lack of progress by area and by crew. Likewise, regional managers could see which districts were moving forward and which were lagging. The files and reports were continually updated, so managers could monitor situations; they could move quickly to remedy problems. For example, the manager of Chicago's regional census center saw quickly that certain districts in his three-state region were moving slowly in followups, and he decided to replace district managers in the the least productive offices. Strangely enough, at the district level, managers might be displeased by reports of very high productivity. If a manager saw that a crew or an enumerator was exceptionally productive, he or she would wonder whether someone was fudging the data. In this situation, too, a manager would be inclined to act quickly.

One particularly clumsy feature of the 1970 and 1980 censuses was that each district office retained all of its finished questionnaires until all procedures were completed and the office was closed. Questionnaires just stayed at the offices in sorting bins. When the office was finally closed, the questionnaires were packed and shipped to processing centers. Thus no data were "captured" until late summer. Furthermore, storing the questionnaires at district offices made them vulnerable to accidents. In 1980 a district office burned down in Brooklyn's Bedford-Stuyvesant, destroying more than 100,000 questionnaires, thus necessitating a whole new census of that district late in the year.

In 1990, the new systems captured questionnaire data soon after each completed form was received by a census office. In Type 2 and Type 3 district offices, clerks checked in the questionnaires by "wanding" the barcodes, thus recording the fact that a return had been received for that specific address. The next step was for clerks to edit the questionnaires to determine that answers to all questions were complete and legible and that no question with FOSDIC circles had more than one circle filled. Most editing operations were automated at processing offices, but at district offices they were all clerical. Questionnaires that passed the edit were sent on to be microfilmed. Those that failed the edit were sent for telephone followup. If a phone number was available, a clerk called the household to obtain answers to the blank questions and the ones with illegible answers. Also, if a respondent indicated that his or her usual home was elsewhere, a phone clerk called to verify that information. If phone clerks could not reach a respondent in order to fix a questionnaire, it was assigned to an enumerator for a regular visit.

In processing offices, envelope barcodes were read immediately by the laser sorters and soon afterwards the questionnaires were filmed. Census officials used the term "flow processing" to refer to this continuous way of handling questionnaires as they arrived. Flow processing offered many advantages, not the least of which was the protection of individual records from accidents similar to the one that occurred in Brooklyn. Flow processing facilitated certain matching operations, such as "UHE" (usual home elsewhere), in which the census attempted to see if it had two returns at different locations for the same persons, for example, a midwestern couple that spent winter and spring in a southern state. Flow processing made it possible for the census to see continually how many questionnaires it had received. Weekly progress reports throughout July and August often showed that data collection and data handling operations were ahead of where they had been in the previous census. For example, this quote from the August 3, 1990 memorandum: "Through July 21, almost 99 million questionnaires converted to computer-readable form passed all edit and repair operations. Thus, questionnaires for over 97 percent of all housing units on our list are ready for final automated processing and analysis, months ahead of where we were at a comparable date in 1980" (C. Jones 1990).

Ultimately, flow processing made it possible for the bureau to tally the results much earlier than it had in previous censuses.

Developing and Maintaining Address Lists

As mentioned above, the address list was the backbone of the census.[2] Viewed from this angle, the main goal of the census was to create a perfect address list, to discover which housing units on the list were occupied, and to get population information from them. For this reason, the census devoted an enormous effort to compiling and correcting these lists. The 1990 method for developing an address list was radically different from the 1980 method. In 1980 address lists were computer printouts in binders, kept at district offices. Any additional information—addresses to be inserted or deleted—was entered in pencil. Thus, although it began as a computer printout, the 1980 address list was basically a paper-and-pencil roster. That approach was scrapped in 1990, replaced by a computerized system.

The basic, national version of the 1990 address list, the address control file, resided on a mainframe computer (UNISYS) in Suitland. District office managers received address lists in the form of computer tapes from Suitland. As the district offices conducted field operations to check and correct the lists, they entered new information—corrections, additions, deletions, and vacancies—into their local computers, which stored it. Then, at the end of each week, the district office computer downloaded the address list and the corrections on a tape that was sent by overnight air express to Suitland. A small staff at the bureau received tapes from all the district offices and worked round the clock to update the master address list. Then they created tapes of all the address lists and sent them back to the district office. Once the district office's computer supervisor got the new tape, updated copies of the local address list were printed.

Converting from the paper and pencil mode to the disk and tape mode had advantages for census managers. It allowed them to make a weekly tally of how many addresses were actually on the list, thus showing what the census's specific target was. In 1980 there was no way of knowing how many occupied addresses were in a district without having clerks count all of the nonvacant entries in all of the address registers. Given the new system along with equally current information on how many completed questionnaires existed, census managers in 1990 knew precisely how much of the job was finished and how much was left to do.

In order to understand the process of building the national address list you must know that the bureau divided the country into four types of enumeration areas.

Tape Address Register (TAR) areas were areas for which a mailing list was purchased from a commercial vendor.[3] Prelist areas describe areas for which an enumerator had listed each residential address and marked its location on a map. TAR and Prelist areas were mostly urban and suburban. These first two types of areas were enumerated by mailout-mailback. Update/leave areas are "primarily rural and seasonal housing areas where an enumerator updates a (previously prepared) address register and map, and leaves a questionnaire at each housing unit to be completed and mailed to the district office." List/enumerate areas are sparsely populated areas where an enumerator lists each residential address, and administers a questionnaire, "collecting a completed questionnaire for each housing unit." As these definitions suggest, address lists were developed differently in each kind of enumeration area. In TAR areas, the bureau reviewed bids from commercial address list vendors and purchased lists. Thereafter, the bureau's staff reformatted the records, which were delivered on magnetic tapes. Then they geocoded the records, so that each address was transformed into a larger computer record, which also included the census geography for that address: state, county, etc., down to district office number, census tract, "ARA" (Address Register Area), census block, and even "walking sequence," this latter detailing the sequence by which the enumerator should travel through the assigned area.[4] (U.S. Bureau of the Census 1988d).

Address lists prepared for TAR areas were checked in September 1988 by post offices in an advance post office check. The first step in this checking process was for census processing offices to print a card for each address in the address file. The processing offices printed about 55 million address cards and delivered them to the postal service (Rivers and Tillman 1991:9). Then, at post offices throughout the country, letter carriers "cased" the cards as though they were letters to be delivered. Casing revealed errors in the address list. Some cards were addressed to nonexistent addresses, some addresses known to the carrier lacked cards, and others had duplicate cards. The postal service notified the census which cards were deliverable, entered corrections on cards with errors, noted undeliverables and duplicates, and filled out new cards for addresses that had been missed.

The Census Bureau did not enter these corrections into the address control file until they verified each one in the field. In an operation known as *APOC reconciliation*, district offices sent enumerators to check adds, undeliverables, and duplicates. Only after such verification did the bureau enter the corrections and add the addresses from the new cards to the address register (U.S. Bureau of the Census 1990h). The advance post office check, then, was the first review of the census address lists and it added 1.3 million addresses (Rivers and Tillman 1991:7). The fact that the census field-checked all of the putative corrections it received from the postal service shows that census administrators recognized that every procedure—even if it is designed to make corrections—has the potential for introducing new errors.

Simultaneously with the APOC reconciliation, district offices were also field-checking address lists in a procedure known as precanvass (U.S. Bureau of the Census 1990h:36). Precanvass was conducted from mid-May to early August, 1989. In this procedure, enumerators were assigned neighborhoods and equipped with maps and printed address registers. In walking (or driving) through the assigned neighborhoods, the enumerators were to verify the addresses on the printed list, to look for addresses that had been missed, and to conduct interviews with residents, attempting to discover additional living quarters that were not apparent. Census planners had injected a deliberate deception in the procedure as a quality control test: certain known addresses were not printed in order to see whether the enumerators would find and add them.

In addition to the regular list, the census compiled a list of "special places." Recognizing that people live in all sorts of accommodations, not just houses and apartments, census administrators defined a catchall term, special places, "that includes colleges and universities, hotels, motels, rooming and boarding houses, hospitals, missions, shelters, flophouses, prisons, jails, nursing homes, and military bases" (U.S. Bureau of the Census 1989b:1). Then, to make the concept more complex, census definitions indicated that within a special place there may be "group quarters." Group quarters were defined as "a type of living quarters found at some special places such as hospital wards, wards at jails, college or university dormitories, and large rooming and/or boarding houses" (U.S. Bureau of the Census 1990i).

From January 17, 1990, to February 12, 1990, there was special place prelisting. By that time the bureau already had a computerized, geocoded list of almost 200,000 special places, but census administrators did not know how accurate it was because it was based on other lists and directories of unknown quality. Personnel in the newly opened district offices, including the special places operations supervisor, began with a "local knowledge update," reviewing the list, looking for omissions and entering new addresses. Then enumerators were to go to all listed special places to verify their existence and their addresses and to collect preliminary information. The point of this story is to show that, while the task of listing the addresses of millions of "ordinary" residences was daunting, the greater job of creating a national address file to include all the different places people live, was even more difficult.

Another precensus check of the address lists took place during the first phase of local government review, from early November 1989, into early January 1990. This unprecedented operation allowed local governmental officials to help catch potential errors prior to the census. District offices distributed to each unit of local government a map of its area and a block-by-block list of housing counts. Having this preliminary information, municipal officials could match their own records with those from the census to look for discrepancies. If local authorities were aware, for example, of a block that had a number of housing units and they noticed that the census lists reported no units, they informed the district office. The district office then sent someone to look at the specified location, check the census list and map, and if the information of the local authorities was confirmed, enter corrections into the address lists.

Then, two weeks before census forms were mailed out in March 1990, post offices reviewed census address lists in TAR areas a second time. Once again processing offices prepared address cards (88 million) to be cased. This second casing check added another 800,000 addresses, bringing to 2.1 million the number of adds from the postal service. As noted by Rivers and Tillman (1991:7), "the total number of addresses added to the census address list (by postal checks) represents 2.8 percent of the total number of housing units in TAR areas."

Address lists for prelist and update/leave areas were made from scratch. Lists were made for address register areas (ARAs) one at a time. A crew leader sent an enumerator to a specific ARA with a map of the area and a blank address register. The enumerator was instructed to enter the address of each of the living quarters on a line in the register and also to mark the location of each of the living quarters on the map. Prelisting was done twice, in spring 1988 and again in early fall 1989. Enumerators' handwritten address registers were keyed into computers to be added to the main national address register.

Finally, in sparsely settled list/enumerate areas, address lists were developed in yet another way. By March 1990, the census had no address lists for these areas—this was according to plan. Then, about a week before Census Day, post offices were to deliver a variant of the short form to every known housing unit. Instructions on those forms said that recipients were to complete them and to hold them for pickup by an enumerator. Then, just before Census Day, an enumerator was to visit every house in his or her address register area. The enumerator was to be equipped with a map, a blank address register, and a supply of long forms.[5] The enumerator was to conduct a long form interview at certain households that fell into a sample. Altogether, the enumerator's task was to collect a completed form from each household, to enter its address on the register, to mark its location on his or her map and, if necessary, to conduct a long form interview. Thus in list/enumerate areas, the address list was not created until the enumeration itself was conducted.

Theoretically then before Census Day the Census Bureau's computers contained an address list for the entire nation (except the sparsely populated List/Enumerate areas). But the job was not yet finished; addresses were added, subtracted, and corrected through all ensuing phases of the census until tabulation began. The census continued to work on the address lists, attempting to discover whether there were actual dwellings that were not yet included on the lists (and to add them), whether the lists included nonexistent addresses, and whether there were errors in the lists, wrong addresses or wrong apartment numbers, for example.

In order to work toward a "perfect" address list, all followup operations included attempts to check on addresses. One census planning document listed a dozen operations that could generate changes in the address control file (U.S. Bureau of the Census 1990b:10). The list included nonresponse followup (the door-to-door visits following mailback), field followup (a later followup), post-census local government review recanvass, search/match, and count review at the end. So, every operation that took enumerators into the field was directly or indirectly an attempt to perfect the address control file. It would not be an exaggeration to say that it took more than two and a half years to develop the address lists. The bureau acquired addresses for special places in 1987, and they started acquiring regular address files in February 1988. Additions, deletions, and other corrections to the files continued into August 1990.

TIGER

The development of a detailed, national computerized mapping system called *TIGER* represented a major investment in the 1990 census. TIGER was a geographical information system and cartographic system that took ten years to plan and carried a $300 million price tag.

There were so many problems with maps and geographical systems in 1980 that the bureau conducted an inquiry right after the census (U.S. Bureau of the Census 1983). A committee, based in the bureau's geographic division, concluded that it had been an error to maintain three discrete geographical systems. There were redundancies between them and their information was not always consistent. Furthermore, they relied too heavily upon clerical input of data. After consulting widely with experts inside and outside the government, the geography division planned a new system that would minimize clerical inputs and consolidate all geographical files into a single, integrated system. By 1981, the geographers resolved to automate the full range of geographic and cartographic operations for the 1990 census (Marx 1990).

TIGER was designed to be a state-of-the-art geographical

information system incorporating an extraordinarily large data base, representing the entire United States, in detail. Geographical information systems—computerized systems that incorporated spatial data and software for mapmaking, together with other data that could be spatially arrayed—were not a new concept in 1981; such systems had existed for more than ten years. Nonetheless, as geographer Robert Marx, who took the lead in developing TIGER, has noted, such systems were typically not oriented toward storing and displaying information about people. TIGER was planned to store, retrieve, and plot (map) a great deal of information about the geographical points and areas and also about population. Planners of the new geographical information system anticipated also that it would be useful to many data users and for many purposes, such as for legislative redistricting with census data.

The geographers' original plan anticipated that it would take twenty years to map the entire country. TIGER would cover the major metropolitan areas for the 1990 census and ten years later it would cover the rest of the country. The geographers were not given that much time; higher administrators at the bureau decided to build the entire national system in time for the 1990 census (Melnick 1987). Funding for TIGER began in fiscal year 1984.

In order to capture geographic information about the entire country, the bureau entered into an agreement with the U. S. Geological Survey, which had produced the nation's "most accurate single set of detailed maps" (Marx 1990). The two agencies had to compile detailed data files that included the location, configuration, and name of every topographical feature—highway, road, street, alley, bridge, railway track, embankment, river, creek, lake, shore. Such information was necessary in order to identify the location of the address of every dwelling. Furthermore, the files had to divide each of these lines into identifiable segments— a block of a street between two intersections, a stretch of shoreline between two piers—and show the range of address numbers that would fall within that segment. In addition, the computer programs had to be able to make combinations of these segments so that they would form the boundaries of conventionally recognized areas: city blocks, townships, counties, and the like. Except for newly built areas (subdivisions, for example), these areas had to be numbered and conform to areas that had been used in 1980 and earlier censuses.

Miraculously TIGER was ready in time for the 1990 census. That accomplishment was notable in three ways: first, the partners were able to write many new computer programs to accept and format the varieties of data that would have to go into the system. Second, the partners had to collect and correct mountains of data from disparate sources, including hundreds of municipalities, throughout the country. Third, the bureau had to acquire the powerful, expensive equipment that supported TIGER. By census time there was a computer-based geography unit at each regional census center. Each unit had a minicomputer and a collection of computer tapes containing TIGER files for the appropriate areas (U.S. Bureau of the Census 1988a:3-3). One task that was carried out at such centers was entering corrections and other update information into the region's TIGER files. Staff members in the regional census center sat before video display terminals and entered corrections or new information into TIGER files. For example, at the Chicago regional census center, I watched staff members enter political geography—wards and precincts—into TIGER files so that they would be ready for redistricting. It was remarkable to me that the census could quickly hire temporary staff and train them to do such technical work.

Each regional census center's geography unit had large, powerful, high speed electrostatic plotters that printed a variety of kinds of maps. The maps literally rolled off the printers. It was a big job just to cut and fold them. They produced maps at various scales tailormade for each operation. Any time an enumerator went out to an assigned area, he or she had to have a precise map of it. Before the census there were prelist ARA maps, precanvass ARA maps, and list/enumerate ARA maps. Later there were postal locator maps, precensus local review maps, postcensus local review maps, and many others. There were also general purpose products including an atlas of ARA maps for every district office, along with district office wall maps and county locator maps. All maps took advantage of the detail in TIGER's vast databank. Unfortunately, the first widespread public notice of TIGER came during precensus local review, accompanied by a blizzard of complaints. When city officials previewed TIGER files and maps for their areas they discovered more than a few glitches. Dozens of city administrations complained.

The loudest complaints against TIGER came from New York City. Geographers in the city's Department of City Planning scrutinized TIGER maps for a sample of forty-one census tracts and discovered dozens of errors (Mann and Salvo 1989). There were seven types of errors: misaligned streets, missing street segments, street segments that were misnamed or had no names, extra street segments, tract boundary misalignments, wrong block numbers, and redundant street segments. Some types of errors could have fouled up later efforts at redistricting because the errors would have put population into areas where they did not reside. In May 1989 New York's Mayor Edward Koch wrote to the secretary of commerce to complain about these errors and to demand that the TIGER file be corrected (Koch 1989). As of June 12, the bureau refused to make corrections before the census, saying that their budget made no provision for the correction of errors in TIGER files. Census officials contended that most of the errors were trivial or that they would be corrected in the ordinary course of field operations. Within six weeks, the bureau yielded; on July 24, Peter Bounpane, Assistant Director, Decennial Census, announced that "we have revised our plan and will update the TIGER file earlier than originally planned" (U.S. Congress 1989).

Notwithstanding these early complaints, TIGER proved to be a major asset to the census, providing high-quality maps on a timely basis.

Mailout-Mailback

Mailout-mailback, the census's first major attempt to collect information about households and individuals, should be seen as one of the census's biggest, most fundamental operations. Even printing the forms and addressing the envelopes was a formidable task. According to a press release from the bureau's "census promotion office," the government had contracted with Moore Business Forms, Inc., to print eighty-six million short forms for $18 million, "the largest single-product contract in Government Printing Office history" (Green and Mersch 1991). Contractors would stuff each questionnaire into a census mailing packet that would also include "instructional guides," "motivational inserts," and return envelopes. After all the packets were addressed, there were enough of them to fill 500 large trucks, which delivered them to the postal service. Questionnaire production work was to be complete by early March, and the postal service was asked to begin delivering on March 23.

Right after mailout, the bureau garnered a good deal of negative publicity as a result of a service improvement—telephone inquiry lines. The bureau installed phone banks at a number of processing offices in order to answer questions from the public, but they were instantly overwhelmed by more calls than they could answer. Hundreds of thousand of callers were frustrated by busy signals. As Barbara Bryant explained on April 19, "The volume of calls . . . significantly exceeded all expectations" (U.S. Congress 1990:10). Notices printed on mailout packets said that people could call an 800 number if they had a question. There were also eight other 800 numbers through which to get information in languages other than English and a number for the hearing impaired. Spanish-speakers were particularly peeved by the phone situation. Anyone who wanted a Spanish-language questionnaire had to call to request one. Spanish-language TV networks ran trailers across their screens for several days before the census, encouraging participation and giving the 800 number. In response, people called in and failed to get through, so they complained to journalists, to city hall, and to Congress.

At the same time, mailout itself ran into trouble when a number of questionnaire packets could not be delivered by the postal service. On April 19 Barbara Bryant testified that the bureau had mailed questionnaires to about 90 percent of the nation's housing units (U.S. Congress 1990:9). Postal carriers delivered approximately 89 million packets between March 23 and March 27 (Rivers and Tillman 1991:24). By and large, this operation proceeded smoothly, but it also had a ragged edge; "4.8 million questionnaires were returned to us [by the Postal Service] as undeliverable, or 5.5 percent of the total mailout." Later, a more complete reckoning showed that 5.8 percent were returned to the bureau (Ibid.:24). Many of the undeliverable packets had been addressed to specific street addresses, but the residents of those addresses actually received their mail at post office boxes. There are entire towns that get their mail at post office boxes. Also many of the undeliverable packets had been addressed to "vacant, demolished, nonexistent, and condemned dwellings" (Ibid.:28). Other packets had incorrect addresses, especially wrong apartment designations and zip codes. There were some duplicates (two packets addressed to the same address), and carriers were instructed to return duplicates to the Census Bureau, but in fact, some households received two packets.

Having received 4.8 million rejects, the census instantly responded with an attempt to deliver the packets themselves. Naturally, they created a procedure with a name: the "PMR (postmaster return) Questionnaire Delivery Project." They dispatched enumerators to hand deliver the packets and succeeded in delivering 1.8 million (U.S. Congress 1990:10). Afterwards, the director told the subcommittee there remain "only" three million undelivered packets. She promised that the census would visit all of those addresses, but, she said, "these will mostly prove to be vacant housing units."

Despite the fact that the 1990 rate of undeliverable packets was approximately half of what it had been in 1980, census critics and the press clobbered the census. On April 13 *USA Today* ran a page-one headline, " 'Hitch' in Census May Cost Cities." The newspaper quoted Representative Charles Schumer of New York, who became the census' most persistent and vitriolic critic. In New York City, 172,000 questionnaires were undeliverable because of faulty addresses, according to Schumer, who added "some of our worst fears have been realized." The article also said that 2,000 households did not get forms in Milwaukee and that "cities nationwide have reported similar problems." Two days later, a *New York Times* headline asked, "What Can Go Wrong in Census? 2.3 Million Undelivered Packets." Newspapers continued to feature the mailout problem. On April 14, a *Washington Post* headline stated, "Census Mailing Missed Thousands in Area, Officials Struggle to Deliver Forms by Hand." On April 18, a headline in the Palms Springs *Desert Sun* said, "Census Makes It Tough to Stand Up and Be Counted." An editorial in the *Desert Sun* asked, "why . . . have we had so many complaints from long-time residents who simply haven't received forms?" and concluded that "the system collapsed."

On April 12 a new, big story materialized: the low mail return rate. Once again the *New York Times* ran a first-page headline: "Federal Officials Report the Census Significantly Lags." The newspaper quoted Director Bryant, who said that "55 percent of the forms had been returned and that the final return rate would be 'solidly in the mid-60s.' " Yet census plans had anticipated a 70 percent mail return rate, down from 83 percent in the previous census. Newspapers across the country highlighted the problem. On April 13 the *Chicago Tribune* ran a headline: "Census Returns Fall Way Behind." Journalists began to look for reasons for the low return rate. A *Washington Post* article on April 18 said the problem was that people are too busy, they get too much junk mail, they found the questionnaire too complicated and intrusive, and they harbor "anti-government sentiment." Ironically, it was the new systems that enabled census administrators to recognize the rate of return so quickly. Computerized check-in of barcoded questionnaires in conjunction with the computerized address control file revealed the return rate instantaneously. So the new, improved systems yielded timely information, leading to instant criticism.

Actually, the extent of the drop-off in mail return was not entirely clear because there are two ways of calculating the return rate. Initially, the bureau is able to calculate a *mail response rate*, which is the number of completed questionnaires received divided by the number of questionnaires mailed out. Later in the census, the bureau calculates a *mail return rate*, which is the number of completed questionnaires received divided by the number of questionnaires mailed to occupied housing units. Before calculating the mail return rate, statisticians subtract the number of questionnaires that had been mailed to addresses that represented vacant or nonexisting housing units. Thus, of the two rates, the mail return rate is the more accurate indicator of how people behaved after they got their questionnaires. It is estimated that the 1980 mail return rate was 83 percent and the 1990 mail return rate was between 73 and 76 percent (Fay, Bates, and Moore 1991; Bryant 1991). Thus, the decline in public cooperation from 1980 to 1990 was somewhat less than it appeared at first. Although it appeared at first that the drop-off was 10 to 12 percent, it was actually from 7 to 10 percent.[6]

In order to learn more about the return rates, the bureau

conducted sample surveys on census awareness and participation and compared the results of these surveys with a similar survey that had been conducted ten years earlier. Survey results failed to support some popular suppositions: there was no indication that people lost their packets in a flood of junk mail or that any increase in antigovernment sentiment accounted for the drop in cooperation. Indeed, people who received lots of junk mail were more likely to return their forms. Also, persons who said that they had been aware of the census and had been anticipating the questionnaire were likely to have returned it. There were some demographic characteristics associated with nonresponse: persons with low levels of education (those who did not complete elementary school) were less likely to return their questionnaires, as were black people, and young people (under age 30). Household composition was very important; as compared with single-person households and households in which all the persons were related to each other, households with some unrelated persons were far less likely to return their questionnaires. Finally, postal problems were very important; as compared with 1980, more people reported that they never received a questionnaire. Also many households—14 percent in a New York City sample and 10 percent in Cleveland— reported that they received two or more forms (Dingbaum and Thomas 1991). Households that claimed to have received multiple forms were less likely than others to have returned them.

The unexpectedly low rate of return meant that enumerators would have to visit millions more households. Each percent of unreturned questionnaires represented almost a million households to be visited and an additional $10 million to the cost of the census. The low return rate meant that the census would have to hire additional enumerators. Indeed, the bureau had to appeal to Congress for a "dire emergency" appropriation of $110 million, which it granted, in order to fund the additional field staff, along with other planned field operations.[7]

In the meantime, across the country, processing offices and district offices were receiving tens of millions of completed forms, checking them in, editing them (checking to see whether all questions had been answered and whether responses were legible), microfilming their data, and transforming it into electronic records.

Nonresponse Followup:
Enumerators Hit the Streets

After mailback, the next major operation was nonresponse followup. Its purpose was "to obtain a completed questionnaire from households for which a questionnaire was not received by mail" (U.S. Bureau of the Census 1990h:28).

During nonresponse followup, enumerators visit each nonresponse unit and determine the occupancy status of the unit on Census Day. Based on the status, enumerators complete the appropriate items on the census questionnaire, even if the householder says he or she returned a questionnaire by mail [because census records still lack information from that housing unit]. . . . Enumerators also clear up any discrepancies that result from the mix up of mail delivery of census questionnaires in apartment buildings. (U.S. Bureau of the Census 1990a:12-1)

Beginning on April 26, nonresponse followup represented the door-to-door interview phase of the census. It also represented the census's peak manpower; in May and June, district offices across the country employed approximately 270,000 clerks and enumerators. Nonresponse followup was so complex that just explaining it required eighteen different manuals, including, for example, "Nonresponse Crew Leaders' Guides for Training," "Assignment Control Manual," and "Nonresponse Enumerators' Job Instructions." These examples are illustrative of the bureaucratic complexity and detail of carrying out a census procedure.

A review of the nonresponse followup chapter in the *Field Operations Manual* shows the variety of activities encompassed by this one large procedure. The chapter covers supplies, staffing and assignments, and training—how to train supervisors, crew leaders, and enumerators; how to review and collect enumerators' work; how to review daily and work records, report progress, and "keep on schedule"; how to fire a crew leader and reassign his or her work. It also explains the use of dozens of different forms.

In order to conduct the followup, each enumerator was given a list of nonresponse units to visit. In the ideal case, an enumerator visits the dwelling, finds that it is occupied and that it was occupied by the same people on Census Day, and obtains an interview from a household member who was at least fifteen years old. If that does not happen, the enumerator is supposed to leave a copy of "Form D-26" to inform the household of the visit, and then, if necessary, to call by phone three times and visit again two more times "at different times of the day, including evenings and weekends" to obtain an interview.

An enumerator who failed to get an interview after making the required number of callbacks could collect last resort information by talking with a neighbor, janitor, or the like and asking about the people who live in the unit. "Last resort data represent the minimum amount of information that must be obtained for each household resident and the household unit."[8] At minimum, the enumerator had to get three out of these four facts about each person in the household: sex, race, marital status, and "relationship," as well as also recording the number of housing units in the building and whether the unit was owned or rented.

Supervisory staff had numerous tasks during nonresponse followup. Crew leaders were to meet their enumerators daily to collect their work and their daily pay and work records. Enumerators were supposed to refer all sorts of problems to their crew leaders. For example, an enumerator who discovered that an address on the list was actually a special place or group quarters was to notify the crew leader, who was to refer the listing to the assistant manager for field operations. The assistant manager was to find an experienced person to enumerate such a place or to enumerate it personally. Problems with persons who refused to cooperate were also to be referred to crew leaders.

How did the district office prevent enumerators from curbstoning—fabricating data without conducting interviews? In each district office, the field operations supervisor for other operations was responsible for quality control over enumerators' work. The district office drew a sample of each enumerator's questionnaires and reinterviewed someone at each household in the sample. "The purpose of reinterview is to detect data falsification as quickly as possible. During reinterview, a reinterviewer verifies the occupancy status and household roster for a sample of each enumerator's forms. The reinterviewers conduct the reinterviews primarily by telephone. Personal visits are kept to a minimum" (Ibid.:13-1). If an enumerator's work attracted suspicion, for example, by including too many households without telephone numbers, three additional cases were reinterviewed.

In the event that reinterview detected fabricated data, the *Field Operations Manual* told the supervisors exactly what to do (Ibid.:13-27). The field operations supervisor for other operations must pull all of the enumerator's completed interviews and call those households to ascertain whether an enumerator had visited them. "If data falsification is confirmed, the enumerator must be released according to procedures in Form D-501." The supervisor must also meet with the enumerator to "confiscate" all of his questionnaires and other materials. Finally, a replacement enumerator must take the enumerator's assigned work to continue nonresponse followup. Regarding the falsified questionnaires, "Repair is conducted after regular enumeration . . . is completed by the replacement enumerator. Enumerators who are known to have good enumeration skills should conduct repair." Throughout nonresponse followup, a group in the district office (the assignment control unit) was receiving, checking, editing, and accepting (or rejecting) questionnaires brought in by enumerators (U.S. Bureau of the Census 1990:9-64). After that review, the completed questionnaires were shipped to processing offices for data capture.

In July 1990 it was time to finish nonresponse followup. District offices had to ascertain that 95 percent of the cases had been resolved. In order to wrap up the operation, the district office had to close-out the unresolved cases. District managers were given a new set of instructions telling them to redistribute unfinished cases among enumerators and crew leaders and even to lower the standards on last resort cases, accepting fewer than three facts about each person counted. Close-out was a period of intense activity, and by July 30, all district offices had finished nonresponse followup.

After a national campaign known as *Were You Counted?*, the field staff began field followup, which required another visit to each housing unit that had been deemed vacant, uninhabitable, or nonexistent. The 1980 census had shown that a late recheck of vacant dwellings and deleted addresses was an effective way to detect earlier errors, adding 1,724,000 persons to that census (U.S. Bureau of the Census 1986:5-29). The bureau's deputy director, Louis Kincannon, explained 1990's field followup as follows: "The vacant and delete check is a verification of the occupancy status of housing units initially identified as vacant or deleted. It improves the coverage of the census by adding persons living in housing units that have been incorrectly deleted or incorrectly identified as vacant during earlier operations" (U.S. Congress 1990d:21).

The last field operation was postcensus local review, which gave local officials an opportunity to review census maps and preliminary housing counts before the conclusion of the census. Presumably, close scrutiny by local officials would help the census to catch and correct errors. By the end of August, regional census centers were to mail listings showing the number of housing units and the group quarters population count on each block. The bureau gave local officials fifteen work days to respond to the listings. When local officials claimed, with adequate documentation, that they had discovered discrepancies between census listings and other data, district offices had to review the situation. District offices disregarded blocks where reported differences were less than 2 percent of the number of housing units. District staff recanvassed all blocks that met this criterion, proceeding from house to house, to identify whether there were any housing units missed. If they found such a unit, they had to complete a questionnaire. They might also find housing units that were misallocated, that is, assigned to the wrong map block. In such cases, the address control file would have to be corrected so that those units were assigned to their correct block. Likewise, if a field visit revealed that a special place or group quarters had been missed, it would have to be added to the address list and population information would have to be collected.

Concurrently with postcensus local review, district offices carried out another late field operation, known as housing coverage check (U.S. Bureau of the Census 1991c).

In August the Census Bureau searched its data bases to identify any blocks or communities where there were any indicators of a possible low count. . . . The Census Bureau looked at its data on areas of new construction . . . for possible missed new subdivisions. . . . We looked at media reports or local complaints of missed buildings or blocks. . . . [We] decided to recanvass blocks where problems might exist. These blocks represented 15 percent of the Nation's housing units. (Bryant 1991:11)

This operation yielded an additional 300,000 persons in the census (Ibid.:7, table 1).

Starting on April 1 and continuing throughout the field work period, the census was trying to deal with cases who had been contacted in one place but who claimed to reside elsewhere. A major operation known as search/match was designed to examine special forms referring to persons in situations such as those who were in the military or on a ship.[9] Completed military and shipboard forms included the address of the person's usual home. The search/match operation compared the information about persons and addresses on the forms in question with information in the address control file and the questionnaire for the address of the usual residence. The goal was to assign the person or household to its correct place. In handling such forms, clerks at the Baltimore processing office were to geocode the address and to check the address control file to verify that it was listed. Clerks would also search microfilmed questionnaire images and, if they found a form for the household in question, they would attempt to ascertain whether the person on the shipboard or military form had already been included. If not, the clerk could add the person and his or her characteristics to the record. Search/match also applied to questionnaires on which someone marked that their whole household had a "usual home" elsewhere. In applying search/match to such a questionnaire, the clerk attempted to find the address of usual home in the address control file. If found, the file was to be corrected to indicate that the housing unit where the household was enumerated was vacant. The information from the completed questionnaire was entered at the address of the usual home.

Unfortunately, search/match did not always work correctly. In my own case, on Census Day my wife and I were on sabbatical from our university and were staying in a building in Washington, D.C. that rented apartments by the month. We filled out a short form and indicated that our usual home was elsewhere, in Champaign, Illinois. A year later, after a search of Washington and Champaign census records, I learned that we were in the census at both locations. Thus, search/match had the potential for double counting.

Other Coverage Improvements

Three coverage improvement programs were designed explicitly to count the urban poor: urban update/enumerate, for blocks of mostly abandoned buildings; urban update/leave, for public housing projects; and S-Night, for homeless people.

Census planners recognized how inadequate mailout-mailback would be for city blocks that had large numbers of abandoned buildings. How could you get a mailing list for such a block? Urban update/enumerate was devised to cover such blocks. District offices sent enumerators with maps, special address registers, and "enumerator friendly questionnaires" to designated areas. If an enumerator could not find a housing unit at a listed address, he was to fill out a deletion record in order to remove it from the address list. If he found a housing unit that was not on his address register, he was to enter its address (as an "add") in the register. If he found occupants in a unit, he was to "conduct an interview . . . obtaining both population and housing data" (U.S. Bureau of the Census 1989a:9-36).

Urban update/leave was a new approach to enumerating persons in public housing projects. Census planners anticipated that commercial mailing lists would be unsatisfactory and that mail delivery would be undependable in public housing projects. They anticipated also that many enumerators would be afraid to work in such areas. So they devised urban update/leave, which would employ project residents as enumerators. Two weeks prior to the census, these enumerators were supposed to begin work in their areas, hanging posters, distributing pamphlets, attending meetings, and answering questions (Ibid.). Then, for the enumeration itself, they would update address lists, check apartment numbers, hand deliver questionnaires to residents, and instruct them to complete the forms and hold them for pickup. The enumerators then returned to collect completed questionnaires and to conduct interviews at households where no one filled in the form. Municipal officials in some cities, most notably New York City, asked census officials not to use urban update/leave in their cities. Officials in other cities, such as Chicago, chose to have update/leave in their public housing facilities. The press had nothing to say about these first two programs, but they blasted S-Night.

S-Night

Travelers and homeless persons present a special problem to census takers. Since at least 1940, the census has designated special nights on which to count persons in hotels and those who occupy a variety of cheap accommodations. The 1980 Census conducted "M-Night" ("M" as in mission). On April 8, 1980 enumerators went to places where the nightly price of lodging was free or less than four dollars, including skid-row flophouses and missions, railroad and bus stations, and all-night movie theaters. Enumerators conducted interviews from 4 p.m. until midnight, and they left individual census returns for individuals checking in after midnight to be collected the next day. In May 1980 they also conducted a daytime operation, called *casual count*, in selected cities. Its purpose was to enumerate "'street people' and other highly transient persons, who, because of their life styles," might be missed (U.S. Bureau of the Census 1986, B:5-49). Enumerators were sent to places where such persons might be found, such as employment, food stamp, and welfare offices, street corners, pool halls, and bars. M-Night and the casual count in 1980 were barely noticed by the media.

Recognizing the large growth in the number of homeless persons during the 1980s and the tremendous interest in this social problem, census administrators planned a major effort to enumerate them in 1990, called *S-Night*. In addition to the former objectives of counting persons living in inexpensive or temporary accommodations, S-Night had two new objectives: to count people who sleep in shelters for the homeless and to count people who spend the night in other places not intended for habitation. The Census Bureau did not claim to be able to count all of the people on the streets, but promised to provide information on "components of the homeless population." Cynthia Taeuber, of the bureau's Population Division, said:

We expect that the street count will be conservative in most areas because we can't enumerate people who are moving about or who are so hidden that their whereabouts are unknown even to local people who work with them. Also, there are the obvious physical dangers ... which is why census takers won't search cars, enter abandoned buildings, or climb up onto roofs or into dumpsters. (Milstrey 1989)

Cynthia Taeuber said also that a major strength of the census operation would be to provide national data that has been collected in a uniform manner and that could be compared across states and regions.

The first step in S-Night was to acquire, for every city of 50,000 or more, lists of shelters and other places where homeless persons are known to sleep. The bureau asked city governments to supply such lists. New York City's list, for example, shows the variety of places where homeless persons spend their nights. The city supplied a list of more than 2,100 locations: 326 shelters and 1,687 other sites, including ferry terminals, bus terminals, airports, train stations, and subway trains and stations. The city's list included 963 "off-street locations," including parks, playgrounds, vacant lots, government buildings, bridges, railroad trestles, and piers. It also specified certain doorways, sidewalks, heating grates, and abandoned buildings, schools, and theaters. The bureau used city-supplied lists to generate work assignments for enumerators on S-Night.

The second step in S-Night was to recruit and train enumerators. Including supervisors, 22,600 census employees worked on S-Night (U.S. Senate 1991:57). District offices were instructed to hire some homeless persons for S-Night, if possible. Enumerators received 3.5 hours of training. They were given assignments, some being sent to specific shelters, to work from 6 p.m. to midnight. Others were sent to conduct street enumerations from 2 a.m. to 4 a.m. and to observe abandoned and boarded-up buildings from 4 a.m. to 8 a.m. Enumerators worked in pairs, although trios could be assigned in hazardous areas. Those who were assigned to streets and boarded buildings were given a precise route to follow.

Those who worked from 2 a.m. to 8 a.m. were instructed to enumerate anyone they saw "regardless of age, except the police, persons in uniform, and persons engaged in employment or obvious money-making activities other than begging or panhandling" (U.S. Bureau of the Census 1989a:9-51). Enumerators were instructed not to awaken anyone who was asleep; just "estimate age, race, and sex." Otherwise, the enumerator was to approach the person and ask all the questions in a short form individual census report. Enumerators were not to ask anyone if he or she was homeless. Those who were assigned to abandoned buildings were to station themselves outside and to watch who entered or left. If someone left the building, the enumerator was to try to obtain information from that individual about the number of persons remaining inside (Ibid.).

In planning S-Night, census administrators were concerned about enumerators' safety. Soon after S-Night, Charlie Jones reported that happily no one was hurt. Director Bryant reported, however, that "there were a few incidents, including an enumerator team being fired on in New York City" (U.S. Senate 1991:57). On S-Night, the census counted approximately 179,000 persons in shelters and 50,000 at street locations (Ibid.:52). From the time S-Night was announced, advocates for the homeless tended to be critical. Robert M. Hayes, chair of the New York Coalition for the Homeless, said the city's list of locations was incomplete but added, "the more New Yorkers who are homeless are counted, the better it is for all New Yorkers, homeless or otherwise." On the other hand, he said he was apprehensive that the census numbers would be far smaller than the true numbers. Hayes predicted that "cynical politicians who want to ignore the massive scale of homelessness" will misuse the numbers (Dunlap 1990).

The late Mitch Snyder, leader of Washington, D.C.'s Community for Creative Nonviolence, which operated a large shelter, was less restrained. In January 1990, when census officials arrived at his shelter, he burned census forms and announced that homeless people should not cooperate with the census. Snyder said: "You can just as easily count grains of sand on the beach . . . as you can the homeless people" (Vobejda 1990). He also tried to persuade shelter managers in other cities not to cooperate with the census, but only a few followed his lead. Barbara Bryant later reported that the census had, in fact, counted the occupants of Snyder's and other noncooperating shelters. "We sent census enumerators to these shelters later to count unobtrusively occupants as they came out in the morning" (U.S. Senate 1991:54).

The bureau retained sociologists and anthropologists in five cities to monitor the S-Night enumeration. Two experienced sociological researchers at Tulane University were hired in New Orleans. A year later, one of them, Joel Devine, testified at a congressional hearing revealing fundamental deficiencies. The bureau's list of locations lacked certain places where homeless persons spend the night. New Orleans has a class of "businesses, typically small, out-of-the-way bars or 'drinking clubs' . . . where homeless people regularly spend the night . . . curled up in a booth or sprawled out on the floor or an available pool table" (Devine and Wright 1991:92). Also, many homeless persons spend the night in the waiting room at Charity Hospital, which has seats for "several hundred." Although it is not labelled as such, "Charity is, in effect, the second largest shelter for the homeless in the city." The Tulane researchers also tested the completeness of the early-morning street count. They hired approximately sixty persons and put them on the streets as observers and decoys.

The number and exact placement of the observation teams was not known to the district offices nor to the enumerators who actually conducted the street count. . . . The objective of these experiments is transparent and simple. As the census enumeration teams combed their assigned areas, they would be expected to encounter the decoys as well as "real" homeless people. . . . Since the decoys were deployed in areas known to be frequented by the homeless during the time the enumeration was taking place, then the number of decoys actually found and enumerated would give a direction indication of the completeness of the census count. (Ibid.:87–88)

The New Orleans sociologists reported that census enumerators located and counted nineteen of the twenty-nine teams of decoys, for a "hit rate" of about two-thirds. Furthermore, they noted that the same test in four other cities yielded lower hit rates. Testifying before the House oversight committee, Devine and Wright criticized the S-Night enumerators. As an extreme case of incompetence, they reported that a team of enumerators walked past a block-long median strip "heavily landscaped with shrubbery" in the middle of a street. The Tulane researchers observed that approximately twenty persons were camped on the benches and grass there, but apparently were not counted. Furthermore, many of the enumerators "appeared extremely hesitant and fearful"; in the late-hours environment, they "stuck out like sore thumbs" (Ibid.:101).

Devine and Wright explained that concealment at night is a

survival strategy for the homeless. They "have very good reasons to 'lay low' at night—not to elude the census, but to avoid the police, thugs, and others that would constitute a potential threat to their well-being" (Ibid.:98). They seek safe, out-of-the-way places, such as in "dumpsters, under abandoned vehicles, beneath shrubbery, in protected, non-visible doorways," and the like (Ibid.:98). What chance would inexperienced enumerators have of finding them? Devine and Wright made one concession to the accuracy of S-Night. They reported that the bureau's list of shelters was reasonably complete, and the enumeration of those who stayed in the shelters was accurate.

Public reaction to S-Night was uniformly negative, especially on the part of homeless advocates. Testimony at the May 9, 1991 hearings shows how politicians, researchers, and advocates rejected S-Night's results (U.S. Senate 1991). Bruce Vento, a member of Congress, from Minnesota, asserted that "the S-Night number is seriously flawed." It was "a blurry snapshot of the shelter and street population on one night in 1990" (Ibid.:8). Anthropologist Kim Hopper, who has conducted important studies of homelessness, said that the enumeration "fell far short of a true census" (Ibid.:105). Louisa Start, director of Phoenix's Community Housing Partnership, concluded that "any numbers resulting from the count must be regarded as invalid and inaccurate" (Ibid.:245). Michael Cousineau, representing the Los Angeles Homeless Health Care Project, suspected "that thousands were not counted" in his city (Ibid.:119).

Maria Fosconarinis, representing the National Law Center on Homelessness and Poverty, leveled a variety of charges against S-Night. "S-Night was flawed in design and implementation. . . . [Implementation] was haphazard at best, chaotic at worst. The result was a grossly inadequate count" (Ibid.:230–232). Likewise, Fred Karnas, Jr., director of the National Coalition for the Homeless, charged that S-Night was "a dismal failure" (Ibid.:222).

Parolee and Probationer Program

One unprecedented feature of the 1990 census was the parolee and probationer coverage improvement program. This program responded to the facts that minority males are disproportionately undercounted and that disproportionate numbers of these men are on parole or probation. The idea for a special effort to enumerate parolees and probationers was proposed by a psychologist, Jerusa C. Wilson, Dean of Graduate Studies at Baltimore's Coppin State College (Wilson 1990). It was endorsed by the bureau's minority advisory committees (U.S. Congress 1990c:14).

The parolee and probationer coverage improvement program had not been included in census plans; it was a last minute addition to the census. The program was not approved by the Office of Management and Budget until February 1, 1990, and specifications for the operation were not announced in the bureau until April 6, five days after Census Day (U.S. Bureau of the Census 1990d:2).

Initial plans for the program called for the bureau to write to the governors of all the states and to the heads of state corrections departments, asking them to cooperate and to designate a person who would take responsibility for enumerating parolees and probationers. (Prisoners would be counted routinely as occupants of special places.) The plan called for individual parole and probation officers to ask each parolee or probationer to complete a special census form that would ask for his or her Census Day address, along with basic demographic characteristics. Completed forms were to be forwarded to processing offices by June 8 (Ibid.).

Since very few states opted into the program, census administrators redesigned it late in the summer.[10] The redesigned program was targeted toward 220 urban counties that had large numbers of persons on parole or probation plus other counties with populations that were at least 20 percent black and Hispanic. The redesigned program relied upon administrative records. Census enumerators were sent to parole and probation offices to read lists and files and to copy names, addresses, and demographic characteristics into census forms. After these census forms were completed, they were checked at district offices and forwarded to processing offices for search/match processing in order to discover whether these individuals had already been counted. If not, the processing offices added them to the census. On November 14, the census director reported that "over 1.3 million parolees/probationers have been identified so far." Information on 729,000 parolees and probationers had been processed, yielding 247,000 additional persons in the census (U.S. Congress 1990c:15). This means that about two-thirds of the records were not used.

The parolee and probationer coverage improvement program represented a serious violation of the bureau's organizational culture. The program was entirely unplanned and untested. It violated the tradition of testing new procedures in surveys or pretests before using them in a decennial census. The program required the use of a special kind of data for a special category of persons. It violated the tradition of using nationally uniform procedures. Perhaps worst of all, it collected information from records of dubious accuracy, months after Census Day, thus posing a risk of introducing errors into the census. One field worker noted that the basic data were deficient. Given a low level of literacy among the parolees and probationers, she said that many of the street names in their addresses were spelled incorrectly. Many of the phone numbers they had supplied failed to correspond with usable addresses. The program raised the possibility of counting the parolees and probationers twice, if someone in their household had enumerated them already. Search/match was supposed to prevent this from happening. The effect of search/match was to discard two-thirds of the names collected in the new program.

From another point of view, census officials were overly fastidious in applying regular search/match standards to the data on parolees and probationers. One administration official, a political appointee, argued that the goal of the census was to overcome the differential undercount by coming closer to counting all of the black and Hispanic population. Given this goal, the census should have included all or almost all of the parolees and probationers. He said that census administrators made the wrong decision in applying strict search/match criteria. In so doing, they threw away information about many persons who had been "found" in the program. (In my opinion, census administrators made the correct decision in this matter.)

A year after Census Day, Director Bryant reviewed the yield of the various coverage improvements not including S-Night (Bryant 1991b:7, table 1; also pp. 2 and 13). She acknowledged that the persons and households garnered by the coverage improvements were expensive, costing "far more to enumerate than the overall average cost." She concluded that they added at least 5.4 million persons, or 2.2 percent, to the count. From first to last, the procedures were vacant/delete, 2.1 million; "Were You Counted?" campaign, 0.2 million; parolee and probationer, 0.4 million; housing coverage check, together with post-census local review, 0.3 million. Other operations, combined, including field followup, exclusive of vacant/delete, added 2.4 million. The director reported these numbers with pride, calling the coverage improvement techniques "extraordinary," and the overall coverage "phenomenal."

Counting

By mid-summer, census officials could begin to count the people. Flow processing made it possible to count and recount on a daily basis until the census was finished. Census administrators produced national population totals, showing how many persons had been counted at that point, on a daily basis throughout the summer. These numbers were of no scientific interest, but they showed how close the count was coming to precensus estimates. By early July, the census had counted 243.2 million persons. Later coverage improvement procedures added 5.5 million.[11] In August, the bureau released preliminary counts of housing units and population by state. These counts had been prepared for the local government review. Printouts were distributed to governors and heads of state congressional delegations and to local governments. These preliminary counts were distributed also in the form of press releases. At that point, the census showed a preliminary national total of approximately 245.8 million (Barringer 1990). Corrections and additions were made to the basic data files as a result of local government review and other procedures in the fall. Then files had to be prepared in order to make final counts. Basic files were edited, and imputation was done on them to put data into unanswered questions. Files on households were merged with another file that held counts from group quarters to create the 100 percent edited detail file, the main population file for the nation.

By December 26, 1990, the bureau was prepared to issue final counts. At that point, they reported to the secretary of commerce, who reported to the president, that the national count was 249,632,692. The final counts also provided totals for each state and the District of Columbia. At that point, the census had fulfilled its basic constitutional function. Also, having run the numbers through the formula that allocates congressional seats to states, the bureau reported which states would gain and which would lose.[12] Arizona, Georgia, North Carolina, Virginia, and Washington gained one seat each; Texas gained three, Florida four, and California seven. California's gains brought its House delegation up to fifty-two, the largest in history. Iowa, Kansas, Kentucky, Louisiana, Massachusetts, Montana, New Jersey, and West Virginia lost one seat each; Illinois, Michigan, Ohio, and Pennsylvania lost two each, and New York lost three. Thus, the census reflected a population shift toward the Sunbelt and, correspondingly, a shift in political power.

They continued to count the population in order to supply small-area statistics to states for use in redistricting. On January 15, 1991, Vermont was the first state to receive such data—population counts, numbers of persons eighteen years of age and over by race and by Hispanic origin. The numbers were tabulated by county, minor civil division, place, census tract, block group and block. Week by week, state by state, the bureau delivered such counts to governors and state legislatures, and by March 8, with Alaska the last state to get its numbers, the job was done. Then, in April and May, the bureau released additional information about the populations and housing of states, counties, places, and tracts tabulated from short forms. In the meanwhile, the bureau continued to count population characteristics on the basis of information collected from a sample of households on long forms. Those results would be released in 1992.

Summary

This chapter tells how the Census Bureau counted the people in 1990. The story begins with a plan to conduct the census basically as it was done in 1980, with a handful of refinements. The basic strategy was to develop an address list of housing units and group quarters across the nation. Then, in most areas, to mail a questionnaire to each housing unit and ask the recipient for a self-enumeration of the household. This mailout-mailback was then supplemented with a house-to-house, face-to-face interview survey to collect information from housing units that did not return their questionnaires. The 1990 census was built upon the same strategy of deliberately redundant operations as had been used in 1980. The census consisted of a series of operations, each of which was supposed to catch and correct omissions and errors that might have been committed in earlier operations. The census's questionnaire was changed very little from 1980, still in a clumsy, difficult-to-use format. There was a short form, with seven population questions and seven housing questions, sent to about five-sixths of the housing units, and a long form, including all short form questions plus another twenty-six population and nineteen housing questions, sent to a sample of about one-sixth of the housing units.

Computerization represented a fundamental innovation. TIGER, an expensive, powerful geographic information system, generated census maps by the hundreds of thousands. Early complaints against it from urban officials failed to recognize how effective TIGER would be. Far superior to the hand-drawn maps used in 1980, these new computer-drawn maps were used at all stages of the census. A network of minicomputers was dispersed among all decennial census offices. These minicomputers were used for routine personnel functions, updating address lists, and data capture. The computer network supported a new management information system that allowed managers at all levels to have daily reports on operational progress. It also allowed the census to stop saving questionnaires at district offices and processing them in batches, as they had in 1980. With the new equipment, the census shifted to flow processing, checking in questionnaires as they arrived and quickly capturing their data. The new computer system also supported search/match, which was designed to prevent counting the same person twice and also to assign certain categories of households to their correct addresses.

The census included several features in an effort to count every housing unit and every person. Conventional procedures were refined and elaborated, in order to look for housing units, to list them correctly, to determine whether they were occupied on Census Day, and to get information about their occupants. Post office checks and a vacant/delete check were used again. There were several operations designed to contact and count the difficult to enumerate, especially in large central cities. New procedures applied to areas with large numbers of abandoned buildings and public housing projects. There was a special effort to enumerate homeless persons on the streets and in emergency shelters. The 1990 census also introduced a new procedure for counting persons on probation and parole.

In one sense, the census worked fabulously well. TIGER produced beautiful, detailed maps for all purposes. The management information system provided excellent, timely reports for managers at all levels. The census succeeded in recruiting and training an enormous workforce of temporary employees. Many of them were skilled individuals who worked on specialized technical tasks. Others were skilled at the difficult tasks of coordinating and supervising temporary workers. Still others had the guts to go door-to-door in the various field procedures. Some temporary employees washed out right away, but the ones who stayed worked hard and effectively.

At the end, the census counted 249,632,692 persons, a great accomplishment.

In another aspect, though, the census failed to accomplish its mandated task, to count all of the people, including the difficult to enumerate. As will be shown, the undercount was still there with the same racial differential as before. The advertising and outreach program failed to reach and motivate the last 2 percent. And the various coverage improvements could not count them either.

11 The Decision Not to Adjust

As I HAVE illustrated, the scene was set for a decision. Before the 1990 census began, a stipulation and order ("settlement") was in place in *New York* v. *Department of Commerce*. Under the terms of that agreement, the department agreed to consider de novo the question of adjusting the 1990 census counts. The department agreed to conduct the Postenumeration Survey (PES) according to the newly developed methodology. The department agreed to appoint a special advisory panel of outside experts to advise the secretary on an adjustment decision. And the department agreed to publish a disclaimer on all census numbers, stating that they might be revised if the secretary decided to adjust the counts. The department accepted a deadline of July 15, 1991, for a decision.

PES was to be a large-scale survey, which was to generate interviews that would be matched against census records. The purpose was to find households and individuals that had been counted (a) in both the census and the survey, (b) in the census but not in the survey, (c) in the survey but not in the census. Results of this matching were to reveal the rate at which individuals with certain characteristics had been missed in the census. Results would also reveal correct enumerations and erroneous enumerations. PES was designed so that its results could be used, in the context of a statistical model, capture-recapture, known in this context as Dual Systems Estimation, for the purposes of adjusting census counts. In order to adjust, the PES sample was to be divided into more than a thousand segments known as poststrata, classified by region, type of community, race-ethnicity, and renting vs. owning. An example of a poststratum is: West-Mountain region, central city of large metro area, renters, Hispanic. PES was designed to generate an adjustment factor, by age and sex, for each poststratum. The goal of the entire PES adjustment was to adjust the census counts for all of the blocks in the United States. Thus adjustment was inextricably bound to PES and bureau publications often use the shorthand PES to refer to the survey and adjusting together.

I have recounted the story of the 1990 census itself, exclusive of the PES, and concluded with the release of the first census counts at the state level in December 1990 and at the block level in the first months of 1991. I will now cover the events leading toward the secretary's decision not to adjust.

The postenumeration survey began interviewing in July 1990, right after the conclusion of field followup. Other PES operations continued at a furious pace throughout 1990 and into the spring of 1991, in order to evaluate census coverage and to adjust for undercounting. PES revealed a differential undercount in the 1990 census. Census coverage was also evaluated by means of demographic analysis, which also showed a differential undercount. Demographic analysis and PES themselves were evaluated to see how accurate they were. The PES worked wonderfully well, and its results were actually utilized as the bureau adjusted the census counts so that the adjusted numbers would be ready in case the secretary decided in favor of adjustment.

PES was subjected to a series of intensive evaluation studies. Results of those studies were scrutinized by census officials, by the undersecretary of commerce, and by the panel of experts, all of whom prepared recommendations for the secretary. Although it is not apparent how the secretary made his decision, it is clear that he received two conflicting sets of advice representing two entirely different interpretations of the statistical evidence. Proponents of adjustment, especially the panel's New York City contingent, concluded that the results of PES could and should be used for the purpose of adjustment. Opponents of adjustment, including the undersecretary and the panel's other faction, came to the opposite conclusion. Ultimately, the secretary made his decision not to adjust.

Demographic Analysis

Demographic analysis has been defined as follows:

The demographic estimates of net coverage of the 1990 census are based on the comparison of the 1990 census counts with independently derived demographic estimates of the total . . . population. These estimates are based on the compilation of historical estimates of the components of population change: births, deaths, immigration, and emigration. . . . The demographic data used to develop the component estimates come from a variety of sources: births and deaths are based on tabulated records from the birth and death registration systems, adjusted for underregistration; legal immigration is derived from administrative data from the Immigration and Naturalization Service. (Robinson et al. 1991:1)

The bureau's Population Analysis and Evaluation Staff got a quick start on the 1990 demographic analysis. By mid-October 1990, while some census field operations were still underway, these demographers already had preliminary estimates of the national population, by race. At a meeting of the census advisory committees they distributed a paper in which they estimated that the national population on Census Day was 253.4 million, having grown about 10 percent since 1980. Demographic analysis also showed that the 1990 population included 32.4 million blacks and 221.0 million "nonblacks." Demographic analysis was used only to make estimates for the total nation and for blacks and nonblacks. In October the census field operations were almost done and the remaining field procedures were unlikely to enumerate many more persons, so the implications of demographic analysis were immediately obvious: once again the census produced a net undercount and, more important, it produced a differential undercount.

Census Bureau demographers had been refining their techniques of demographic analysis. They suspected that one methodological flaw was distorting their estimates of the black undercount. One of their major tasks was to discover whether the size of one particular cohort within the black population—males born between 1925 and 1945—was being measured incorrectly. In demography, a cohort represents all the individuals entering the population at the same time, in this case by birth. Using cohort analysis, demographers can watch the experience of a cohort as it ages.

Coverage estimates for every census, 1940 through 1980, showed that black men in the 1925–1945 birth cohorts had been disproportionately undercounted. In census after census no other cohort, female or male, white or black, had been disproportionately undercounted. Ordinarily, it is expected that undercounts follow a predictable age profile, high for children under age ten, followed by a drop for teenagers, a rise for persons in their twenties, and declining after age thirty. The 1925–1945 cohorts failed to conform to that pattern, while all others did. Demographers could find no historical reason for that cohort's distinctiveness, and they began to reexamine their methodology. They focused upon one key component of their estimate of the "true" number of persons in the cohort, the birth registrations occurring in the period 1935–1945. They suspected that they were using inflated numbers of births for black males during those years.

Demographers had been relying on a 1940 study for their estimates of black births. They assumed that birth registrations understated the real numbers of births. Many black births were not registered because they occurred outside of hospitals and because some localities had inadequate registration offices. In 1940, demographers conducted an intensive analysis of birth registration (U.S. Bureau of the Census 1943). They searched that year's census records for enumerated infants under four months of age. Then they attempted to match those census records to birth certificates. They found that only 82 percent of black births had been registered. Based upon that finding, demographers have been inflating black birth numbers by about 18 percent for the cohorts in question. Recent reevaluations of the 1940 study suggest that it tended to underestimate the number of births that were registered and that consequently, demographers have been overinflating the numbers of black male births for those cohorts (Robinson et al. 1990). Based upon that conclusion, demographers made new, smaller estimates of the numbers of black male births in those cohorts. The demographers recomputed their demographic analyses by race for census years from 1940–1980. They also used the revised birth numbers in their demographic analysis for 1990. In the newly revised demographic analyses, the age profiles of undercounts were more credible than they had been.[1] But more important, the new estimates of black male undercounts were slightly smaller than the old ones.

By early 1991, the demographers had produced 1990 coverage estimates based upon demographic analysis. The bottom line was that the census counted 98.2 percent of the population, while 1.8 percent were not counted (U.S. Bureau of the Census 1991d:5). Demographic analysis showed that the census missed more males (3.5 percent) than females (0.9 percent), and more blacks (5.7 percent) than nonblacks (1.3 percent). Overall, the demographers estimated that the census missed 4.68 million persons. About three-fourths of the persons omitted were male; two-fifths were black (Robinson, et al.:1991). Actually, these "point estimates" (single numbers representing undercounts) imply an unwarranted degree of precision. The demographers also generated ranges of estimates for the undercounts, suggesting that there was a 95 percent likelihood that the true number lay within each range.[2]

black males	5.9 to 12.7%
black females	0.7 to 7.4%
non-black males	0.8 to 4.2%
non-black females	−0.4 to 3.0%.

(A negative number represents a possible overcount.) The pattern of the ranges is the same as that of the point estimates: male undercounts exceed female and black undercounts exceed nonblack.

These figures imply two main points, both of which were useful to critics of the census. (1) The net undercount in 1990, almost 2 percent, was greater than that of 1980. Each of the previous four censuses had a lower net undercount than the preceding one. Thus, with a higher undercount than in 1980, the new census broke the trend. It also broke three years of promises from the Department of Commerce that the 1990 census would be the most complete ever. (2) The racial differential was not diminished. Despite all of the advertising and outreach programs targeted toward poor minority groups, and despite all of the coverage improvements, the census failed again to count the difficult to enumerate. Furthermore the black-white difference expanded somewhat. Census critics insisted that both of these points supported their demand for a statistical adjustment of the counts.

The Postenumeration Survey (PES)

The Postenumeration Survey represented years of planning and testing, based upon innovative statistical thinking. It was one of the biggest, most complex, and, at a cost of $57 million, most expensive surveys ever conducted by the bureau. Despite its scope and complexity, it was executed smoothly. Indeed, PES received high praise even from key players who opposed adjustment. Undersecretary Michael Darby, the most implacable and influential opponent of adjustment, wrote, "the PES was a generally high-quality survey that operationally was well-executed" (Darby 1991:12). Likewise, Kenneth Wachter, a member of the Special Advisory Panel, who wrote a detailed and powerful argument against adjustment, said, "The quality of the Postenumeration Survey appears, on the whole, to be high" (Wachter 1991).

In late 1989 staff members at census headquarters drew a sample of 5,300 block clusters for the survey. (A block cluster consisted of a block or a collection of blocks.) In February 1990, experienced interviewers were sent to those block clusters to make lists of all housing units and group quarters. They listed approximately 170,000 housing units, 143,000 of which had been occupied on April 1. They also listed 661 occupied group quarters. In May and June 1990, interviewers and supervisors were selected and trained. PES interviewers were recruited from among the best census enumerators. They were trained in late June and early July. Interviewing began on June 20 and was finished by September 4 (Erickson et al. 1991, App. C:4). PES administrators became concerned about the level of nonresponse in certain geographical areas and decided to mount a special effort to try to conduct interviews in nonreponse households. In September they employed teams of experienced interviewers from regular Census Bureau surveys and sent these interviewers to contact nonresponse households. The field staff managed to interview 99 percent of the sample, a remarkable achievement.

PES incorporated a survey within a survey, an unusual feature. The smaller survey, known as *evaluation followup*, was designed to explore problems arising from E-sample cases.[3] Evaluation followup had a sample of 11,000, most of which were to get a questionnaire that probed address misreporting. The sample also included 300 households where PES failed to get interviews. Staffed with the best PES interviewers, the evaluation followup frequently obtained an interview where PES had not.

In order to keep PES separate from the census, it was administered from the bureau's regular regional offices, not from 1990 field offices. Administrators who worked on the decennial staff were not supposed to work on PES, which was administered by others, mostly permanent bureau staff. As finished questionnaires were received by regional census centers, they were edited in a quality control procedure. After they passed quality control, they were forwarded to processing centers for matching to census records.

The computer matcher proceeded to match information from survey interviews to census records—name, address, and selected demographic characteristics. This operation also worked remarkably well; "the computer matcher was able to match about 80 percent of the P-sample persons to their corresponding original enumeration" (Ibid.:2).

There were survey records, including some from persons who had moved into the sample blocks after Census Day, that could not be matched by the computer matcher. Such cases were referred to a trained team of clerks and statisticians who examined the information collected in the census and in the survey interview. They had to decide whether the person listed in the survey was matched, not matched, or "match status unknown" (Ibid.). Census records from the E-sample were also matched to the survey records. If it was not possible to make such a match, additional field work was called for. Unmatchable E-sample households were recontacted by field workers for the purpose of collecting enough information to designate the enumeration as "correct" or "erroneous" (Ibid.:2–3). Concurrently, all P-sample persons who were designated as "match status unknown" were recontacted by the same field workers for the purpose of collecting enough additional information to designate the person as enumerated or not enumerated in the original census. These followups were particularly difficult for the field staff. They conducted interviews by phone and with home visits to resolve differences between census and PES information. For example, a failed match might show the same set of persons living in the same building, but grouped into different households. The interviewer might discover, for example, that after Census Day a woman had a fight with her mother in her original household and moved upstairs and was living with her brother at the time of the PES interview. Eventually the matching, in tandem with the intensive fieldwork, eliminated almost all of the match status unknowns. Ten years earlier, 8 percent of the cases in PEP had unknown match statuses, which helped render the study useless. So in 1990–1991, the bureau had solved one of the most intractable problems of postcensal surveys.

The Undercount   Like demographic analysis, PES yielded an overall national undercount estimate, 2.1 percent, but the survey's strength was its ability to estimate undercounts for population subgroups. According to PES, the 1990 black undercount was 4.8 percent, the nonblack, 1.7, the Hispanic undercount was 5.2 percent, Asian (including Pacific Islander) 3.1, and American Indian, 5.0 (Hogan 1991: table 3.1). For the nation as a whole and for each racial subgroup, male undercounts were higher than female. In particular, black males were undercounted by 5.4 percent, Hispanic males by 5.8 percent, and American Indian males by 5.6 percent. Blacks and Hispanics, as poor, urban minorities, were disproportionately undercounted once again.

The PES was subjected to the intense scrutiny of twenty evaluation studies. One group of studies attempted to measure different sources of error in PES, including missing data, misreported Census Day addresses, fabrications (curbstoning), matching error, erroneous enumerations, correlation bias, and random error (Bateman et al. 1991:1). Results of these evaluation studies repeatedly confirmed the high quality of the PES. For example, one study produced twenty-three different undercount rates based upon alternative methods for imputing missing data. The study produced twenty-two national undercount rates within the range 2.02 to 2.16, with one "outlier" at 1.65. Thus, the study showed that the initial choice of an imputation technique did not influence PEP's resulting undercount number. Another study (designated P-18), which analyzed the effects of "late late" census data on PES confirmed the strength of the survey's results. There was some concern that the addition of names to the census after PES through last minute coverage improvements (mainly the parole and probationers program) might degrade the quality of PES results. Study P-18 concluded, "The results of the study show that the exclusion of the small number of [late late] census data from the PES has only a small effect and would have decreased the undercount slightly if it had been included" (Alberti 1991). Results of some of the evaluation studies were more ambiguous.

Erroneous Enumerations   One study explored the prevalence of erroneous enumerations in the census (as shown through the E-sample.) Examples of erroneous enumerations are people who died before Census Day, but were listed in census returns; people born after Census Day; fictitious people; and duplicated people. Study P-9 showed that "Total erroneous enumerations account for 3.97 percent of the total weighted E-sample" (U.S. Bureau of the Census 1991a). The most common type of erroneous enumerations is individuals who died before Census Day, were born after Census Day, or should have been counted elsewhere. The second most common type was duplicates. In my opinion, 3.97 percent erroneous enumerations is a lot.

The Scientific Struggle over Adjustment

Proponents and opponents of adjustment used the results of PES and the evaluation studies to support their broader arguments. Indeed, they sent hundreds of documents to the secretary of commerce in the last month before he rendered his decision. Controversy revolved about differences between the results of PES and demographic analysis, correlation bias, effects of smoothing, and loss functions—whether adjusting would do more harm than good. Some of these issues are interconnected.

Differences between PES and Demographic Analysis   Overall, the results of demographic analysis and the PES were quite similar. For the whole country both showed a net undercount of about 2 percent: 1.8 percent from demographic analysis and 2.1 percent from PES. Both showed that blacks were more likely to be undercounted than nonblacks (demographic analysis, 5.7: 1.3, PES, 4.8: 1.7) and that males were more likely than females (demographic analysis, 3.5: 0.9, PES, 2.4: 1.8). Considering how different the two methods are, it is remarkable and perhaps reassuring that the results resemble each other so closely.

One evaluation study, P-17, was designed to probe the internal consistency of PES estimates by analyzing population distributions by age and sex. The study was to determine whether the age-sex distributions in PES and in the census were "reasonable." In other words, PES generated an estimate of the U.S. population by age and sex. The census produced counts of the population by age and sex. In P-17, staff members examined these numbers, category by category, and asked whether they were internally consistent. Also the study assessed the PES estimates of undercount (also by age and sex) by comparing them with the results of demographic analysis.

Project P-17 revealed certain differences between the results of PES and demographic analysis. The study showed that PES indicated an unreasonably high undercount of persons aged 10 to 19. The study's authors surmised that college students in that age group were liable to be double counted and that PES failed to detect enough of those duplications. Second, the report stated that PES indicated a higher undercount in the census than demographic analysis did for females in general. "No sound explanation for this difference between the PES and demographic analysis is available" (Adlakha et al. 1991:ii). Third, P-17 came up with an expected conclusion: "The PES estimates of undercount for black males over age 20 are lower than the DA [demographic analysis] estimates. The differences are large and are likely the result of the presence of correlation bias in the PES (Ibid.:ii).

Proponents and opponents of adjustment used these results quite differently. Eugene Ericksen and three others on the Special Advisory Panel formed a group that consistently argued in favor of adjustment. They said that PES had correctly detected an undercount of black males but that it had failed to measure its full extent. This meant that if census counts were adjusted with PES results, the adjusted numbers would be more accurate than unadjusted ones because the new numbers would reflect as much of the black male undercount as PES had been able to measure. Adjustment would be helpful because it would correct for at least part of the undercount. The bureau's Undercount Steering Committee concluded that adjusted counts would be more accurate than unadjusted ones; "the adjusted counts will not fully correct for the black male undercount, but will move the counts in the right direction" (U.S. Bureau of the Census 1991b).

Opponents of adjustment, including a minority of the committee, emphasized differences between the results of PES and demographic analysis. Michael Darby claimed that an adjustment based upon PES would add too many persons in some categories, too few in others. Furthermore, it would delete persons in categories that should get additions, according to demographic analysis (Darby 1991:E2).

Arguing against adjustment, panel member Kenneth Wachter asserted that it was possible to use the discrepancy between demographic analysis and PES results to estimate how many persons, particularly black males, had been missed by the census and PES. "These numbers are very imprecise. But they suggest that hundreds of thousands, perhaps half-a-million people missed net by the census are not accounted for by the adjustment based on the PES" (Wachter 1991:8). Wachter asserted that these discrepancies between PES and demographic analysis undermined the feasibility of adjustment: "The comparisons between Demographic Analysis and the PES just discussed implied that 1990 census adjustment, as it affects minority members, is subject to a huge 'fudge factor.' As much as one quarter of the actual net census misses, male and female, could easily be outside the scope of the adjustment process altogether" (Ibid.).

Correlation Bias   Wachter went on to argue that estimates from PES of the number of adult males were considerably smaller than the estimates from demographic analysis. He concluded that the PES had failed to capture these men, just as the census had. Thus, there was correlation bias. Proponents and opponents of adjustment agreed that correlation bias represented a serious problem. "Correlation bias appears to have been the major source of error in the PES" (Ericksen et al.:15). Likewise, William Kruskal, who was also a member of the Special Advisory Panel, wrote: "The major gap in our knowledge . . . is our uncertainty about the capture-recapture method. . . . The usual assumptions on which capture-recapture analysis rests include several that are clearly not factual; of these the most troublesome is perhaps the assumption of uniform capture probabilities within the strata around which the whole system is organized" (Kruskal 1991).

This represented a weakness in dual systems analysis. Study P-13 examined correlation bias and concluded, "There is evidence of significant correlation bias for black males twenty and older, and for nonblack males thirty and older." Study P-17 compared undercounts from PES and from demographic analysis and reached the same conclusion, "The PES estimates of undercount for black males over age twenty are lower than the Demographic Analysis estimates. The differences are large and are likely the result of the presence of correlation bias in the PES" (Adlakha et al. 1991:2).

Wachter gave correlation bias a new name, "catchability error." He noted that dual systems analysis is based upon the assumption that members of the population in question are equally likely to be captured in the first and second samples, in this case, in the census and in the PES. Reverting to the origin of this method, in sampling animals in the wild, and using the example of counting the trout in a pond, he wrote, "Among nettable fish, some are harder to net than others. Among all fish, some 'wily trout' are not to be netted at all." By analogy, in the context of the U.S. census, "there is also some number of 'unreachable' people who avoid or outstretch all attempts to record them." Wachter praised the bureau's statisticians for developing new statistical tools with which to estimate correlation bias and its effects, but he concluded that ultimately, correlation bias necessarily remains an unknown. Estimates are based upon persons who are captured in PES who were missed in the census. But, Wachter said, "Counts of people in places that list-makers mostly find don't tell much about how many people there may be in improbable, inaccessible places." He concluded that it would be a mistake to adjust census counts on estimates of undercount that are based upon such weak data and statistical models. "I believe it is better not to attempt any formal allocation of unreached people to local jurisdictions" (Wachter 1991:18–20).

It is not surprising that Ericksen and his group offered a different interpretation of correlation bias. They acknowledged its presence, noting that "correlation bias is an important source of error in the PES." But its main effect was to cause the estimated undercounts for many cities to be too low (Ericksen et al. 1991, App. C:21, 22). Correlation bias was probably a bigger problem in cities than elsewhere. "If so, the undercount differentials between central cities and other areas have been underestimated by the PES." This interpretation buttressed their overall argument for adjustment on the grounds that undercounting represents a fundamental injustice against cities. Implicit in this argument, again, is that even if PES has failed to detect all of the undercount, it detected enough of it so that adjusting would push the counts closer to the truth.

Smoothing   Kenneth Wachter based much of his argument against adjustment on problems in smoothing. "The smoothing has turned out to be the most problematic part of the adjustment calculations. The most serious problem occurs in an arcane and technical aspect of the calculations known as *variance presmoothing*" (Wachter 1991). Wachter explained the statistician's rationale for using this procedure, saying that it would remove some of the effects of random variability from the raw adjustment factors. He surmised that they expected the presmoothing to have little overall effect on final adjusted counts. "Unfortunately, it turned out to have a large effect on the final adjusted counts. . . . The issue of variance presmoothing becomes, now, one of the key issues in the accuracy of adjusted counts" (Ibid.). Wachter noted that the bureau's statisticians could make reasonable choices among procedures for smoothing—indeed, they did so as they scrutinized PES results—and those different procedures yielded sets of adjustment factors "differing in many cases by two or more percentage points." Wachter concluded that this much uncertainty in the smoothing process, and thus in the adjustment process, was unacceptable (Ibid.:33–36).

In their report to the secretary, Ericksen's group explained that smoothing was a necessary procedure and that it did not undermine the usefulness of adjusted numbers. Relying upon the work of a statistical consultant (Hoaglin), they evaluated the impact of various alternative decisions in the smoothing process and concluded that they did not make a major impact upon the adjustment factors (Erickson et al. 1991:17–19).

In the last days before the July 15, 1991, deadline, Census Director Barbara Bryant prepared for the secretary an argument in favor of adjustment. In that argument she conceded that smoothing had been a problem. She admitted that the smoothing model did prove to be sensitive . . . to variations in handling of the small number of unusually large variances. There is also concern that different sets of predictor variables could produce a different set of adjustment factors. Thus, the weakness of the prespecified PES adjustment model is in its sensitivity to changes in the smoothing procedure. (U.S. Bureau of the Census 1991d:21)

Nonetheless, she asserted that those problems were not sufficient to undermine the overall advantages of adjusting. She relied on the advice of the Undercount Steering Committee; "On balance, the majority [of the Census Bureau's Undercount Steering Committee] finds there is no evidence to conclude that concerns about the smoothing model would affect their overall assessment about the accuracy of the adjusted numbers" (Ibid.:22).

Loss Functions   One evaluation study, known as loss function analysis, was designed to determine whether adjusted counts offer an improvement over census counts in the distribution of population among states and places. This study was to produce a "loss function," showing at the subnational level whether adjusting would do more harm than good. The study's main conclusion was that "adjustment is better than the census for apportionment. It is more likely that the corrected apportionment based on an adjusted count would be closer to the truth than further from the truth" (Ibid.:15).

According to the loss function analysis, twenty-nine states gained in accuracy of proportion of population, while twenty-one states possibly lost accuracy. Inaccuracy could make a state have more or less than its "true" proportion of the national population. The authors of the loss function analysis report noted that "The states where accuracy would be improved contain two-thirds (67 percent) of the nation's population enumerated in the census" (Ibid.:13). They went on to say that "Adjustment will improve the accuracy of the 1990 population for the majority, but not for all places" (Ibid.:14). In summary Bryant wrote: "The Census Bureau's nine member Undercount Steering Committee majority judges that the improvement in counts on the average for the Nation, States, and places over 100,000 population outweighs the risk that the accuracy of adjusted counts might be less for smaller areas" (Ibid.:15). Thus, proponents and opponents of adjustment differed in their interpretations of all four aspects of the evaluations of PES: differences between demographic analysis and PES estimates of undercount, correlation bias, smoothing, and loss functions. They differed also on other major statistical issues, including whether the strata were sufficiently homogeneous to justify applying a single adjustment factor to all the blocks in each stratum and whether the statistical model used to evaluate the PES altogether, the "total error model," actually measured the problem correctly.

Releasing the PES Results

Backtracking from July 1991 to April, we can see the political impact of the PES. On April 18, 1991, the Census Bureau issued a press release containing the preliminary results of PES for every state and the District of Columbia; the results formed an unanticipated pattern. The big surprise was that the worst undercounts were in Sunbelt states, including Florida and California. The results showed that midwestern and northeastern states that had complained the loudest were undercounted at about the same rate as the nation as a whole. Some of those states, including Pennsylvania and Ohio, had been undercounted less than the national average. Redistricting experts quickly fed these new data into their computer models and discovered that if census counts were adjusted, Pennsylvania and Wisconsin would each probably lose one additional congressional seat. The reallocation based upon the regular counts had taken two seats from Pennsylvania and none from Wisconsin. A reallocation based upon adjusted counts would take three seats from Pennsylvania and one from Wisconsin. Furthermore, one of the seats would move to 1990's big winner, California, bringing its congressional delegation to fifty-three seats. New York State stood neither to lose nor to gain. As the *New York Times* stated: "New York State would not be a big winner, at least in terms of Congressional representation, if there is an adjustment based on these numbers" (Barringer 1991a).

On June 14, 1991, a month before the secretary's decision deadline, the bureau issued another press release, reporting "refined estimates" from PES. These numbers reflected the effects of smoothing. The press release included a series of tables with numbers for states and for counties and cities over 100,000. Now that smoothing and other operations were finished, these numbers represented statistically adjusted census counts, the first the nation had ever seen. Featuring the new numbers on page one, the *New York Times* drew dramatic political inferences. "The industrial states of the Midwest and Northeast that had hoped an adjustment would bolster their anemic growth rates would end up after an adjustment with a smaller share of population and political power than they had at the end of the census" (Barringer 1991b). The adjusted numbers also showed the differences between outcomes for cities and states. *New York Times*'s Felicity Barringer noted that "big cities would be relative winners," even in states that would not gain from adjustment. "New York City would profit from adjustment; New York State would lose. Chicago would gain; Illinois would lose. Detroit would gain handsomely; Michigan would lose" (Ibid.). New York City's adjustment advocates claimed that the PES results supported their demands. New York City's corporation counsel called the results "a vindication" (Levine 1991).

One political effect of the results was to divide congressional Democrats, many of whom had advocated adjustment. Once it became apparent that adjustment would deprive Pennsylvania and Wisconsin of one seat each in the House of Representatives, their congresspersons and senators had deep second thoughts about the wisdom of adjustment. Senator Herbert Kohl, from Milwaukee, chair of the subcommittee that has oversight over the census, opined that there were "basic flaws" in the PES, which is "fraught with error" (Barringer 1991b). The senator concluded that we ought to leave well enough alone "until we have a real solution" (Vobeja 1991).

The real effects of adjustment became apparent at this point because the new numbers showed that adjustment's power derived from differences in distribution, not just from absolute differences between raw and adjusted census numbers. Thus, for example, since adjustment would have increased the whole country's population by 2.1 percent and the state of New York's by 1.7 percent, the state would have gained nothing proportionately. New York City, with a 3.1 percent upward adjustment, would have gained at the expense of the rest of New York state—suburban, small town, and rural.

An economic analysis of the effects of adjustment appeared at about the same time as the adjusted numbers, and it, too, emphasized the effects of distribution and redistribution. Under contract to the Department of Commerce, economist Michael P. Murray, of Bates College, calculated estimates of the extent to which the distribution of federal dollars would be affected by census adjustment (Murray 1992). Murray applied the funding formulas for five major programs to adjusted and unadjusted census counts, looking for the differences between allocations to states and localities that would result from the two sets of calculations. He used the two sets of population numbers in the formulas for five major programs that distributed more than $50 billion in 1989. Then he computed estimates for an aggregate of ninety-six programs that distributed an additional $6.9 billion.

He grounded his analysis in the assumption that "all formula based grants have a fixed pot of money to distribute." This means that adjustment is a step in a zero-sum game. Any place that gains dollars does so at the expense of some other place. "As population count rises [by adjustment] the amount available for each person shrinks." Murray also pointed out that many grant formulas include several determinants, of which population is only one. Finally, he noted that some formulas actually penalize places for population growth; "adjustment's effects on grants from these programs can offset some gains a community might receive in other programs that reward population increases" (Ibid.).

Murray's calculations showed that census adjustment would have a small impact upon the distribution of federal funds. Less than one-third of 1 percent of the federal dollars would pass from one community to another if the 1990 census were adjusted. He concluded that a place that gained population by adjustment would get an increment of approximately $56 per miscounted person per year. This number is obviously far smaller than the imaginary $400 that had been mentioned in 1980. The benefit to big cities would not necessarily be trivial. Presumably, the mayors would be pleased to see the additional income. Murray's analysis did not take account of state moneys that are distributed within states on the basis of population. Nonetheless, the mayors had always suggested that their cities were losing far more than $56 per undercounted person per year.

A Summary of the Arguments

By mid-June, 1991, both sides had set forth their main arguments. The argument for adjustment was most fully developed in the documents prepared by Eugene Ericksen and his three colleagues on the panel. The argument of Ericksen's group began by asserting that the 1990 census was replete with errors. They noted that the net undercount rate, as measured by demographic analysis, was greater than the 1980 rate, and that this was the first time in the history of the modern census that a census had an undercount higher than that of the previous census. They noted also that the 1990 enumeration failed to make a dent in the racial and ethnic differentials. New York City's attorneys pointed out that these results finally showed how foolish the Department of Commerce's precensus promise of a complete enumeration had been.

Ericksen's argument highlighted certain deficiencies in census data collection and in the data themselves, particularly the prevalence of last resort cases and of erroneous enumerations. It also emphasized the low quality of data generated by some of the coverage improvements such as Were You Counted? and the parolee and probationers count that occurred late in the census process. Their argument showed that there were excessive numbers of errors, thereby weakening the credibility of the census itself. In dealing with the racial and ethnic differentials, Ericksen's argument shows that it was the poor, urban minorities, especially blacks, Hispanics, and Native American Indians, who were most severely undercounted. All of these points militate toward the necessity for a statistical correction.

Ericksen's group strongly supported the PES. After intensive study of the survey, matching, adjusting, and evaluation processes, they concluded that the numbers were sufficient to the task of adjusting census counts. They acknowledged the deficiencies of PES, such as its failure to overcome correlation bias and the unpredicted effects of smoothing. Still, they clearly stated that adjusting according to this system produced a set of counts that were superior to the raw census counts; the adjusted numbers were closer to the truth. Two other proponents of adjustment were the Census Bureau's Undercount Steering Committee and the director, Barbara Bryant. They would not agree that the census was as badly flawed as Ericksen's group said, but otherwise, they endorsed the same argument about the usefulness and applicability of PES results.

In opposition to adjustment, the most forceful voice on the panel was Kenneth Wachter's. In his recommendation to the secretary of commerce, he concentrated on the weaknesses of PES, not discussing the census itself. Wachter argued that we will not have an acceptable device for census adjustment until we overcome correlation bias. He said that the PES had failed to overcome correlation bias so it is not adequate to the task of adjustment. Furthermore, he said, problems in smoothing also undermined the usefulness of PES. Choosing among different smoothing routines, all of which were statistically defensible, could make a difference in the allocation of three congressional seats. Wachter said it would be unreasonable to make such a weighty governmental decision—which states got the congressional seats—based upon a technical decision about smoothing.

Wachter questioned the entire intellectual underpinning of the adjustment process. He asserted that the logic of survey sampling is ordinarily to facilitate the creation of estimates of population level parameters. For example, statisticians take a sample of the labor force to discover what proportion is unemployed, then they make an estimate of unemployment for states and the nation as a whole. But the PES takes a sample and then uses it to make estimates for small areas, which is to use sampling for a new and unexplained purpose. Since the census is so important, it is unwise to use a new technique on it. Buttressing this argument, he questions the logic of adjusting within the PES poststrata. He is not convinced that the blocks within poststrata are sufficiently homogeneous so that the sample data can be applied to all of them for the purpose of adjusting.

Undersecretary of Commerce Michael Darby also recommended not adjusting; his statement employed all of the same points as Wachter. Darby's recommendation emphasized the effects of adjusting on individual population segments and on particular places, arguing that an adjustment would inject errors into the census counts. At least for certain groups and places, adjusted numbers would move further from the truth. Darby also speculated on adverse political effects of adjusting, for example by making people think they didn't need to participate in future censuses because adjustments would be made.

The Secretary's Decision

On July 15, 1991, Secretary of Commerce Robert Mosbacher announced his decision—he would leave the census counts as they were; there would be no adjustment. A week later the *Federal Register* published his decision, which took up sixty-one pages (U.S. Department of Commerce 1991). The text provided a point-by-point justification of the decision, including attempts to refute many of the points that had been made earlier in the Ericksen group report to him. The text, which was organized according to the eight guidelines (see chapter 9), borrowed heavily from Undersecretary Darby's recommendations.

Mosbacher opened his statement by saying that the decision was among the most difficult in his life. He worried about abandoning "a two hundred year tradition of how we actually count people. Before we take a step of that magnitude, we must be certain that it would make the census better and the distribution of the population more accurate. After a thorough review, I find the evidence in support of an adjustment to be inconclusive and unconvincing" (U.S. Department of Commerce, Office of the Secretary 1991).

He offered several reasons for his decision. In the political realm, he says that the census is not the right tool with which to solve problems of equity. Furthermore, a statistical adjustment now would open the door to "political tampering with the census in the future." He concedes that "political considerations played no role in the Census Bureau's choice of an adjustment model for the 1990 census" (Ibid.).

The secretary reiterated the department's old line that 1990 would be the best census ever, saying that "the 1990 census is one of the two best censuses ever taken in this country." And he suggested that there was not enough research and evaluation into the quality of the PES and the adjustment. Because of the July 15 deadline, he wrote, the bureau had to rush through the evaluation studies. More time was needed for analysis. "The analysis has not been subject to the full professional scrutiny that such important research requires and deserves." Fundamentally, though, his rationale for the decision was scientific. He was not convinced that the methodology was adequate to the task of improving the numbers. He worried that the statistical models "depended heavily on assumptions, and the results changed in important ways when the assumptions changed." The secretary emphasized the issue of distribution of population across states and places, with and without adjustment. He referred to a paradox, "that in attempting to make the actual count more accurate by an adjustment, we might be making the shares less accurate." He was disinclined to adjust the numbers because it would make them less accurate in areas of the country where one third of the people live (Ibid.).

The secretary emphasized that he received conflicting scientific advice. He noted that he received advice from the panel, whom he thanked, and from professionals in the Commerce Department and the Census Bureau. Unfortunately, "there was a diversity of opinion among my advisers." The panel split evenly, he mentioned, without recognizing that it was designed to do so. There was "disagreement among the professionals" in the department and the bureau. Furthermore, the experts raised fundamental questions about an adjustment, thus convincing him that an adjustment would rest on "unstable ground." Given such division among these experts and professionals, he concluded that the only wise course was not to use this untested method (Ibid.).

So, the story of PES ended ironically. After more than ten years of research, testing, development, and implementation, it worked. The census yielded a differential undercount that was amenable to statistical adjustment. And the secretary of commerce decided not to adjust.

12 Conclusions

THE UNITED STATES has an excellent census that counts almost everyone. Consider the U.S. census in the context of the censuses of the nations of the world. It is not difficult to list the U.S. census' strong points. The U.S. conducts its census every ten years with perfect regularity, having done so for two hundred years. This series of censuses has produced an ongoing historical record of the American people.

The U.S. census counts almost everyone, approximately ninety-eight out of every hundred persons. There is a handful of countries with higher census coverage rates (lower undercounts) but they are either smaller than the U.S., which makes it easier for them to count their people, or they have substantially different governmental traditions, which I will discuss presently. Canada, in 1986, actually had a larger undercount than ours, 3.6 percent, despite having an excellent national statistical agency and a population one tenth the size of ours. (Ordinarily, Canadian undercounts are lower than that.) Indeed, the inventory numbers of large corporations probably have greater margins of error than the U.S. census undercount. So, recent U.S. census undercounts, ranging between 3.3 percent in 1960 and 1.4 percent in 1980, do not signify a poor census. Censuses, like all large and small data collection efforts, are subject to error. People make mistakes in the answers they give. Census workers and those who help them, such as postal workers, make errors. Given the scale of the U.S.

census, there is no way to expect to eliminate error. We should be surprised that the census contains as few errors as it has.

The form and conduct of the census fit the kind of society we have; the U.S. census reflects U.S. society. More generally, every country's census corresponds to that country's social conditions and patterns; ours is no exception. How is the U.S. census isomorphic to U.S. society and social patterns? American society affords great personal freedom to citizens and aliens alike. This freedom sets a major condition for censustaking. Persons are free to move from place to place at will, without notifying any governmental authority. Persons are free to avoid contact with governmental agencies. Conversely, except in time of war, the government is unable to register the people or to assign personal identity numbers or cards.

Freedom is a major obstacle to censustaking. In a highly regimented society, governmental officials can restrict people for the purpose of taking a census.[1] There have been cases in which officials ordered everyone to stay at home on census day until an enumerator visited. After collecting information, the census taker would mark each person's hand to show that he or she had been counted.

Even modern democracies such as the Scandinavian nations maintain ongoing population registers. Usually maintained at the community level, these registers list every person from birth to death. Typically, in such countries, every person is assigned a lifetime identification number. In those countries where registers are kept perfectly, if a person migrates from one community to another, he or she must notify local authorities so that his or her record can be deleted from one register and added to another. This implies that every person "belongs" to one and only one address. A census in such a country counts each person in the community to which he or she belongs. In such a system, it would be difficult to count one person twice, even if he or she were residing away from home temporarily.

High-quality population registers greatly simplify the censustaker's work. Most of the registers have been computerized; they can be tallied in order to create national population statistics, in lieu of taking censuses. When the national statistical agency conducts a census, the register not only provides an address list, but also a list of persons. Starting with the register, the censustaker can contact every person and collect population information. The register also provides a benchmark against which to measure census coverage.

Leaving aside international comparisons, we can find that our way of conducting censuses is anomalous within our own governmental traditions. While most local functions are decentralized, the census is centralized. Typically, local government is handled by state and community structures. In the case of the census, while the work is highly localized, the constitutional strictures require that the federal government come in and do the work. At the outset, since every state had an interest in the outcome of the census, no state could be trusted to do its own census. Now, every community also has an interest in the outcome, so neither states nor communities can be trusted to do censuses. Otherwise every place might be expected to produce an overcount. The inability of the U.S. federal government to maintain ongoing registers or to assign personal identification numbers and the requirement that the federal government conduct the census, greatly influence the way in which we conduct our censuses. Being unable to delegate the task to state and local governments, the census bureau throws together a temporary nationwide organization every ten years to count the people. The bureau exercises a good deal of ingenuity in planning detailed procedures for recruiting, training, and supervising hundreds of thousands of temporary workers to perform meticulous and sometimes unpleasant tasks, such as knocking on strangers' doors and asking personal questions.

The basic strategy is to look for people and, after finding them, to count them. In the absence of population registers, the census bureau makes a list of all the dwellings. Since there is no existing complete list of the dwellings, the bureau makes one more or less from scratch every ten years. In 1990 that list had approximately 100 million entries. Having made a list of dwellings, the bureau attempts to get population information about their occupants. It first mails questionnaires to them and then, it goes door to door to conduct interviews with those who fail to return them.

Given the multiplicity of ways in which errors can enter such an operation, the census employs a strategy of redundant procedures. This strategy sequentially uses each operation as a way to collect additional information and also to correct errors that were made in previous operations. When the strategy works correctly, the data get progressively improved—more and more information with fewer and fewer errors—as the data collection moves from beginning to end.

The undercount is not a feature of the census; it is a feature of our society. Changing the census has not eliminated the undercount. In order to eliminate the undercount we would have to change the society. Our society abides great material inequality. Despite the nation's wealth, every city has destitute homeless people. Furthermore, freedom and inequality conspire to create disorder. Poverty and disorder are great obstacles to censustaking. Persons who sleep on the streets, in parks, or in dumpsters must conceal themselves at night, for their own protection, so they cannot be counted fully; ethnographic studies conducted on S-Night demonstrated this. Also, persons who live outside the law— drug dealers, professional thieves, prostitutes—must avoid contact with representatives of the government.

What other aspects of disorder are relevant to censustaking? People in certain situations have good reasons to avoid contact with the government. No amount of advertising and community relations work will convince all of them that it is safe and in their own interest to disclose themselves to the census. Illegal immigration is perhaps the simplest and most obvious case; undocumented immigrants live in fear of being found and deported. Millions of persons entered the United States from and through Mexico during the 1970s and 1980s. Others arrived by air with tourist and student visas and overstayed their visas. All such persons have a powerful incentive to avoid any contact with the government. In this regard, we may compare the United States with some nation that has tight control over its borders, perhaps an island nation. Assuming that this hypothetical nation has good immigration controls and a good records system, it is unlikely to harbor aliens who are unknown to the government. Without saying anything about the political morality of different immigration policies, we can say that the U.S. situation mitigates against the censustaker's work.

Rules governing housing occupancy may provide disincentives to census cooperation. Municipalities have zoning and occupancy regulations. If a homeowner has an extra unapproved apartment in his house, in violation of local zoning rules, he may attempt to conceal it. If two families are doubled up in a public housing unit, in violation of their lease, they may attempt to conceal some of the occupants. If people live in a condemned building, they have an incentive to conceal themselves from the authorities. Likewise, AFDC welfare rules also create disincentives to accurate census reporting; if a woman is living with a man and she receives AFDC payments, she must conceal this fact from the welfare department. She has no reason to disclose that fact to the census.

Each one of these social conditions has defied solution. Each one—crime, drugs, welfare, homelessness—is deep and difficult. If society cannot solve them, why does anyone imagine that the census can overcome them as obstacles to enumeration? Given these circumstances, it is not surprising that there is an undercount. What is surprising is that the census manages to count as many as it does.

Politically, there is less at stake than meets the eye in the undercount-adjustment issue. Much as I sympathize with their problems, I think that the big city mayors have misunderstood the impact of the census. Cities of the northeastern and midwestern regions stopped growing by 1950; thereafter they lost population. After more than a century of explosive growth, this stasis or decline was shocking and hard to accept. Nonetheless, instead of facing facts, the mayors chose to criticize the census for "failing" to count their people.

Then, in 1980, when they sued the Census Bureau and the Department of Commerce, complaining about undercounts and demanding adjustment, they made extravagant claims about the injuries their cities were suffering due to the census. New York claimed that they lost a seat in congress. Press reports frequently reported that cities were losing $400 per year per uncounted person, $4000 over a decade. Eventually, it was shown that both claims were false.

There are several reasons why neither New York City nor any other city could realize major financial gains by means of a census adjustment. First, most of the federal grant programs add up to fixed national totals for all the cities together, so redistribution represents a zero-sum game. If New York got more dollars, they would have to come from allocations for Cleveland and St. Louis. But poor minorities were undercounted in those cities, just as they were in New York. Furthermore, as the General Revenue Sharing program was being phased out around the time of the 1980 census, there were fewer federal dollars to distribute.

For years, there was a lack of research on the redistributive effects of census adjustment, but once the results of the new PES were released in April 1991 it was possible to calculate them. Economist Michael Murray quickly analyzed the financial impacts on the city and he showed how small they would be. Like other undercounted cities, New York City stood to gain about $56 per uncounted person per year. Given a PES-measured undercount of about 229,000, that would give the city an annual increment of about 12.8 million federal dollars. New York City does have a legitimate claim on those dollars, but they represent a trivial fraction of the city's budget and would not go far towards solving the problems of poor minorities.

Likewise, the release of the PES numbers also showed how congressional allocation would be affected by adjustment. The most unanticipated result of PES was to show that the greatest undercount occurred where there was the greatest population growth, in southern California. So, adjustment implied that two House seats would be reassigned and one of them would go to the the state that already had the biggest delegation and that had already benefitted most from the unadjusted census! At the same time, adjustment would have taken two seats from from frostbelt states, Wisconsin and Pennsylvania.

A brief digression on the process by which congressional seats are reapportioned every ten years. Acting on behalf of the president, the census bureau applies a mathematical formula to census results in order to assign each state its seats in the House of Representatives. That formula, which has been used after every census since 1930, is sensitive to small differences between state populations, especially when it is allocating the last few seats in the House. In 1990 differences of fewer than 10,000 persons determined which states got the 434th and 435th seats (and which did not).

Census procedures can produce state-level differences of that magnitude. In 1980, the state of Indiana lost the 435th seat to Florida. The governor of Indiana sued the government, protesting that the census bureau's imputation procedure, particularly regarding vacant housing units, created so many imputed (but not counted) persons in Florida that it illegitimately boosted its population to the point where it got the last seat. Likewise, in 1990 the state of Massachusetts lost the 435th seat by a small margin. The governor of Massachusetts sued the government, protesting that the census bureau's decision to include foreign-based military personnel in state population numbers was illegal. Massachusetts's case is still pending.

There has been speculation about the interests of political parties in adjustment and there has been less attention to the regional dimension. Some critics of the Department of Commerce allege that the secretary rejected adjustment because it would be bad for the Republican party. Likewise, I have heard speculation that adjustment was an issue for Democrats. Neither of these observations illuminates the situation. Reallocation of congressional seats affects states as states. Therefore, when it became apparent in 1991 that a PES-based adjustment would take one seat each from Pennsylvania and Wisconsin, the congressional delegations from those two states—Democrats and Republicans alike—were unified in their opposition to adjustment. In that situation, adjustment was not a party issue.

Politically, adjustment makes its biggest difference within states. In any state containing one or more major urban centers, adjustment would have shifted power slightly away from the rural and suburban sectors, toward central cities. If small area census counts were adjusted, then cities would be more heavily represented in congressional districts and in state legislative districts. Rural and suburban areas, which were not disproportionately undercounted, would not gain from adjustment and in some cases would be adjusted slightly downward. So, one may speculate that the Democratic party would gain from an adjustment because big city areas tend to vote Democratic. This being the case, it appears that the National Republican State Legislators Association anticipated the benefits correctly when they wrote their antiadjustment letters in early 1990. The other dimension that becomes apparent at this scale is that of region. Contrary to what had been anticipated in the 1980 lawsuits, the 1990 PES revealed that adjustment would benefit sunbelt states, at the expense of the rest of the country.

There are good arguments on both sides regarding adjustment. Proponents say that the methodology, while not perfect, is excellent, sufficient to the task, and that it would bring the census numbers closer to the truth. Opponents say that adjustment would be a big change in the census that should not be introduced until the methodology is watertight. (I reject that argument.)

Good Arguments for Adjustment

Despite decades of sincere and expensive efforts on the part of the census bureau to eliminate the differential undercount, it is still there. Efforts to improve the census (coverage improvements) and to communicate with and persuade the difficult to enumerate groups have failed. There is an ongoing need to generate more accurate numbers that would overcome the differential undercount. Statistical adjustment appears to be the only possibility.

Research and development at the census bureau leading to the new PES represented a genuine accomplishment in statistical science. The new PES has solid theoretical grounding. It solved fundamental problems that undermined the 1980 Postenumeration Program by developing a new survey sample design along with new procedures for matching records between a census and a survey. The new PES was field-tested in 1985–1987 and then implemented on a national scale in 1990–1991—and it worked. The subsequent adjustment of census counts in spring 1991 also worked, yielding a set of adjusted numbers for all places in the country, down to the block level. These adjusted numbers were ready on time to meet the agreed upon deadline of July 15, 1991. Altogether these accomplishments were remarkable.

The conduct and results of the new PES and the adjustment were subjected to intensive scrutiny. Dozens of evaluation studies demonstrated that the new PES was conducted to a high standard. Furthermore, a number of statisticians, including a large majority of the bureau's top officials—who were not necessarily predisposed toward adjusting and who were in danger of offending their superiors at the Department of Commerce—concluded that adjusted numbers were superior to the raw census counts. Although adjustment would degrade the census numbers for some places, on balance they would improve more numbers for more places. After studying the data and the evaluation studies, the census administrators voted in favor of adjustment.

Good Arguments against Adjustment

Even though adjusting would improve the numbers for some places, it is known that it would also inject errors into the numbers for other places that were accurately counted. There is no justification for doing so.

The new PES has not yet solved two fundamental problems. The method relies upon the creation of strata (categories of persons in designated types of places) within which adjustments are to be made. A sample of cases within each stratum determines the adjustment factor for that whole stratum. It is not known whether those strata are sufficiently homogeneous so that the adjustment factor for the sample can be accurately applied to all places in the stratum. A more important unsolved problem is correlation bias. It is known that some of the same types of persons are missed by the census and the PES. Thus, even after the execution of a high-quality PES, the results cannot compensate for undercounts of those types of persons. By definition, those types represent some of the hard to enumerate persons who are at the heart of the differential undercount.

PES results and the adjusted numbers that resulted from them were somewhat unstable. Errors were discovered by the bureau's statisticians after July 15, 1991; they were then corrected. These corrections to the PES would have produced adjusted numbers that were different from the first set of adjusted numbers. This shows that small corrections may make big differences. It also implies that with a new methodology like the PES, it is unwise to work quickly in order to meet a short deadline. More generally, it would have been premature to apply the method of the new PES to create officially adjusted numbers in 1990–1991.

When the secretary of commerce announced his decision on July 15, 1991 not to adjust the census counts, he justified it on the grounds that he had received conflicting advice. He said that since qualified statisticians disagreed on the issue, the only prudent act on his part would be not to adjust. Otherwise he might be making the situation worse. He was cognizant of the legal standard of judgment that required him not to be arbitrary or capricious. Given the conflicting advice from credible sources, he said, it was best not to act.

If events had taken their normal course (i.e., if the Department of Commerce had not bludgeoned its way into the center of the issue) the bureau would have introduced adjustment techniques into the census in 1990–1991. Those adjustment techniques would have brought the numbers closer to the truth. The modern history of the census shows that the bureau continually introduces innovations, minor and major. Major changes since 1940 have included sampling; household forms to replace person-by-person, line-by-line rosters; self-enumeration to replace face-to-face interviews; optical scanning machines to extract data from questionnaires; "hot deck" imputation to assign values for missing data; and extra field checks to reexamine apparently vacant dwellings. This list could be extended considerably. These innovations were rarely introduced without extended tests. The 1970 vacancy check would be a major exception to that generalization. Innovations were typically introduced through a regular process. Census officials perceived a problem in the conduct of the census and proposed a possible future solution. During an intercensal period they tested, evaluated, and modified the solution. Then, they either phased it into a series of censuses (as they with self-enumeration); or they introduced it all at once into a census.

Invariably, these innovations have been developed within the census bureau. The bureau would have informed the Department of Commerce of the innovations and the department would have treated them without interest. The bureau's director would also have informed the house oversight committee of the innovations and would not have proceeded without its approval. The main point, though, is that the department and the subcommittee delegated such decisions to the bureau.

Undoubtedly several of these innovations made differences in census counts that were sufficient to determine which state received the 435th seat in the House of Representatives. As mentioned above, one procedure that had an effect of that magnitude was imputation. In 1980 the state of Indiana lost the 435th seat to Florida. The governor of Indiana sued the government, protesting that the Census Bureau's imputation procedure, particularly regarding vacant housing units, created so many imputed (but not counted) persons in Florida that it illegitimately boosted its population to the point where it got the last seat. After a trial, a federal district judge rejected Indiana's claim, ruling that, under delegation of authority from the secretary of commerce, the census director had the responsibility to decide on the technical procedures to be used in a census.

What was radically different about the 1990–1991 adjustment decision was that the Department of Commerce took it away from the bureau and held onto it tightly. Starting in 1987 when the undersecretary announced unilaterally that there would be no adjustment in 1990, the department retained control over the decision; the department "undelegated" it from the bureau. Department of Commerce officials and their supporters argued that this issue's public policy dimensions were too great for it to be left to the discretion of technical bureaucrats. The historical precedents show, however, that for decades census officials had been making decisions with equally weighty numerical implications. Census bureau officials had made those decisions responsibly. Secretaries of commerce had been satisfied to leave them to the discretion of the "technical bureaucrats." On occasion, when such decisions were challenged, they were supported by the courts.

The big loser in the undercount-adjustment issue has been the Census Bureau. It has lost its autonomy. Since at least 1979, because of the undercount adjustment issue, the Census Bureau has been kicked around. Applying unrealistic standards as to the conduct of a census, newspapers, led by the *New York Times*, have publicized every glitch in the conduct of the 1980 and 1990 censuses and have given voice to the bureau's adversaries. Likewise, ethnic leaders, attorneys, mayors, and congresspersons have criticized the Census Bureau mercilessly. Simultaneously, various parties have encroached upon the bureau's autonomy. By increasingly using its statistical oversight authority, based upon minimizing respondent burden, the Office of Management and Budget has curtailed the bureau's discretion over surveys and censuses. As shown in the 1987 questionnaire approval imbroglio, OMB has at times acted capriciously toward the bureau. Likewise, the Congress has not hesitated to micromanage the census. This was shown most clearly when members of the House of Representatives insisted that one question in the 1990 census be written and designed as they preferred, in rejection of the bureau's research-based design for that same question. Overall, the Department of Commerce has been the worst offender. By seizing control of the bureau in 1987 and retaining that control, they have deprived the agency of its well-earned autonomy.

The bureau's diminished autonomy may have deleterious effects in two ways. One is that the agency's subordination to the Department of Commerce may inject an atmosphere of caution into the bureau's scientific work. Census administrators, aware that their superiors are looking over their shoulders, may hesitate to attack politically sensitive questions. And, as scientists, census staff members may feel that they are constrained in their contacts with outside colleagues. They may feel that there are certain results, facts, thoughts, issues, that may not be readily disclosed outside the bureau. Thus, the free flow of scientific ideas is impeded. Another deleterious effect is the damage to the bureau's reputation. The Census Bureau has enjoyed a reputation for producing accurate, high-quality statistics. That reputation has been bolstered by a public trust in the agency's nonpartisan, nonpolitical, impartial stance. The worst thing that could happen to the bureau would be to lose that reputation.

Notes

1. INTRODUCTION

1. By April 1991 the plaintiffs were joined by fifteen other cities, four counties, five states and the District of Columbia, the Council of the Great City Schools and the Navajo Nation, as plaintiff-intervenors.

2. SCIENCE AND POLITICS IN THE CENSUS

1. Japanese-Americans and civil libertarians have criticized the Census Bureau for cooperating with the War Department in its effort to round up Japanese-Americans on the West Coast in 1942. As noted in a 1943 report to the War Department, "The most important single source of information prior to the evacuation was the 1940 Census of Population." The Census Bureau provided punched cards and tabulations pertaining to Japanese persons. In defense of the bureau's actions, Director Vincent Barabba wrote in 1980:

Officials at bureau headquarters prepared a duplicate set of punch cards which were used to tabulate information on the geographic concentrations of Japanese-Americans, primarily in California. These cards contained no names or other identifiers for individuals, but provided sufficient geographical information to use for planning purposes in the evacuation program. . . . The punch-card tabulations undoubtedly provided aggregate data on the numbers of Japanese-Americans for small geographical areas." [Letter from Vincent Barabba to Mr. Raymond Okamura, December 16, 1980]

Essentially, the bureau's defense was that it provided aggregated small-area statistics, including racial or ethnic variables. These were the same statistics that are routinely published after each census. Even though no individual's name or address was mentioned in the tables, they were still harmful to the members of that group.

3. PRELUDE TO THE 1980 CENSUS

1. "Assistance to States for State Equalization Plans," under P.L. 93–380, Education Amendments of 1974, as amended.

4. MEASURING AND OVERCOMING THE UNDERCOUNT

1. This matter of purpose and design became extremely contentious in the context of *Cuomo* v. *Baldridge* because expert witnesses for the plaintiffs asserted that the results of PEP were adequate for the purpose of making adjustments for states and cities, while the bureau said that PEP had not been designed for that purpose and was clearly not adequate for that task.

2. In 1986 the government of Somalia conducted a post-enumeration survey by sampling people as they visited watering holes with their cattle (Cowan et al. 1986).

3. The bureau also instituted a research program to attempt to measure the results of this effort. See Moore 1982.

5. HOW THEY DID THE CENSUS

1. Group quarters were defined as "any single-family home or apartment, rooming/boarding house, or similar type of residential unit occupied by 10 or more unrelated persons" (U.S. Bureau of the Census 1986:5–39).

2. In the 1990 census these files were superseded by a new geographic information system, TIGER (Topologically Integrated Geographic Encoding and Referencing).

7. THE NEW YORK CASE

1. When it was filed in 1980, the case was known as *Carey et al.* v. *Klutznick et al.* The plaintiffs were "the State of New York and its Governor [Hugh L. Carey], the City of New York and its Mayor [Edward Koch], and eight other New Yorkers of diverse ethnic-racial heritage" (Plaintiffs-Appellees 1981:1). The defendants were the secretary of commerce (Phillip Klutznick), the director of the Census Bureau, two regional census directors

and one assistant regional director, the Department of Commerce, the Census Bureau, and the clerk of the U.S. House of Representatives.

2. The forms were published in several languages, but still not enough for New York. Mann recalled that the forms had not been provided in appropriate languages for immigrants from Yugoslavia and Romania.

3. Typically, such a search showed that the person had already been enumerated. Nationwide, 67,000 persons were added by means of "Were You Counted" forms (U.S. Bureau of the Census 1986:5–51).

4. In addition to the Cravath attorneys, the plaintiffs' legal team included Robert Abrams, Attorney General of the State of New York, and three of his staff, along with Frederick A. O. Schwarz, Jr., who had become Corporation Counsel of New York City, and Mary McCorry, Assistant Corporation Counsel.

5. As the editors of *Statistical Science* indicate, "This paper describes statistical work done in connection with a lawsuit. . . . Freedman gave expert testimony on behalf of the defense." Although Freedman makes the same points in his testimony and in the paper, I relied upon the paper because it is more cogent than a court transcript (Freedman and Navidi 1986).

8. RESEARCH TOWARD ADJUSTMENT

1. Citro and Cohen note that "The Internal Revenue Service provided a sample of tax returns to the Census Bureau for the analysis but had no access to the census data for these returns" (1985:183).

2. The original plan for TARO included a second sample, predominantly African-American, in Compton, California. However, the bureau closed the Compton district office and dropped that sample when mail-return rates were far lower than planned and census administrators decided that it would require too much time and money to complete that part of the test.

3. See reproduction of letter in U.S. Congress 1987:49–50.

4. David Whitford's notes from the July 17, 1987, meeting, along with those of other participants, were entered into evidence in *New York v. Department of Commerce*.

9. THREE ATTACKS ON THE CENSUS

1. Refer to two documents in Jones 1988: (1) Attachment 5, letter, Wendy L. Gramm to Katherine M. Bulow, Sept. 16, 1987, p. 2; and (2) Attachment 2, U.S. Bureau of the Census, "Observations Concerning the September 16, 1987, Reply by the Office of Management and Budget to the Census Bureau's Initial Request to Clear Questionnaires for the 1988 Dress Rehearsal," p. 6.

2. See Advisory Committee minutes of April 14–15, 1988 (U.S. Bureau of the Census 1988b:6–7).

3. Testifying before the House Oversight Subcommittee on March 3, 1988, Ortner argued against adjustment and promised "the best count and the best coverage in history" (U.S. Congress 1988:5). He also submitted for the record a copy of his October 30, 1987, press release! Ignoring the accomplishments of the Undercount Research Committee, Ortner based his argument on the uncertain results of the 1980 PEP.

4. The *Washington Post* also published an extended summary of her testimony (Bailar March 6, 1988).

5. This new panel was completely distinct from the preexisting Panel on Decennial Census Methodology (of the National Research Council/ Committee on National Statistics). Indeed, the creation of the new Special Advisory Panel led to the dissolution of the Panel on Decennial Census Methodology.

6. Copies of their letters were available to be read at an office of the U.S. Department of Commerce in Washington, D.C.

10. CENSUS YEAR 1990

1. There were an additional thirty-five "Type 4" offices that worked on outreach activities plus some minor data collection. Each Type 4 office was essentially a satellite to a regular district office. The Type 4 offices extended the field organization to every congressional district.

2. Using a different metaphor, one census administrator referred to the address list as the "foundation." "The ACF [Address Control File] is the foundation of the census" (U.S. Bureau of the Census 1990b:1).

3. Here is one technical definition of TAR: "A type of enumeration area having city-type mail delivery for which a vendor list is obtained and subsequently geocoded through the use of the TIGER address range files" (U.S. Bureau of the Census 1988c:2).

4. Two definitions: An ARA or Address Register Area was "a geographic area established for data collection purposes. It usually consists of several neighboring census blocks." A block or census block was "A geographic area bounded on all sides by visible features such as streets, roads, railroad tracks or rivers; or by invisible features, such as city limits or a county or property line" (U.S. Bureau of the Census 1989a:B1–B2).

5. Every sixth line or every second line in the address register was marked, indicating that the housing unit that "fell" onto that line was in the sample for a long form. Whether the sample called for every second or every sixth household depended upon the population size of the community being canvassed.

6. Charles Jones's tables distributed at meeting of Census Advisory Committees, April 19, 1990.

7. The appropriation was included in PL101–302, signed on May 25,

1990, which included appropriations for a number of other departments and programs.

8. All of the material about nonresponse followup comes from chapter 9 in U.S. Bureau of the Census, *Manager's Handbook (Type 1 Office)*, *21st Decennial Census, 1990*, Manual D-506–1, July 1989:9–76.

9. Other records that were subjected to search/match were individual census reports, parolee-probationer forms (described later in this chapter), and "Were You Counted?" forms (U.S. Bureau of the Census, Susan M. Miskura, March 18, 1990c).

10. U.S. Bureau of the Census, 1990 Decennial Census Informational Memorandum No. 142, Susan M. Miskura, "Parolee/Probationer Coverage Improvement Program, Nonresponse Follow-up—Targeted Areas," Sept. 14, 1990. Also, 1990 Decennial Census Informational Memorandum No. 145, Susan M. Miskura, "The Decennial Census Parolee/Probationer Coverage Improvement Program Followup Program," Oct. 1, 1990.

11. Ibid.

12. "1990 Census Population for the United States Is 249,632,692; Reapportionment Will Shift 19 Seats in the U.S. House of Representatives (*U.S. Department of Commerce News*, Dec. 26, 1990).

11.   THE DECISION NOT TO ADJUST

1. Kenneth Wachter, a member of the panel, accepted the revisions of the older estimates of black births as an improvement. He noted, though, that "the treatment of this anomaly [the incorrect estimate of black male births] has, however, necessarily been ad hoc, and we cannot be confident that other, less conspicuous errors in the corrections for birth registration completeness do not remain." See his recommendations to the secretary (1991:16).

2. Eugene P. Ericksen, Leobardo F. Estrada, John W. Tukey, Kirk M. Wolter (members, Special Advisory Panel, referred to hereafter as Ericksen et al. 1991), Report on the 1990 Decennial Census and Post-Enumeration Survey, 11.

3. See Chapters 4 and 8 for definitions of E-sample and P-sample.

12.   CONCLUSIONS

1. Turkey and Iraq have imposed one-day curfews, keeping everyone at home for censuses (*New York Times*, Nov. 26, 1980; Littman 1979).

Bibliography

Adlakha, Arjun, Howard Hogan, and J. Gregory Robinson. 1991. "A Report on the Internal Consistency of the Post-Enumeration Survey Estimates," part of an appendix to "Decision of the Secretary of Commerce."

Advisory Committee on Problems of Census Enumeration, Division of Behavioral Sciences, National Research Council. 1972. *America's Uncounted People*. Washington, D.C.: National Academy of Sciences.

Alberti, Nicholas. 1991. "The Evaluation of Late Late Census Data in the 1990 Post-Enumeration Survey." U.S. Bureau of the Census. unpublished.

Alonso, William, and Paul Starr, eds. 1987. *The Politics of Numbers*. New York: Russell Sage Foundation.

American Statistical and Federal Statistics Users' Association Conference. 1973. *Maintaining the Professional Integrity of Federal Statistics*. Photocopy.

Anderson, Margo J. 1988. *The American Census: A Social History*. New Haven, Conn.: Yale University Press.

———. January 20, 1990. Letter to Undersecretary of Commerce Michael Darby.

Bailar, Barbara. 1983. "Affidavit," in *Cuomo et al.* v. *Baldridge et al.* New York: U.S. District Court, Southern District of New York.

———. March 6, 1988a. "Census 1990, The Miscounting of America." *Washington Post*, C-3.

———. 1988b. "Affidavit," in *Notice of Motion, City of New York et al.* v. *United States Department of Commerce et al.* New York: U.S. District Court, Eastern District of New York.

———. 1988c. "Testimony." In *The Decennial Census Improvement Act*. U.S. Congress. House. Committee on Post Office and Civil Service, Subcommittee on Census and Population. Washington, D.C.: Government Printing Office:76–125.

———. March 13, 1990. Interview with author, Washington, D.C.

Barabba, Vincent P. December 16, 1980. Letter to Raymond Okamura.

———. July 26 and 27, 1984, Interview with author, Rochester, N.Y.

Barringer, Felicity. August 30, 1990. "Census Data Show Sharp Rural Losses." *New York Times*, A-1.

———. April 19, 1991a. "Federal Survey Finds Census Missed 4 Million to 6 Million People." *New York Times*, A-8.

———. June 14, 1991b. "Census Revisions Would Widen Political Gains of Three Big States." *New York Times*, A-1.

Bateman, David, Jon Clark, Mary Mulry, and John Thompson. 1991. "1990 Post-Enumeration Survey Evaluation Results." Presented at meeting of the American Statistical Association, Atlanta, Ga.

Bates, Nancy, and David C. Whitford. 1991. "Reaching Everyone: Encouraging Participation in the 1990 Census." Presented at meeting of the American Statistical Association, Atlanta, Ga.

Bounpane, Peter. February 18, 1983. Interview with author, Suitland, Md.

Bounpane, Peter A., and Thomas A. Jones. 1988. "Automation of the 1990 U.S. Census." *Chance: New Directions for Statistics and Computing* 1:28–35.

Bounpane, Peter, and Clifton Jordan. 1978. "Plans for Coverage Improvement in the 1980 Census." Presented at meeting of the American Statistical Association, 1978.

Bryant, Barbara E. 1991a. "The 1990 Census: Protecting Confidentiality While Striving for Complete Population Coverage." Unpublished.

———. 1991b. "The Last 2 Percent Counted in the 1990 Census: Undercount Research and Taking a New Look at Census Taking for the Year 2000." Presented at meeting of the American Association of Public Opinion Research, Phoenix, Ariz.

Citro, Constance F., and Michael L. Cohen, eds. 1985. *The Bicentennial Census New Directions for Methodology in 1990*. Washington, D.C.: National Academy Press.

City of New York. 1988. "Complaint," in *City of New York et al.* v. *United States Department of Commerce et al.* New York: U.S. District Court, Eastern District of New York.

———. 1988. "Memorandum of Law in Support of the Plaintiffs' Motion for a Preliminary Injunction," in *City of New York et al.* v. *United States Department of Commerce et al.* New York: U.S. District Court, Eastern District of New York.

Coale, Ansley J. 1955. "The Population of the United States in 1950 Classified by Age, Sex, and Color—a Revision of Census Figures." *Journal of the American Statistical Association* 50:16–54.

Coale, Ansley J., and Norfleet W. Rives, Jr. 1973. "A Statistical Reconstruction of the Black Population of the United States, 1880–1970: Estimates of True Numbers by Age and Sex, Birth Rates, and Total Fertility." *Population Index* 39:3–36.

Coale, Ansley J., and Melvin Zelnik. 1963. *New Estimates of Fertility and Population in the United States: A Study of Annual White Births from 1855 to*

1960 and of Completeness of Enumeration in the Censuses from 1880 to 1960. Princeton, N.J.: Princeton University Press.

Cohen, Patricia Cline. 1982. *A Calculating People: The Spread of Numeracy in Early America.* Chicago: University of Chicago Press.

Conk, Margo A. 1987. "The 1980 Census in Historical Perspective." In *The Politics of Numbers,* ed. William Alonso and Paul Starr, 155–186. New York: Russell Sage.

Council of Professional Associations on Federal Statistics. August–September 1987. "OMB 'Unable to Approve' Dress Rehearsal, Proposes Alterations." *News from COPAFS,* 1–10.

Cowan, Charles D. 1983. "Affidavit," in *Cuomo et al.* v. *Baldridge et al.* New York: U.S. District Court, Southern District of New York.

Cowan, Charles D., William R. Breakey, and Pamela J. Fischer. 1986. "The Methodology of Counting the Homeless." In *Proceedings of the Section on Survey Research Methods,* 170–175. American Statistical Association.

Cowan, Charles D., Anthony G. Turner, and Karen Stanecki. 1986. "Design of the Somali Post-Enumeration Survey, 1986–1987." Presented at meeting of the Population Association of America.

Darby, Michael R. 1990. "Statement of Michael R. Darby, Under Secretary for Economic Affairs." In *Press Release, United States Department of Commerce.* Washington, D.C.:

———. 1991. "Recommendation to the Secretary on the Issue of Whether or Not to Adjust the 1990 Decennial Census from Michael R. Darby, Under Secretary for Economic Affairs and Administrator of the Economics and Statistics Administration." Unpublished.

DeBarry, Marshall. May 26, 1983. Interview with author, Suitland, Md.

Defendants. 1980. "Defendants' Post-Trial Brief," *Young et al.* v. *Klutznick et al.* Detroit: U.S. District Court, Eastern District of Michigan, Southern Division.

Defendants. 1984. "Defendants' Post-Trial Memorandum," in *Cuomo et al.* v. *Baldridge et al.,* 80 Civ. 4550. New York: U.S. District Court, Southern District of New York.

Defendants-Appellants. 1981. "Brief for Defendants-Appellants." New York: U.S. Court of Appeals for the Second Circuit.

Dellenback, John. 1971–1972. Correspondence with census officials.

Devine, Joel A., and James D. Wright. 1991. "Counting the Homeless: S-Night in New Orleans." In *Joint Hearing on Quality and Limitations of the S-Night Homeless Count,* 82–103. Washington, D.C.: Government Printing Office.

Diffendal, Gregg. 1987. "1986 Test of Adjustment-Related Operations: Procedures and Methodology." Prepared for the Census Advisory Committee of the American Statistical Association and the Census Advisory Committee on Population Statistics.

Dingbaum, Tamara L., and Kathryn F. Thomas. 1991. "Telephone Survey of Census Participation." Presented at the Joint Statistical Meetings.

Duncan, Joseph W., and Willian C. Shelton. 1978. *Revolution in United States Government Statistics, 1926–1976.* Washington, D.C.: U.S. Department of Commerce.

Dunlap, David W. January 22, 1990. "Listing Shows Homeless Sites to Aid Homeless." *New York Times,* B-1.

Eckler, A. Ross. 1972. *The Bureau of the Census.* New York: Praeger.

Ekanem, Ita. 1972. *The 1963 Nigerian Census.* Benin City, Nigeria: Ethiope Publishing Corp.

Ericksen, Eugene P., Leobardo F. Estrada, John W. Tukey, Kirk M. Wolter. 1991. Report on the 1990 Decennial Census and the Post-Enumeration Survey.

Fay, Robert E., Nancy Bates, and Jeffrey Moore. 1991. "Lower Mail Response in the 1990: A Preliminary Interpretation." Presented at the Annual Research Conference of the U. S. Census Bureau.

Fein, David J., and Kirsten K. West. 1988. "The Sources of Census Undercount: Findings from the 1986 Los Angeles Test Census." *Survey Methodology* 14:223–240.

Freedman, D. A., and W. C. Navidi. 1986. "Regression Models for Adjusting the 1980 Census." *Statistical Science* 1:3–39.

Gilmore, Judge Horace. 1980. "Opinion in *Young et al.* v. *Klutznick et al.*" *Federal Supplement* 497:1318–1339.

Green, Somonica L., and Michael L. Mersch. 1991. "Quality Program and Results of the Creation of the Short-form Mailing Packages for the 1990 Decennial Census." Presented at meeting of American Statistical Association.

Hansen, Morris H., William N. Hurwitz, and William G. Madow. 1953. *Sample Survey Methods and Theory.* New York: Wiley.

Harvard Law Review. 1981. "Demography and Distrust: Constitutional Issues of the Federal Census." *Harvard Law Review* 94:841–863.

Hauser, Philip M. 1972. "Statistics and Politics." In *Proceedings of the Social Statistics Section, American Statistical Association,* 95–98. Washington, D.C.: American Statistical Association.

———. 1981. "The U.S. Census Undercount." *Asian and Pacific Census Forum* 8:1–2, 7–10.

Heer, David M., ed. 1968. *Social Statistics and the City.* Cambridge, Mass.: Joint Center for Urban Studies of the Massachusetts Institute of Technology and Harvard University.

Herriot, Roger A. September 1979. "The 1980 Census: Countdown for a Complete Count." *Monthly Labor Review* 102:3–13.

Hill, Robert B. 1980. "The Synthetic Method: Its Feasibility for Deriving the Census Undercount for States and Local Areas." In *Conference on Census Undercount,* Washington, D.C.: Government Printing Office: 129–141.

Hill, Robert B., and Robert B. Steffes. 1975. "Estimating the 1970 Census Undercount for States and Local Areas." *Urban League Review* 1:36–45.

Hogan, Howard. 1983. "The Forward Trace Study, Its Purposes and Design." Presented at meeting of the American Statistical Association.

———. 1989. "Nine Years of Coverage Evaluation Research: What Have We Learned?" Presented at meeting of the American Statistical Association, Survey Methods Section.

———. 1991. "The 1990 Post-Enumeration Survey: Operations and Results." Presented at meeting of the American Statistical Association, Atlanta, Ga.

Holden, Constance. 1987. "Census a Public Burden?" *Science* 237:839.

Jones, Charles D. 1988. "Documents Concerning Content and Sample Design for the 1990 Census of Population and Housing." U.S. Bureau of the Census. Unpublished.

———. August 3, 1990. "Progress on the 1990 Census." Bulletin. U.S. Bureau of the Census.

Jones, David R. May 16, 1986. Interview with author, Brooklyn, N.Y.

Jones, Thomas. April 26, 1983. Interview with author, Suitland, Md.

Kadane, Joseph B. 1984. "Review of *The 1980 Census: Policymaking Amid Turbulence* by Ian A. Mitroff, Richard O. Mason, and Vincent P. Barabba." *Journal of the American Statistical Association* 79:467–469.

King, Benjamin. May 26, 1987. Letter to John G. Keane.

Klutznick, Philip M. 1980. "Memorandum for Vincent Barabba." *Federal Register* 45:82879.

Koch, Edward I. May 3, 1989. Letter to Secretary of Commerce Robert A. Mosbacher.

Kruskal, William. June 13, 1991. Letter to Secretary Robert A. Mosbacher.

———. 1983. "The Census as a National Ceremony." In *Federal Statistics and National Needs*. Washington, D.C.: Government Printing Office:177–180.

Lee, Anne S. 1984. "The Census Under Fire: The Press and the 1890 Census." Presented at meeting of the Population Association of America, Minneapolis, Minn.

Levine, Daniel. April 12, 1983a and April 20, 1983b. Interview with author, Washington, D.C.

Levine, Richard. April 22, 1991. "Gain Seen for New York If Census Adjusts Tally." *New York Times*, A-13.

Lieber, Sheila. February 15, 1983. Interview with author, Washington, D.C.

Littman, Mark S. September 1979. "The 1980 Census of Population: Content and Coverage Improvement Plans." *Journal of Consumer Research* 6:204–212.

McLaughlin, Joseph M. 1989. "Memorandum and Order." New York: Eastern District of New York, United States District Court.

Magnet, Myron. February 9, 1981. "Behind the Bad-News Census." *Fortune*:88–93.

Mann, Evelyn S. August 20, 1980. "Affidavit," in *Carey et al. v. Klutznick et al.* New York: U.S. District Court, Southern District of New York.

———. April 15, 1983. Interview with author, New York, N.Y.

Mann, Evelyn S., and Joseph Salvo. June 1989. "Inspection of Tract Maps Reveals Numerous Errors." *APDU News* (Association of Public Data Users) 13:1–8.

Mann, Nancy R. 1988. "Why It Happened in Japan and Not in the U.S." *Chance: New Directions for Statistics and Computing* 1:8–15.

Marks, Eli S. 1978. "The Role of Dual System Estimation in Census Evaluation," in *Developments in Dual System Estimation of Population Size and Growth*, ed. Karol J. Krotki, 156–166. Edmonton, Alberta, Canada: University of Alberta Press.

Marks, Eli S., William Seltzer, and Karol J. Krotki. 1974. *Population Growth Estimation: A Handbook of Vital Statistics Measurement.* New York: Population Council.

Marx, Robert W. February 6, 1990. "Seminar Presentation at Georgetown University, Department of Demography."

———. 1990. "Developing an Automated Geographic System for Future Censuses." Presented at meeting of American Statistical Association, Anaheim, Calif.

Melnick, Daniel. 1987. *The Census Bureau's Plans for Using Computerized Maps in 1990: Fact Sheet.* Congressional Research Service Report No. 87–206.

Melnick, Daniel, and David Huckabee. 1989. *Adjusting the 1990 Census for Miscounts: An Analysis of the Implications of the Stipulation Agreed to in the New York Court Case.* Testimony before the Subcommittee on Census and Population. Congressional Research Service.

Melnick, Daniel, and Alexander Lurie. 1987. "Census Questions and OMB's Review of the Census Bureau Proposal: A Summary and Brief Analysis." In *OMB Proposals for Severe Cuts in the 1990 Census.* Washington: Government Printing Office.

Milstrey, Susan. 1989. "Census Bureau Plans to Count Homeless Persons in 1990." *Access*, 4.

Mitroff, Ian I., Richard O. Mason, and Vincent P. Barabba. 1983. *The 1980 Census: Policymaking amid Turbulence.* Lexington, Mass: Lexington.

Moore, Jeffrey C. 1982. "Evaluating the Public Information Campaign for the 1980 Census—Results of the KAP Survey." 1980 Census, Preliminary Evaluation Results Memorandum No. 31. U.S. Bureau of the Census, Center for Social Science Research.

Mulry, Mary, Howard R. Hogan, John R. Walker, David W. Chapman, Judy Evand, and Roger H. Moore. 1981. "A Research Proposal for a Study of Methods for 1980 Decennial Census Coverage Evaluation," unpublished. U.S. Bureau of the Census.

Murray, Michael P. 1992. "Census Adjustment and the Distribution of Federal Spending." *Demography* 29:319–332.

Myers, Robert J. 1940. "Errors and Bias in the Reporting of Ages in Census Data." *Transaction of the Actuarial Society of America* 41, Part 2:395–415.

New York Times. December 31, 1980. "Court Votes 7–1 to Stay Judge Werker's Order," sec. II–1.
———. Nov. 26, 1980. "Letter," A-18.

Ortner, Robert. 1987. "Statement of Robert Ortner, Under Secretary for Economic Affairs, on the 1990 Census." In *Press Release, United States Department of Commerce*. Washington, D.C.
———. 1988. "Declaration of Robert Ortner."

Panel on Decennial Census Plans, Committee on National Statistics, National Research Council. 1978. *Counting the People in 1980: An Appraisal of Census Plans*. Washington, D.C.: National Academy of Sciences.
Passel, Jeffrey. 1983. "Affidavit" in *Cuomo et al. v. Baldridge et al.* New York: U.S. District Court, Southern District of New York.
———. Oct. 25, 1989a, and Nov. 8, 1989b. Interview with author, Washington, D.C.
Plaintiffs. 1980. "Post-trial Brief," in *Post-trial Brief Filed on Behalf of Coleman A. Young and the City of Detroit. Young et al. v. Klutznick et al.* Detroit: U.S. District Court, Eastern District of Michigan, Southern Division.
———. 1984. "Plaintiffs' Reply Memorandum after Trial on Remand: *Cuomo et al. v. Baldridge et al.*, 80 Civ. 4550." New York: U.S. District Court, Southern District of New York.
Plaintiffs-Appellees. 1981. "Brief for Plaintiffs-Appellees." New York: U.S. Court of Appeals for the Second Circuit.
Price, Daniel O. 1947. "A Check on Underenumeration in the 1940 Census." *American Sociological Review* 12:44–49.
Pritzker, Leon, and N. D. Rothwell. 1968. "Procedural Difficulties in Taking Past Censuses in Predominantly Negro, Puerto Rican, and Mexican Areas," in *Social Statistics and the City*, ed. David M. Heer, 55–79. Cambridge, Mass.: Joint Center for Urban Studies of the Massachusetts Institute of Technology and Harvard University.

Rich, Spencer. January 15, 1988. "Ex-Aide Says Republicans Killed Census Adjustment." *Washington Post*, A-19.
Rivers, Emilda B., and Amy L. Tillman. 1991. "The Role of the United States Postal Service During the 1990 Decennial Census." Presented at meeting of the American Statistical Association.
Robinson, J. Gregory. 1988. "Perspectives on the Completeness of Coverage of Population in the United States Decennial Censuses." Presented at meeting of the Population Association of America, New Orleans, La.
Robinson, J. Gregory, Bashir Ahmed, Prithwis Das Gupta, and Karen A. Woodrow. 1991. "Estimating Coverage of the 1990 United States Census: Demographic Analysis." Presented at meeting of the American Statistical Association, Atlanta, Ga.

Robinson, J. Gregory, Prithwis Das Gupta, and Bashir Ahmed. 1990. "A Case Study in the Investigation of Errors in Estimates of Coverage Based on Demographic Analysis: Black Adults Aged 34 to 54 in 1980." Presented at meeting of the American Statistical Association, Anaheim, Calif.

Rockwell, Richard C. 1989. "It's No Burden, It's Our Right." *Chance: New Directions for Statistics and Computing* 2:36–37, 44.

———. 1990. "The Paperwork Reduction Act: Scourge of Social Statistics?" Presented at meeting of the American Statistical Association, Anaheim, Calif.

Sedler, Robert. Sept. 2, 1983. Interview with author, Detroit, Mich.

Senate Committee on Governmental Affairs, Subcommittee on Government Information and Regulation and House Committee on Post Office and Civil Service, Subcommittee on Census and Population. 1991. *Joint Hearing on Quality and Limitations of the S-Night Homeless Count.* Report No. 102–11.

Simon, Julian L. 1969. *Basic Research Methods in Social Science.* New York: Random House.

Slater, Courtenay. May 24, 1983. Interview with author, Alexandria, Va.

Sudman, Seymour, Monroe G. Sirken, and Charles D. Cowan. 1988. "Sampling Rare and Elusive Populations." *Science* 240:991–996.

Taeuber, Conrad. November 12, 1987. Letter to author.

Takei, Rich. May 6, 1983. Interview with author, Suitland, Md.

Thernstrom, Abigail. 1987. "Statistics and the Politics of Minority Representation," in *The Politics of Numbers.* ed. William Alonso and Paul Starr, 303–328. New York: Russell Sage Foundation.

Tippett, Janet. May 6, 1983. Interview with author, Suitland, Md.

Tuck, James A. September 1, 1983. Interview with author, Detroit, Mich.

Tukey, John W. 1983. "Affidavit," in *Cuomo et al.* v. *Baldridge et al.* New York: U.S. District Court, Southern District of New York.

U.S. Bureau of the Census. 1943. "Completeness of Birth Registration, United States, December 31, 1939 to March 31, 1940. Part 1, Studies in Birth Registration Completeness." *Vital Statistics—Special Reports* 17.

U.S. Bureau of the Census. 1976. *Procedural History, 1970 Census of Population and Housing,* PHC(R)-1. Washington, D.C.: Government Printing Office.

U.S. Bureau of the Census. 1980. *Report of the United States Bureau of the Census in Response to the Judgment of the Court Entered September 30, 1980. Young et al.* v. *Klutznick et al.,* 80 Civ. 7130. Detroit: U.S. District Court, Eastern District of Michigan, Southern Division.

U.S. Bureau of the Census. 1980. *Conference on Census Undercount: Proceedings of the 1980 Conference.* Washington, D.C.: Government Printing Office.

U.S. Bureau of the Census. 1980. *District Manager's Manual, Decentralized.* Technical Manual D-507.

U.S. Bureau of the Census. 1980a. *Followup 1 Crew Leader's Manual, Decentralized.* Technical Manual D-554.

U.S. Bureau of the Census. 1980b. *Followup 1 Enumerator's Manual, Decentralized.* Technical Manual D-548.

U.S. Bureau of the Census. 1980c. *Followup 2 Enumerator's Manual, Decentralized.* Technical Manual D-558.

U.S. Bureau of the Census, Stanley D. Matchett. 1983. "1990 Geography Planning Committee Issues Report." 1980 Decennial Census Information Memorandum No. 4.

U.S. Bureau of the Census. 1986. *History, 1980 Census of Population and Housing.* Washington, D.C.: Government Printing Office.

U.S. Bureau of the Census. 1987. *Framework for Census Design Incorporating Adjustment Operations.*

U.S. Bureau of the Census. Apr. 9 and 10, 1987. "Minutes and Report of Committee Recommendations." Census Advisory Committees of the American Statistical Association, on Population Statistics, of the American Marketing Association, and of the American Economic Association. Washington, D.C.: U.S. Bureau of the Census.

U.S. Bureau of the Census. Oct. 8 and 9, 1987. "Minutes and Report of Committee Recommendations." Census Advisory Committees of the American Statistical Association, on Population Statistics, of the American Marketing Association, and of the American Economic Association. Washington, D. C.: U.S. Bureau of the Census.

U.S. Bureau of the Census. 1988a. *1990 Decennial Census Geographic Handbook.* D-519 (Revised June 1988).

U.S. Bureau of the Census. Apr. 14 and 15, 1988b. "Minutes and Report of Committee Recommendations." Census Advisory Committees of the American Statistical Association, on Population Statistics, of the American Marketing Association, and of the American Economic Association. Washington, D. C.: U.S. Bureau of the Census.

U.S. Bureau of the Census. Susan M. Miskura. June 20, 1988c. "Operations Requirement Overview: 1990 Address List Acquisition." 1990 Decennial Census Information Memorandum No. 83.

U.S. Bureau of the Census. Susan M. Miskura. July 8, 1988d, "Operations Requirement Overview: Tape Address Register (TAR) Geocoding." 1990 Decennial Census Information Memorandum No. 84.

U.S. Bureau of the Census. 1989a. *Manager's Handbook (Type 1 Office) 21st Decennial Census, 1990.* Manual D-506–1.

U.S. Bureau of the Census. Susan M. Miskura. July 26, 1989b. "1990 Special Place Prelist Requirement Overview." 1990 Decennial Census Information Memorandum No. 81, Revision 2.

U.S. Bureau of the Census. 1990a. *Field Operations Manual* D-530.

U.S. Bureau of the Census. Susan M. Miskura. 1990b. "Operations Requirement Overview: 1990 Address Control System Requirements Overview." 1990 Decennial Census Information Memorandum No. 117.

U.S. Bureau of the Census. Susan M. Miskura. March 18, 1990c. "1990 Search/Match Requirements Overview." 1990 Decennial Census Information Memorandum No. 124.

U.S. Bureau of the Census. Susan M. Miskura. April 6, 1990d. "The 1990

Decennial Census Parolee/Probationer Coverage Improvement Program." 1990 Decennial Census Information Memorandum No. 131.

U.S. Bureau of the Census. Susan M. Miskura. Sept. 14, 1990e. "Parolee/ Probationer Coverage Improvement Program, Nonresponse Followup— Targeted Areas." 1990 Decennial Census Information Memorandum No. 142.

U.S. Bureau of the Census. Susan M. Miskura. Oct. 1, 1990f. "The Decennial Census Parolee/Probation Coverage Improvement Program Followup Program." 1990 Decennial Census Information Memorandum No.145.

U.S. Bureau of the Census. 1990g. *21st Decennial Census, 1990, Census Awareness and Products Program.* Reference Manual D-599.

U.S. Bureau of the Census. 1990h. *21st Decennial Census, 1990, Glossary of Census Operations.* Technical Manual D-529.

U.S. Bureau of the Census. 1990i. *21st Decennial Census, 1990, Manager's Handbook (Type 1 Office).* Technical Manual D-506–1.

U.S. Bureau of the Census. May 31, 1991a. "Post-Enumeration Survey (PES) Project P9: Accurate Measurement of Census Erroneous Enumerations." Appendix to Secretary's Recommendation of July 15, 1991.

U.S. Bureau of the Census. 1991b. "Technical Assessment of the Accuracy of Unadjusted Versus Adjusted Census Counts." Report of the Undercount Steering Committee.

U.S. Bureau of the Census. Susan M. Miskura. January 15, 1991c. "Processes Used to Identify and Select Recanvass Areas." 1990 Decennial Census Information Memorandum No. 138.

U.S. Bureau of the Census. Barbara E. Bryant. 1991d. "Recommendation to Secretary of Commerce Robert A. Mosbacher on Whether or Not to Adjust the 1990 Census," unpublished.

U.S. Congress. House. 1970. Committee on Post Office and Civil Service, Subcommittee on Census and Statistics. *Accuracy of 1970 Census Enumeration and Related Matters.* Hearings.

U.S. Congress. House. 1972. Committee on Post Office and Civil Service, Subcommittee on Census and Statistics. *Investigation of Possible Politicization of Federal Statistical Programs.* Report No. 92–1536.

U.S. Congress. House. 1977a. Committee on Post Office and Civil Service, Subcommittee on Census and Population. *The Census Reform Act.* Report No. 95–46.

U.S. Congress. House. 1977b. Committee on Post Office and Civil Service, Subcommittee on Census and Population. *Pretest Census in Oakland, California, and Camden, New Jersey.* Hearings, Report No. 95–42.

U.S. Congress. House. 1978. Committee on Post Office and Civil Service, Subcommittee on Census and Population. *The Use of Population Data in Federal Assistance Programs.* Committee Print No. 95–16. Washington, D.C.: U.S. Government Printing Office.

U.S. Congress. House. 1986. Committee on Post Office and Civil Service, Subcommittee on Census and Population. *1990 Census Adjustment Procedures and Coverage Evaluation.* Serial No. 99–65.

U.S. Congress. House. 1987. Committee on Post Office and Civil Service,

Subcommittee on Census and Population. *Problem of Undercount in 1990 Census.* Hearing Serial No. 100–19.

U.S. Congress. House. 1988. Committee on Post Office and Civil Service, Subcommittee on Census and Population. *The Decennial Census Improvement Act.* Hearing 100–51.

U.S. Congress. House. 1989. Committee on Post Office and Civil Service, Subcommittee on Census and Population. *Hearing: Plans for Conducting 1990 Census in New York.* Report No. 101–19.

U.S. Congress. House. 1990a. Committee on Post Office and Civil Service, Subcommittee on Census and Population. *Proposed Guidelines for Statistical Adjustment of the 1990 Census.* Report No. 101–43.

U.S. Congress. House. 1990b. Committee on Post Office and Civil Service, Subcommittee on Census and Population. *Hearing: Reviewing the Status of Census Operations.* Report No. 101–48.

U.S. Congress. House. 1990c. Committee on Post Office and Civil Service, Subcommittee on Census and Population. *Hearing: Review of Final Coverage Improvement Programs and Other Census Operations.* Report No. 101–85.

U.S. Congress. House. 1990d. Committee on Post Office and Civil Service, Subcommittee on Census and Population. *Hearing: Status of Census Operations in the State of Pennsylvania,* Report No. 101–72.

U. S. Congress, Joint Economic Committee. 1987. *OMB Proposal for Severe Cuts in the 1990 Census.* Hearing.

U.S. Congress. Senate. 1973. Committee on Post Office and Civil Service. *Reappointment of Robert E. Hampton to be U.S. Civil Service Commissioner and Nomination of Vincent P. Barabba to be Director, Bureau of the Census.*

U.S. Congress. Senate. 1991. Committee on Governmental Affairs, Subcommittee on Government Information and Regulation. *Joint Hearing on Quality and Limitations of the S-Night Homeless Count.* Report No. 102–11.

U.S. Court of Appeals for the Second Circuit. 1980. "Joint Appendix" (transcript), 80–8198. *Carey et al.* v. *Klutznick et al.* Vols. VI, VII, VIII, and IX. New York: U.S. Court of Appeals for the Second Circuit.

U.S. Court of Appeals, Sixth Circuit. 1981. "Decision." *Young et al.* v. *Klutznick et al. 652 Federal Reporter, 2d Series:* 617–641.

U.S. Department of Commerce, et al. 1988. "Defendants' Memorandum of Law in Support of Defendants' Motion to Dismiss, or, in the Alternative, for Summary Judgment, and in Opposition to Plaintiffs' Motion for Preliminary Injunction." *City of New York et al.* v. *United States Department of Commerce, et al.* New York: U.S. District Court, Eastern District of New York.

U.S. Department of Commerce. 1989. "Proposed Guidelines for Considering Whether or Not a Statistical Adjustment of the 1990 Decennial Census of Population and Housing Should Be Made for Coverage Deficiencies Resulting in an Overcount or Undercount of the Population." *Federal Register* 54 (236, Part XI): 51002–51005.

U.S. Department of Commerce. 1990. "Final Guidelines for Considering

Whether or Not a Statistical Adjustment of the 1990 Decennial Census of Population and Housing Should Be Made for Coverage Deficiencies Resulting in an Overcount or Undercount of the Population." *Federal Register* 55 (51): 9838–9861.

U.S. *Department of Commerce News.* January 16, 1990. "Production of Questionnaires Needed for Nation's 21st Census Nearly Complete." CB90–N90.01. Press release.

U.S. *Department of Commerce News.* December 26, 1990. CB90–N90.232. Press release.

U.S. *Department of Commerce News.* December 29, 1992. "Census Bureau Director Decides not to Adjust Intercensal Population Estimates." CB92–275. Press release.

U.S. Department of Commerce, Office of the Secretary. 1991. "Decision of the Secretary of Commerce on Whether a Statistical Adjustment of the 1990 Census of Population and Housing Should Be Made for Coverage Deficiencies Resulting in an Overcount or Undercount of the Population." *Federal Register* 56 (140): 33582.

U.S. District Court. "Stipulation and Order." *City of New York et al.* v. *United States Department of Commerce et al.,* 88 Civ. 3773. U.S. District Court, Eastern District of New York, 1989.

U.S. General Accounting Office. 1987. *Grant Formulas: A Catalog of Federal Aid to States and Localities.* GAO/HRD-87-28.

U.S. President's Commission on Federal Statistics. 1971. *Federal Statistics: Report of the President's Commission.*

Valentine, Charles A., and Betty Lou Valentine. 1971. "Missing Men: A Comparative Methodological Study of Underenumeration and Related Problems." Unpublished.

Vobejda, Barbara. March 21, 1990. "Census-Takers Struggle to Tally the Homeless." *Washington Post,* A-1.

———. June 14, 1991. "Adjusting Census: Winners and Losers." *Washington Post,* A-3.

Volner, Martha W. November, 1981. "Congress and the 1980 Census." *American Demographics,* 33–37.

Wachter, Kenneth W. June 17, 1991. "Recommendations on 1990 Census Adjustment to the Honorable Robert A. Mosbacher, Secretary of Commerce, from Kenneth W. Wachter, Member, Special Advisory Panel, 17 June, 1991." Unpublished.

Wallman, Katherine K. January 29, 1990, and February 7, 1990. Interview with author, Arlington, Va.

———. 1988. *The Statistical System Under Stress: Framing an Agenda for Success.* Council of Professional Associations on Federal Statistics.

Wall Street Journal. October 29, 1980. "Census Bureau Says It Counted Several Million More Than Expected." 4.

Warren, Robert, and Jeffrey S. Passel. 1987. "A Count of the Uncountable:

Estimates of Undocumented Aliens Counted in the 1980 Census."
Demography 24 (August 1987): 375–393.

Whitford, David. 1987. "Minutes, Census Redesign Meeting." Unpublished.
U.S. Bureau of the Census.

Wilson, Jerusa C. 1990. "Reducing the Undercount of Black Male Persons
and Young Black Children in the 1990 Decennial Census." *Journal of
Research on Minority Affairs* 1:25–48.

Wolter, Kirk. June 6, 1990. Interview with author, Northbrook, Ill.

———. 1987. *Technical Feasibility of Adjustment*, unpublished. U.S. Bureau of
the Census.

Yagoda, Ben. April 12, 1980. "Who Counts? The Politics of the 1980
Census." *Saturday Review*, 23–26.

Young, Arthur. Aug. 9, 1990. Interview with author, Washington, D.C.

Index

address lists, commercial. *See* mailing lists
address register, 55–57, 72–73, 105; in *Cuomo* v. *Baldridge*, 105, 107–108; in 1990 census, 176–181; "precanvass" of, 55–57, 178
Address Register Area (ARA), 177, 180
adjustment of census counts: arguments against (*see also* Ortner, Robert), 216–218, 224–226, 234–236; arguments in favor of, 6, 8, 114–115, 215–220, 223–224, 233–235; deadline for decision, 155; decision against in 1990, 206–226, 235–238; demands for, 61, 153; economic effects of, 222–223; feasibility in 1990, 125, 128, 130, 133, 146; first discussions of, 61; methodology, 61–64; political effects within states, 233; rejected by census officials, 114; report on, in *Young* v. *Klutznick*, 94–96; small area statistics and, 120; use of 1990 postenumeration survey in discussions of, 214–220
administrative records, use of in censuses, 48, 121–122
advertising, 60, 170
Advertising Council, 60
aliens, illegal, counted in census, 112
American Economic Association, 37
American Marketing Association's Census Advisory Committee, 36
American Sociological Association, 37, 92
American Statistical Association, 23, 35, 37, 92, 129, 131, 148

Anderson, Margo J., 22, 161–162
Arbuckle, Don, 138, 140

Bailar, Barbara, 113–114, 120–122, 124–125, 127, 133, 135, 147, 149–152, 154, 162–163
Baker v. *Carr*, 3, 26
Barabba, Vincent, 36–37, 40, 61, 84, 94, 108, 151
barcoding of addresses, 172–173, 187
Belin, Thomas R., 162
Betts, Jackson, 26–27
Bounpane, Peter, 56, 134, 172, 184
Brown, Clarence, 148
Bryant, Barbara, 5, 168, 185, 197, 202, 219–220, 224
Bureau of the Census. *See* U.S. Bureau of the Census
Butz, William, 140

Camden, N.J., 37–38
Canada, 121–122, 228
Carter, Jimmy, 37, 40
capture-recapture theory and technique, 49, 217; and correlation bias, 49–50, 123–124
"casual count," 52, 195
census administrators, as scientists, 11
Census Advisory Committee on Population Statistics, 129, 131
Census Bureau. *See* U.S. Bureau of the Census
Census Reform Act (1977), 38–39

About the Author

Harvey M. Choldin is a professor of sociology at the University of Illinois, Urbana-Champaign.